ETHNOGRAPHY ESSENTIALS

Designing, Conducting, and Presenting Your Research

JULIAN M. MURCHISON

JOSSEY-BASS
A Wiley Imprint
www.josseybass.com

Published by Jossey-Bass
A Wiley Imprint
989 Market Street, San Francisco, CA 94103-1741—www.josseybass.com

Readers should be aware that Internet Web sites offered as citations and/or sources for further information may have changed or disappeared between the time this was written and when it is read.

Jossey-Bass books and products are available through most bookstores. To contact Jossey-Bass directly call our Customer Care Department within the U.S. at 800-956-7739, outside the U.S. at 317-572-3986, or fax 317-572-4002.

Jossey-Bass also publishes its books in a variety of electronic formats. Some content that appears in print may not be available in electronic books.

Library of Congress Cataloging-in-Publication Data

Murchison, Julian M., 1973–
  Ethnography essentials : designing, conducting, and presenting your research/Julian M. Murchison.—1st ed.
      p. cm.
Includes bibliographical references and index.
ISBN 978-0-470-34389-0 (pbk.)
1. Ethnology   Methodology.   I.   Title.
  GN345.M87 2010
305.8001—dc22

                                                                          2009031953

Printed in the United States of America
FIRST EDITION
PB Printing   SKY10026676_042821

CONTENTS

PART 2
ETHNOGRAPHY IN THE FIELD:
COLLECTING DATA

PART 3
ANALYZING AND WRITING

PREFACE

This book aims to guide the relatively new ethnographer through the research process step by step. Advanced undergraduate students in anthropology, sociology, education, and related fields that employ ethnography will appreciate this text, and it could also prove useful to undergraduate students at the introductory level, more advanced students who want a practical guide to doing research, and even practitioners of ethnography in organizations and institutions outside of academics. The book starts from the premise that you will be engaged in your own ethnographic research over the course of a semester or a similar time period. Some projects may be slightly more concentrated in duration, and some projects may last a year or longer. The same basic principles apply in either case.

The book assumes relatively little prior exposure to ethnography, though previous experience in reading ethnographies or even doing ethnographic research is always a plus. With this working assumption, the book starts at step one in the research process and walks the reader through the entire project in a mostly chronological fashion. Readers who bring some experience with ethnography to the book may find that some sections provide a sort of review. Such a review can help those readers in evaluating their own thoughts about ethnography.

The book was written to maximize usefulness and accessibility. You will find important ideas and concepts (often highlighted as key terms) throughout the text. However, you should find very little jargon or highly specialized terminology. I have aimed to cover important and complex ideas and issues in as simple and straightforward a manner as possible. When the ideas and issues can be covered in relatively plain language, I have preferred that approach over the language used in texts on ethnographic methods intended for a more advanced and specialized audience.

The reader of this book should find the tools and the space to pursue various ethnographic projects. As a research strategy, ethnography encompasses a lot of different approaches and assumptions. There are even fundamental disagreements about what ethnography is or should be. I have aimed to address key questions and critiques that arise in discussions of ethnography without getting sidetracked by topics that will prevent you from completing your task in a relatively straightforward and effective way. Along these lines, I explain why the use of terms like informant and field can be the subject of significant debate, but I choose to use these terms because you will frequently encounter them elsewhere and they make discussion of certain topics, methods, and strategies easier. I expect that you will come to use these terms with some awareness of their multiple layers of meaning and that you will be part of the next generation of ethnographers who will help the research strategy evolve and overcome some of its limitations.

In producing this guide for the ethnographic endeavor, I want to allow, and even encourage, students and other readers to explore multiple possibilities in conducting ethnography. Therefore, the text is intended to include multiple approaches under the umbrella of ethnography. For example, your individual approach may be decidedly scientific or intentionally subjective. Either way, you should find useful information for your work in the text. At times, in order to allow for this multiplicity of approaches, the text has to include multiple possible scenarios and multiple options for you. In these instances, you have to decide for yourself the approach that seems most suitable for you and your research. I have provided suggestions and criteria for making those decisions and emphasized the ways in which decisions and strategies related to research strategies, methods of data collection, and analysis are interrelated.

The topic of ethics is not confined exclusively to the final chapter or an appendix. Ethical issues arise throughout the text. This regular treatment of ethics should help you understand the importance of ethical considerations and the manner in which all ethnographers grapple with and address the issues. The book aims to give you a sense of the underlying ethical questions that ethnography raises and the practical steps that ethnographers take to address ethical concerns.

THE BASIS FOR THIS BOOK

There are a number of good books out there that examine ethnography as a whole or one of its component parts. Relatively few of these books are geared toward an undergraduate audience, and many of them are theoretical rather than practical in focus. Those books that are both practical and accessible to the undergraduate tend to assume a rather narrow sort of project or present a series of separate ethnographic exercises. Therefore, this text assumes that you benefit from designing and carrying out a particular project that employs a combination of methods.

A copy of the syllabus for a course called Ethnographic Research and Writing started the conversation between the publisher and me that ultimately led to this book. I have taught that course on two different occasions. Students in the most recent class read drafts of many of the chapters contained in the final book. Like the book, that course is designed around a semester-long ethnographic research project. Students are expected to choose their own topics and devote considerable time to the project throughout the course of the semester. The class considers the nuts and bolts of ethnographic methods, the strength and limitations of ethnography, and the writing process. There is a strong commitment to the idea of ethnography as writing. Work by the student and the instructor is presented and critiqued in a workshop format that requires the students to write and revise throughout the process. This book reflects that commitment to ethnography as writing intensive. While the ultimate focus is on producing a final written ethnography, this book focuses also on the processual writing that happens in the course of writing from start to finish. Ethnographers write to record information, and they write as a way of analyzing the data they collect. If they are aware of the centrality of writing to the process, they can use writing to their best advantage as researchers and analysts.

This book generally assumes that the final ethnography will be a written ethnography. Many of the principles and methods discussed here also apply to ethnographic film and to other media, but writing ethnography includes its own unique opportunities and challenges, and these are the focus of this book.

Much of the content in the book is based directly or indirectly on my teaching experiences in a number of classes that involve ethnography. From students in Introduction to Anthropology who write a short ethnography to honors students who are writing ethnographic theses of a hundred pages or more, some of the concerns and questions are strikingly similar. The text aims to address as many of these concerns and questions as possible and tries not to make unwarranted assumptions about knowledge or experience.

ORGANIZATION OF THIS BOOK

The book is basically organized chronologically, starting with choosing a research topic and developing research design, then proceeding to consider the practice of ethnography in terms of note taking and specific methods, and finishing with a focus on the writing process that produces a final ethnography. Almost all ethnographies follow this basic progression in one form or another. The chapter on analyzing along the way, though, shows that data collection and analysis should be linked rather than separated. Therefore, embedded in the organization and thoughts about chronology you will find an important idea about connections between different stages of research.

The chronological model for the text can be expanded or contracted and even revised as your situation requires. When or how often you pause to review your progress during the course of your research will depend in part on how long your project lasts. Chapter Eight may apply to the third week of ethnographic research or the third month or both. You may decide to read the chapter on interviews or mapping before you read the chapter on participant-observation if you know that one of the methods is particularly important or pressing for your project. The chapters are presented in this order to suit what is most likely to occur first in the most cases, but many projects will follow a slightly different model. You should make the text your own as you seek the parts that are most helpful for your ethnographic research.

NOTE TO STUDENTS

Ethnographic research should be an exciting opportunity. It takes you out of the library and the laboratory and into the social worlds around you. This project is your chance to learn from others and to gain knowledge about something in the real world about which you have always wondered. This book is designed to guide you step-by-step through that process. This research will probably be different from the research you have done for other classes. Make the most of the opportunity, and make the research process your own. You are the researcher and the research instrument. If you are prepared to think openly and learn from your neighbors and your fellow human beings, you are prepared to start your ethnographic project.

ACKNOWLEDGMENTS

My work on this book and my approach to ethnography are a result of many varied influences. I have benefited immeasurably from assistance and kindness from many people in the course of my career and my ethnographic endeavors. I will never be able to repay all of my debts, but I wish to thank many of the people that have helped me at different points.

I am thankful to Jossey-Bass for the opportunity to write this book and support in the relatively painless process. I am glad that Andy Pasternack approached me with the idea to write this book, and I have enjoyed working with Seth Schwartz, Kelsey McGee, and others in seeing this book to completion.

My first experience doing ethnography of a sort came when I went to live in Argentina in 1989. The Jerez family took me in as one of their own and taught me about life and culture in northern Argentina. They had incredible patience as they taught me Spanish and helped me through a long learning process. I will be forever thankful for their openness and kindness. They probably don't realize it, but they helped kindle my love for studying culture firsthand before I even knew what the word ethnography meant. Thank you, Susana, Periquín, César, Suzy, Martín, Valeria, Javier, Ernesto, Carla, Leandra, and Gastón. I remember the learning experiences with fondness and cherish the time that I got to spend with all of you. My classmates, teachers, and friends in Argentina were equally generous in their giving spirit and their willingness to teach me. My thanks to them all.

Matt Samson was the first person to introduce me to the words and worlds of anthropology and ethnography. He took me to Mexico and Cuba and encouraged me to learn and to engage culture in all its complexity. I did not fully appreciate it at the time, but I do now. Ever since, he has been a wonderful friend, supporter, and colleague. Thank you, Matt, for the trips, the guidance, and the conversations.

Kenyon College was a wonderful place to study anthropology as an undergraduate. I had excellent teachers in Rita Kipp, Ed Schortmann, Pat Urban, Nick Kardulias, and Ken Smail. Dave Suggs was and is an invaluable mentor. From our first conversation on the porch, I knew that Dave was somebody with whom I shared a common intellectual pursuit. I continue to be amazed at the way he guided and supported me while also allowing me to develop my own ideas and convictions about the discipline. I continue to treasure the times when our paths cross.

During my time at the University of Michigan, I was surrounded by people who constantly engaged me in interesting conversations about anthropology and ethnography. I learned so much from my classmates and colleagues, including Veve Lele, Jeff Jurgens, Jen Tilton, Erica Lehrer, Meghan Callaghan, Lourdes Gutierrez, Liz de la

Portilla, Rochelle Davis, Bill Parkinson, and Lars Fogelin. As a graduate student instructor for Holly Peters-Golden, I gained a deep appreciation for ways that undergraduate students can study and learn ethnography with a keen interest. In a class on ethnographic writing with Ruth Behar, I was introduced to the craft of writing ethnography and the importance of detail and skill in communicating what emerges through the ethnographic process. Janet Hart taught me to appreciate the importance of words, narratives, and conversations in ethnography. Kelly Askew and Nancy Rose Hunt both offered helpful feedback on my own ethnographic work that helped me to become a more effective ethnographer and teacher. Conrad Kottak was my guide and mentor throughout my time in graduate school, and he helped me to understand the importance of using ethnography to effectively communicate information and insights concerning the world around us. Rackham, the Department of Anthropology, and the Center for Afroamerican and African Studies at the University of Michigan provided important support that allowed me to do my own ethnography.

The bulk of my own ethnographic work has taken place in Tanzania. There are so many people who have assisted me throughout these endeavors. Without their assistance, I would not be able to speak about ethnography from a firsthand perspective, and I would not be in a position to write this book. I am always amazed by Tanzanians' willingness to share so much of their thoughts, words, and lives with me. I have a deep appreciation and affection for Tanzania as a place and for Tanzanians. I thank all the government workers who helped me, from the national offices that provided me with research clearance and immigration permits to local government offices. So many others have helped me and opened their homes and lives to me at different points. Even though I cannot name you all here, please know that I deeply appreciate your kindness. You were wonderful teachers, hosts, and friends. The Ndumbaro and Nyoni families have provided homes and companionship on too many occasions to count. I will never be able to repay fully your generosity. I will be forever thankful and treasure the ways that you have allowed me to become a part of your families.

When I began looking for a faculty position, I was very lucky to find an opportunity at Millsaps College. I have been blessed with wonderful colleagues, engaged students, and a life partner. George Bey, Mike Galaty, and Ming Tsui have provided exemplary models as undergraduate teachers and the sort of collegiality that makes work fun. The college has provided me with support to pursue my ongoing ethnographic research and the sabbatical during which most of this book was written. My students at Millsaps have taught me many things. I have a better understanding of ethnography from their comments and questions inside and outside of the classroom. Some of my most rewarding teaching experiences come when I guide students through their own research projects. I would not have been able to write this book without the chance to work with students like Chelsi West, Doc Billingsley, Ellen Beilmann, Khyati Gupta, Maggie Morgan, Brian Wallace, Caroline Ficara, Hannah Page, Jon-Mark Olivier, Matt Casteel, Jane Fuller, Mary Mitchell Williams, and many others. You may not always realize it, but working with you pushes me to new thoughts and new questions. I hope that you can see some of our learning experiences contained in this book.

Ben McNair provided bibliographic assistance for this book as a student worker in the department. Erin Jordan has been a wonderful editorial assistant in the process. Her willingness to help with the minutiae of putting a manuscript together has helped keep me sane during the process, and she has also offered cogent critique and useful suggestions along the way. I am truly lucky to have the chance to work with so many wonderful students. The line between student and colleague can be very fuzzy, and that is a good thing.

My family is a constant source of support. My mother, Eloise, and my father, Ken, have always been supportive of my goals and my dreams. Thirty years ago, they almost certainly did not envision their son as an ethnographer working in East Africa, but their support has been unflagging. They are both scholars in their own right and they have been wonderful models for me as I have pursued my own path. My sister, Kathryn, is the real educator in the family. I always find her deep commitment to teaching high school social studies (and to her soccer teams) to be an inspiration. I hope I can approach the sort of meaningful difference in the lives of my students that she makes in the lives of her students. Kathryn and my parents have always helped me find meaning and clarity, even when it did not seem obvious to me.

My biggest thank-you has to go to my wife, Sandra. When we married in 2004, I gained a best friend and someone who inspires me. Her kindness and generosity make me a better person. Her love for making art makes me want to fulfill my own dreams as an anthropologist and an ethnographer. A good portion of this book was written while I was sitting in the printmaking studio working alongside her. Sandra, I cherish your love and your companionship more than I can explain.

October 2009
Jackson, Mississippi

THE AUTHOR

Julian M. Murchison is associate professor of anthropology at Millsaps College in Jackson, Mississippi. He received a BA in anthropology from Kenyon College and MA and PhD degrees in anthropology from the University of Michigan. As a cultural anthropologist, he has extensive ethnographic experience working in Tanzania. After studying at the University of Dar es Salaam as an undergraduate in 1993–94, he has returned regularly to pursue ethnographic research in Tanzania. His work has focused on the intersections of health and religion in southern Tanzania. Many of his presentations and publications have focused on topics including religious identity, spirit possession, HIV/AIDS, and religious and medical pluralism. Recently his thinking and writing have also focused on the nature of fieldwork experiences and an urban law firm as an ethnographic setting. His teaching experiences at Millsaps have taught him the value of ethnography as a learning tool and convinced him of the ability of committed students to conduct significant ethnographic research.

To Sandra, my inspiration and the love of my life

PART

1

THE WHY AND WHAT OF ETHNOGRAPHY

CHAPTER

1

WHAT IS ETHNOGRAPHY?

LEARNING OBJECTIVES

- Define ethnography
- Explain the basic history of ethnography
- Track trends in contemporary ethnography
- Explore the implications of ethnography as firsthand research
- Examine the ethnographer's role as research instrument
- Consider collaboration as the foundation for ethnographic research

ETHNOGRAPHY: THE ENGAGED, FIRSTHAND STUDY OF SOCIETY AND CULTURE IN ACTION

Ethnography is a **research strategy** that allows researchers to explore and examine the cultures and societies that are a fundamental part of the human experience. Unlike many other scientific research strategies, the ethnographer as researcher is not typically a detached or uninvolved **observer**. The ethnographer collects data and gains insight through *firsthand* involvement with **research subjects** or **informants**. With few exceptions, the ethnographer conducts research by interacting with other human beings that are part of the study; this interaction takes many forms, from conversations and interviews to shared ritual and emotional experiences.

From the standpoint of ethnography, the only plausible way to study social and cultural phenomena is to study them *in action*. The complexity of human lives and social interaction cannot be reduced to a sterile laboratory experiment with the strict control of variables characteristic of a scientific experiment. Instead, ethnography aims to study life outside of a controlled environment. As a result, the objects of study are sometimes hard to identify and always subject to change as the result of innovation, conflict, and many other factors. Ethnographers employ a number of different research techniques and methods in a complex research strategy that matches the complexity of their objects of study.

Today, researchers employ ethnography as a research strategy in a number of disciplines, including anthropology, sociology, and education, and as a practical research strategy in marketing, management, and public policy arenas. This breadth of use indicates that the utility of the approach has become apparent in many different circumstances where better understanding of social and cultural dynamics is desirable. Ethnographic research encompasses a number of different research **methods** and **techniques**; this text will introduce many of these techniques and methods and will explain how to design and to carry out effective research that applies these techniques and methods in appropriate situations.

A BRIEF HISTORY

Ethnography originally developed as a research strategy in academic circles, mainly within the discipline of anthropology. Therefore, anthropology provides many of the most famous early ethnographers and many "classic" ethnographies. Names like Bronislaw Malinowski, E. E. Evans-Pritchard, Margaret Mead, and Ruth Benedict, along with ethnographic subjects like the Trobriand Islanders, the Nuer, the island of Samoa, and the nation of Japan are important markers of ethnography's early history. These ethnographers and their works have given us a number of important texts and some films that are important resources for students of ethnography. Before you begin planning to carry out your own research, you should become familiar with the history of ethnography. This section will provide a very brief discussion of that history, but it is not a substitute for exploring ethnographies and their history more deeply. A good ethnography makes for a good read, and reading the work of others broadens the ethnographer's awareness of the possibilities for ethnography as a research strategy. Anthropology and ethnography arose at the end of the nineteenth century and the beginning of the twentieth century in the context of a particular set of historical circumstances that influenced early ethnographic work. These circumstances included European imperialism, American expansionist tendencies, and dominant understandings of race, ethnicity, and gender that usually placed white males in positions of privilege and power and placed others in marginalized or colonized positions of oppression and subordination. Ethnography can offer important insight into situations of suffering and disempowerment, and anthropology has a long history of using ethnography to expose human systems that are taken for granted and to offer implicit or explicit critiques of dominant systems and understandings. Nevertheless, much of early anthropology and ethnography intentionally or unintentionally supported existing systems and structures of power.

Early ethnography consisted mostly of white male ethnographers going from academic and political centers in the United States and Europe to study in geographically distant locales among socially marginalized groups. (There are many exceptions to this general statement: Margaret Mead, Zora Neale Hurston, and many other early ethnographers were not white males.) In some cases, their research projects were directly connected to political endeavors like colonialism—for instance, Evans-Pritchard's work among the Nuer (Evans Pritchard 1940). The byproduct of research in these circumstances was a research situation in which clear foreigners arrived to study the "Other." This dynamic has raised questions about the potential for mutual understanding, the importance of language, the role of intermediaries, and, perhaps most important, the role of power—political, economic, and social—in the research context. Because of the desire to present authoritative accounts that appeared to be suitably objective and scientific and for a variety of other reasons, many of these questions and concerns were not adequately addressed at the time. As a result, at least some of the potential for bias and the potential for multiple perspectives was ignored or left unexamined during an important part of the early history of ethnography.

The ethnographies that appeared in this context tended to present holistic accounts of particular groups of people—for instance, the Nuer (Evans-Pritchard 1940), the Trobriand Islanders (Malinowski 1922), and the Japanese (Benedict 1946)—that appeared to be well defined and relatively homogeneous. Most of these ethnographies provided definitive information about these groups; for example, the reader of Evans-Pritchard's ethnography learns that the Nuer have a segmentary lineage organization, and Benedict identifies the Japanese national character as Apollonian. In a time when cultural difference was the subject of much discussion, consternation, and imagination, these texts helped to establish a sense of cultural essence that defined groups of people. The reader of these texts comes away with the sense that the essence has been discovered and recorded for posterity. This tendency to essentialize cultural groups stemmed at least in part from understandings of nationalism and cultural identity that drew upon essential characteristics and in many cases supported claims of cultural superiority and racism. Understandings of variation and conflict within groups as well as the difficulty in defining clear boundaries came to the fore only in later years.

Because of the desire to define and to describe the group under study, the most common approach to ethnography involved collecting and presenting comprehensive, wide-ranging accounts. Depending on theoretical orientations, these accounts sometimes looked like a catalog or list of cultural traits and sometimes appeared as a report of how the individual pieces worked together to form a coherent whole. Whichever style of presentation was adopted, the ethnographic data collected typically included information about topics like economics, politics, religion, rituals, kinship, and material culture. The ethnographer expected to collect information about everything pertaining to the culture under study. In many ways, these ethnographies are a wonderful testament to the industriousness of these early ethnographers as researchers, but they also sometimes cover up a lack of depth of knowledge and present an ethnographic picture that is partial or mistaken.

Many of these early ethnographies do not address the question of research methods or do so only in a very cursory manner. In other words, many of these ethnographers were not inclined to write about *how* they carried out their research. Some of this reluctance may have stemmed from an uncertainty about techniques and methods and a concern about claims to authority arising from experience-based research that did not readily meet some of the scientific conventions of the time. Still, a number of common understandings and practices emerged out of this early ethnographic work:

1. Starting with Malinowski's (1922) work on the Trobriand Islanders, there was general acknowledgment that ethnography required a lengthy stay in the field— usually a year or longer.

2. There was an increasing recognition of the importance of learning and working in local languages.

3. There was a focus on kinship as the fundamental building block of culture and the construction of kinship charts.

4. It was generally accepted that the researcher should try to become as much a part of the group being studied as possible to gain the insiders' perspective.

Many of these understandings stem from the fact that the researchers were traveling (usually long distances) to study groups that they were not a part of and with whom they therefore did not share a language or prior cultural understandings. These assumptions continue to underlie much of the current understanding of ethnography, though they have been the subject of significant critique as ethnography has evolved as a research strategy and been applied in different circumstances.

Perhaps most notably, this early mode of ethnography meant ignoring a lot of the complexity of human lives and groups. It seemed to assume that groups were well defined and that the members of those groups generally behaved and thought in the same way. Differences between individuals and between groups defined by age and gender were most often ignored or downplayed. In many cases, an individual or small group came to represent the collective whole without proper consideration for how justified that representation was. The ethnographer often assumed that one member of a group—an elder male, for instance—could speak for everyone without questioning how that person's particular social position (and personality) would influence his thoughts, behavior, and interactions with the ethnographer. The ethnographer usually had an easier time **gaining access** and **building rapport** with certain members of a community, but this fact was seldom acknowledged. In fact, the predominance of male researchers almost certainly produced androcentric ethnographic accounts in the initial decades of ethnography. Other forms and sources of bias have also come to light.

The context of ethnography's emergence as a research strategy also meant that it was associated with the study of relatively isolated, small-scale, rural communities. The focus on these sorts of communities stemmed from anthropology's fascination with cultural difference, geographic distance, and a spirit of exoticism, but it also plugged into assumptions that the ethnographer was supposed to be studying everything in the research setting. The ethnographer could at least hope to know everybody and to keep track of events in a village of two hundred people; that goal seemed to become more unreasonable the larger the group under study.

In short, classic ethnography most often involved researchers traveling long distances to study supposedly isolated groups in small communities. (In *Coming of Age in Samoa*, 1928, Margaret Mead offers very little discussion of her research methods or techniques, but she does explain her choice of Samoa as a field site. She suggests that finding a "simple" or "primitive" field site is the next best thing to a scientific experiment. Much of early ethnography was based on assumptions about simplicity or primitiveness and the idea that these sites would offer an easier way to study human society and culture. These ideas and assumptions were fundamentally ethnocentric and have been discarded in contemporary ethnography.) Usually, the ethnographer had little prior knowledge of the group under study, and much of the early research involved learning a language, befriending a local intermediary or informant, observing and participating whenever possible, and employing research techniques like **household surveys, mapping,** and **kinship charts** that were well suited to use by an outsider researcher with limited understandings of languages and local cultural practices. Over time, the underlying approach assumed that the ethnographer's increased familiarity with the language, customs, and individuals would allow the researcher to gain more of an **insider's perspective** and a deeper understanding of behavior and thought. According to Malinowski (1922), this should be the primary goal of ethnography. This need for familiarity and the acquisition of detailed knowledge is one of the main reasons why a lengthy research project became the norm; it took time for the ethnographer to become an effective **participant-observer**.

HOW ETHNOGRAPHY HAS CHANGED: DOING CONTEMPORARY ETHNOGRAPHY

From the beginning, there were exceptions to these general trends in ethnography. For instance, Zora Neale Hurston worked in the southern United States and presented her ethnographic findings in a nontraditional format in the early 1900s (Hurston 1990a, 1990b). Close examination reveals a rich history of ethnographers experimenting with research strategies, research sites, and styles of presentation. This experimentation and variation almost certainly stems from ethnographers' awareness of the tremendous variation in their research subjects and circumstances and the challenge of studying complex social and cultural phenomena in action. Nevertheless, a sustained critique that questioned many of the underlying assumptions of "classical" ethnography did not emerge until later in the twentieth century. This critique appeared as researchers and others began to rethink when and how ethnography was a useful research tool. They began to question whether ethnographers could employ their methods in situations other than small, rural communities. Critics of classical ethnography also asked penetrating questions about ethnography's reliance on models that too often tended to assume homogeneity and stasis. The critique also focused on whether ethnography could and should make claims to **objectivity**. In many cases, the critics argued that ethnographers needed to address some fundamental problems in terms of **perspective** and **bias**, as well as their ethical obligations to the people with whom they worked.

Many of the questions and issues raised within these criticisms have been the subject of vigorous debate. Some have argued that ethnography is an inherently flawed research strategy. Others have called for radically rethinking ethnography, both as a research strategy and a means of presenting information and analysis. These debates have had a tremendous effect on the pursuit of ethnography and have produced significant variety under the umbrella of ethnography. The remainder of this section highlights the most significant and useful ways that this critique and experimentation have helped to shape ethnography in contemporary practice.

In the second and third decades of the twentieth century, the Chicago School adapted ethnography to the study of American communities, especially the city of Chicago. This work produced important ethnographic findings and helped to highlight ethnography's utility in different research circumstances and sites. Most notably, these ethnographic projects demonstrated that researchers could effectively use ethnography in urban and industrialized research settings. This shift made it more acceptable to do ethnography locally. In many cases, ethnography allowed the researchers to study particular groups and topics that were not readily researched using more traditional sociological research methods, like surveys. For instance, homeless populations are notoriously underrepresented in survey data because of the difficulty in identifying them and their wariness of surveillance and intervention. An ethnographic research approach has allowed researchers to understand better the behaviors, thoughts, experiences, and extent of homeless populations. Nels Anderson's *The Hobo: The Sociology of the Homeless Man* (1923) is a classic example from the early years of the Chicago School, and Mitchell Duneier's

CASE STUDY

The Ethnographer as Stripper

Strip clubs may not be the first image of an ethnographer's field site that comes to mind, and the idea of becoming a stripper in order to conduct research may be surprising to some, but Katherine Frank describes her ethnographic research as a stripper in six different strip clubs in *G-Strings and Sympathy* (Frank 2002). Her ethnographic work offers insight into the public performances of (primarily male) sexual desire and the importance of observation as a primary element of these experiences for the men who frequent strip clubs. In discussing her research experiences, Frank refers to her role as "observing the observers" (2002, 1). Feminist understandings inspire Frank's research strategies, and the choice to conduct participant-observation as a stripper allows her to engage questions of male desire in particularly interesting ways.

Frank's work is an excellent example of contemporary ethnography for a number of reasons. Her choice of strip clubs in a southern city in the United States shows the applicability of ethnography as a research strategy to an urban environment that is not necessarily geographically or socially distant from the ethnographer's origins. Because she is a female ethnographer studying mostly male patrons of strip clubs, the variety of perspectives and issues of power and gender occupy a prominent place for Frank. She assumes that the different actors involved in these strip clubs operate with a wide range of understandings and perspectives and attempts to use her ethnography to present the intricate structures and layers of erotic desire and power that she encountered in her field sites.

Sidewalk (1999) is an excellent recent example of the work that comes from this legacy. Other examples of sociological use of ethnography in urban settings include William Whyte's *Street Corner Society* (1943) and Jay MacLeod's *Ain't No Makin' It* (1995).

The Chicago School's embrace of ethnography as a research strategy helped make ethnography a tool that sociologists began to utilize more and more. Today one finds exciting ethnographic work in rural and urban settings across the globe coming from the disciplines of both anthropology and sociology. Ethnography no longer implies traveling to remote villages, and there is increased recognition that cultural and social phenomena are ripe for ethnographic study everywhere we find humans.

In addition to opening ethnography for use by sociologists and in urban and industrialized settings, ethnographers have also revisited the classic ethnographies and the associated field sites in the intervening years. The result has been a host of questions about the way those ethnographies were researched and the findings they presented. In some cases, there have been vehement critiques of the ethnographies and their claims.

Derek Freeman's critique of Margaret Mead's work in Samoa is perhaps the most virulent and famous of these critiques (Freeman 1983). Freeman claims that Mead was misled by her informants and therefore provided a flawed ethnographic picture of life for adolescent girls in Samoa. Freeman was able to talk to some of Mead's informants years later and obtained an understanding that seems very different from Mead's original version. In fact, Freeman's work raises a lot of questions about how informants' perspectives and understandings may change over time and how interactions with different researchers (in this case, a man or a woman) may influence the information gleaned through ethnography. Mead's work in Samoa remains an important early ethnographic source, but students of ethnography are now much more aware of the contestability of ethnographic data and the need to evaluate critically the sources of data and the methods of data collection as well as the role of the ethnographer.

Along similar lines, several decades after Malinowski's work in the Trobriand Islands, Annette Weiner returned for a follow-up study. Her ethnography *Women of Value, Men of Renown* (Weiner 1976) highlights the role of women in everyday economic activities and shows that Malinowski's famous account of the kula ring as an elaborate system of symbolic exchange provides only a partial understanding of economics and exchange in the Trobriand Islands. Malinowski's rather andocentric presentation stemmed from his focus on men and their activities. He did not pay proper attention to the important activities of women, and his authoritative ethnography failed to take full account of gender and women's roles. Many early ethnographies demonstrated similar androcentric tendencies. As more female ethnographers have conducted research and all ethnographers have paid increased attention to gender dynamics within groups and communities, some of these original shortcomings have been addressed and the character of ethnography has changed. Now ethnographers pay much closer attention to the role that gender plays in their research and the role the ethnographer's own gender identity plays.

The work by Weiner, Freeman, and others has helped ethnographers understand the importance of considering the multiple perspectives and subject positions that will almost certainly be encountered in the course of any ethnographic research. Ethnographers are much more circumspect in their claims to speak for collective groups, especially groups like "*the* Trobriand Islanders" and "*the* Nuer." Ethnographers seek to determine the extent to which individuals and groups share common behavior and thought. The result is a new type of ethnography that is much more attentive to internal divisions and different perspectives; often these ethnographies are more focused in terms of the groups and topics that they seek to examine than the earlier, more holistic ethnographies that sought to describe all aspects of the larger whole.

Along these lines, Sharon Hutchinson's *Nuer Dilemmas* (1996) is a fascinating, though often distressing, account of the impact of civil war and other major economic, political, and religious changes among the Nuer in Sudan. In many ways, her ethnography is an important update of the work of Evans-Pritchard and others who have done ethnographic work among the Nuer. She shows how the cattle that Evans-Pritchard recognized as essential to Nuer understandings remain important but have had to be reconceptualized in new ways to meet changing circumstances; for instance, the Nuer now distinguish between the cattle of money and the cattle of marriage.

In many ways, Evans-Pritchard's classic account of the Nuer presented them as a timeless, static entity, and many other classic ethnographies adapted a similarly static approach or perspective. Ethnographies like Hutchinson's have illuminated the fact that cultural and social phenomena are constantly subject to change. *Cultures and societies are dynamic.* With increasing recognition of these dynamic qualities, ethnographies have to attempt to engage and reflect the fundamental realities of change and variation within cultures and societies. Recognition of the dynamic processes being studied has entailed rethinking ethnography as a research strategy and a style of presentation. (In his 1920 essay on the "The Methods of Ethnology," Franz Boas clearly made the case for human societies' dynamism and the need to study history and change. Thus, recognition of this fact arose early in the history of anthropology and ethnography, but it did not become central to general practice until later.)

Ethnographers now have to think about how to recognize and analyze change. In many cases, change itself becomes the research subject. With the central importance of change has come an increasing awareness of the role of history. Many recent ethnographies incorporate considerable historical components, and many ethnographers work regularly with both historical documents and oral histories as part of their research designs.

Ethnographers have also changed their styles of writing and presentation to reflect these shifts in awareness. Most ethnographers today avoid presenting timeless accounts by including historical sections or chapters and using verb tenses to show what has happened recently, what happened in the past, and what happens continuously, as well as pursuing explicit consideration of both long-term and short-term changes. These shifts in the field of ethnography have positioned it as a research strategy that provides important insight through historical comparison and through close firsthand examination of change in action.

Despite these changes and these challenges, many of the early ideas about ethnography have proved to be enduring. Ethnographers still tend to commit to conducting research over rather lengthy periods of time; they still tend to pay close attention to language and its methodological importance; and they still tend to be interested in studying the wide range of cultural and social features of human life and interaction. Ethnography is particularly well suited for researching the connections and interactions between different elements of society and culture (for instance, between economics and religion or politics and gender). In many ways, this ability to uncover and analyze these connections and interactions can be seen in the all-encompassing early ethnographies, but contemporary ethnography now begins from a foundation that recognizes and foregrounds dynamic processes, variation and variability, and the need to consider the different perspectives and biases that may influence the research. As a result, many researchers today utilize ethnography as a primary research strategy to address a wide range of questions.

ETHNOGRAPHY AS FIRSTHAND RESEARCH

From the beginning, starting with the work of Malinowski and others, ethnography has involved a commitment to "**being there**" to conduct research. (The general concept of being there is so pervasive in ethnography that at least two recent books on the subject have used the phrase as a title: Bradburd's *Being There: The Necessity of Fieldwork*, 1998, and Watson's *Being There: Fieldwork in Anthropology*, 1999. See Sluka and Robben 2007 for a discussion of this concept as well.) By moving to their field sites to conduct their fieldwork, ethnographers signaled the importance of their direct connection with the research site and the research subjects. Following Malinowski's lead, these early ethnographers typically went to live in the field for a year or longer, and much of their research data came directly from experiences living in the community under study. Ethnographies are full of accounts of daily life in different communities, as well as stories of ethnographers' experiences of integration into these communities that are often quite humorous.

The underlying assumption in ethnography's commitment to being there is an assumption that certain types of information are only obtainable through firsthand research. A researcher can obtain a great deal of information about a particular place or group of people without engaging in ethnography. For instance, a survey instrument can provide information about demographics, economic activities, political opinions, and many other things. In order to yield useful data, a survey has to be well designed and administered appropriately, but it can often be carried out rather quickly and in some instances can even be conducted at a distance using telephones, mail, or the Internet.

Other disciplines that study human beings, especially psychology, occasionally use detached observation as a research technique. In this approach, the researcher is usually removed or detached (the stereotypical example is observation through glass or a video lens). Often the intent is to make sure that the researcher does not influence the situation and variables under study. Projects like these allow researchers to discover how people respond to certain stimuli, how they make decisions and solve problems, and how they interact in certain circumstances. In controlled experimental situations, the data produced can be very powerful in terms of revealing key variables and parameters for human behavior.

Ethnography, on the other hand, seeks to discover and record different types of information that are not readily obtainable through relatively detached approaches like surveys and observations. In many cases, surveys ask questions and use categories that originate in the surveyors' own cultural understandings or assumptions. Ethnography allows the researcher to discover and analyze the categories and questions that are most relevant for the people being studied and participating in the research. One of the strengths of ethnography as a research strategy is its ability to illuminate locally relevant understandings and ways of operating. In many ethnographies, these local modes of thought and behavior are the primary focus.

Ethnography also allows the researcher to observe and to *experience* events, behaviors, interactions, and conversations that are the manifestations of society and culture in action. The controlled environments of laboratory experiments are absent; ethnography is about the messiness of human lives. This means the ethnographer has to cede a lot of control over the research situation, but it also means ethnography offers the opportunity to study real-life human behavior and to gain a unique understanding of the context and thought that informs such behavior. Ethnography allows the researcher to examine how people's actions compare to what they say about their actions in ideal situations and their thoughts or opinions on particular topics. In many cases, actions and behaviors in particular situations differ significantly from those observed or predicted by other research strategies. In situations like this, important research questions emerge as researchers try to account for apparent discrepancies. In some cases, this involves turning attention to variables or questions that did not seem relevant initially.

In the course of doing this sort of engaged, firsthand research, the ethnographer becomes a participant-observer. The term *participant-observer* emphasizes the different position and role of the ethnographer in comparison to researchers employing more detached research strategies. Detailed consideration of participant-observation as a research method appears in Chapter Six; here it is important to note that this is a distinct approach to research on the part of the ethnographer. It moves beyond observing from afar or behind the glass and moves the researcher directly into the research context as a participant. Ethnography is able to provide insight into a number of different things precisely because of this unique position. It is a powerful research strategy, but this unique approach also carries with it particular issues and questions.

The ethnographer's position in the research venue raises vexing questions about objectivity—both whether it is achievable and whether it should be the goal of ethnography; **replicability**—whether another researcher can duplicate an ethnographer's research; and **ethics**—questions about the influence the ethnographer has on the people and events being studied. All these questions are important topics for consideration both in designing and conducting the research plan. Ethnographers can and do take different stances on these topics. In this text, the goal is to provide warnings about potential problems and concerns that can and should be avoided. The goal is also to allow you to explore the questions that arise and to implement strategies that make the most sense for you and your research goals. These questions and concerns do not imply that ethnography is fundamentally flawed. Its engaged nature means that it is both very powerful and potentially treacherous.

ETHNOGRAPHER AS RESEARCH INSTRUMENT

Because of the ethnographer's unique position as participant-observer, the ethnographer becomes the primary **research instrument** through which information is collected and recorded. Whereas researchers in other disciplines use instruments like micrometers, pipettes, and mass spectrometers to collect data for their research, you make yourself the research instrument. The ethnographer's five senses become the

Ethnographic Field Sites or "The Field"

The original practice of traveling to remote sites to conduct ethnographic research has given way to a much more varied collection of **field sites**, which can range from the local neighborhood or school to the corporate boardroom to a small village in the rainforest to cyberspace. All these locations are legitimate sites of research that offer exciting opportunities and unique challenges. In ethnographic circles, it became commonplace to talk about "the field" as a place that existed separate from the researcher's personal home or academic circles. That idea has been rightfully criticized in terms of its tendency to distance and exoticize the objects of study in relationship to researchers and centers of knowledge. This critique has also raised questions about whether people perceive and act differently in "the field" compared to other human environments that they inhabit. Finally, it has raised questions about the whole idea of traveling or moving into the field and assumptions about the researcher's role as an outsider; more recently there have been a number of important calls for "insider ethnography," with the ethnographer studying a cultural or social unit of which he is already a part.

Talking about "the field" in ethnography is no longer as easy to do as it once was. In a way, the field is everywhere and nowhere at the same time. This text refers to *field sites* as locations for doing research but avoids referring to the field as a monolithic place of research. You should evaluate carefully your relationship to the field site(s) in which you choose to conduct research. Why are you choosing a particular field site for research? Does it have a particular significance for you? Are you an outsider who needs to establish rapport and acquire basic local knowledge? Are you an insider who needs to investigate and question things that you have learned to take for granted? What other issues of perspective and bias might influence your ability to do research in a particular field site? Asking yourself these types of questions will help you build awareness of the field site and your relationship to it as a researcher. Reflecting critically on these ideas will help you avoid making assumptions about field sites that might hamper or limit your ability to conduct effective research.

principal avenue for collection information. For example, the ethnographer might collect information by observing behavior, listening to conversations or interviews, touching textiles and other forms of material culture, tasting local cuisines, and paying close attention to the smells that accompany the primary activities in a given space. You need to record what you perceive and note as relevant. Therefore, you have a lot of responsibility for evaluating and recording information. In many cases, the ethnographer cannot determine which pieces of information will be most valuable until well after they have been recorded.

In much the same way that other research instruments must be calibrated to ensure their accuracy, the ethnographer has to be trained to collect appropriate and relevant data. Subsequent chapters will provide more detailed guidance on particular ethnographic techniques and the art of ethnographic note taking. The ethnographer should always strive to collect as much detailed information as possible while keeping in mind the specific research topic or question. Notes should be extensive and descriptive. In the course of their training, ethnographers have to learn to pay close attention and to notice details. The power of concentration required often means that ethnography can be draining physically, mentally, and emotionally. Like other instruments, sometimes you need time to download information and recharge your batteries, so to speak. These practical concerns are an important consideration when designing a research plan. Doing research is important, but so are the recording, collection, and analysis of information from these research experiences.

The ethnographer's role as research instrument again raises questions of objectivity, **replicability**, and **validity** in the language of scientific research. The information that ethnographers seek and collect is often very personal and occasionally idiosyncratic, but there are ways to counterbalance those types of information with other techniques and to draw on both the power of personal experiences that constitute participation and the more objective forms of data that might be collected through observation. One way to address some of these questions is by comparing results with those of others working on similar projects. Some ethnographers choose to work in teams so that they can pool and compare results from different researchers in similar contexts. Other researchers try to present the raw ethnographic data that they have collected for others to study and analyze. This approach attempts to make the researcher as transparent a research instrument as possible. Still, some ethnographers are more comfortable talking about the "information" they collect and analyze, as opposed to suggesting they are relying on the sort of objective "data" that might be gained through different research methods. In this text, the words *data* and *information* are mostly used interchangeably, but the reader should keep in mind that a researcher's goals or assumptions are often embedded in the words she uses to talk about her research.

COLLABORATION AS RESEARCH MODEL: ETHNOGRAPHER AS STUDENT

In order to be an effective researcher, you have to place yourself in a position to learn from others. The goal of ethnography is to gain insight into cultural and social behavior as well as the cultural understandings and underlying thought processes that produce behavior. A well-trained ethnographer will be prepared to collect different types of information with different techniques. Some of these techniques, like mapping, may depend less on significant input from informants, but all ethnography ultimately depends crucially on the cooperation and input of others.

The people being studied by the ethnographer possess the knowledge and information that the ethnographer seeks to acquire and to record. Therefore, while you may have significant resources and occupy a position of relative social power or privilege in many cases, in the end you must place yourself in a dependent position in the course of research. In a very real way, the ethnographer is a student, and the informants are the teachers (see Spradley and McCurdy 2008). There are situations when you may become teacher or instructor, but you should be prepared to embrace the position of student. This is often a difficult stance for well-educated researchers to adopt, but it helps to highlight the value of the knowledge and information that others possess and that you are attempting to access.

The **ethnographer's role as student** is most obvious in situations when you enter your field site as an outsider without knowledge of the local language and local customs. In cases like these, ethnographers often commit serious faux pas and have to learn from their mistakes. However, even insiders or ethnographers with a strong understanding of language and custom should still seek to learn as students. Placing yourself in this position will allow you to confront your own assumptions by listening to and learning from the experts—your informants. One of the most powerful lessons of ethnography is that the researcher can learn from anyone; research design then often becomes a plan for learning from the appropriate representatives and experts. Who these people are will depend on what you are studying and what you aim to learn.

For a long time, ethnographers have tended to use the term **informant** to refer to the people they learn from and study. The use of this term is important because it distinguishes the research relationship in ethnography from the relationships that accompany other research strategies. The relationship between ethnographer and informant is typically different from that between experimenter and subject or surveyor and respondent. Compared to the terms *subjects* and *respondents*, the term *informants* implies that these individuals play a more active role in guiding and shaping the research process as teachers. The relationship is often much more personal and typically endures for longer periods of time than these other research relationships. Again, much of the power in ethnography as a research strategy originates in this unique research relationship.

Nevertheless, the term *informant* raises concern for a number of ethnographers. Critique of the term has been part of the development of contemporary ethnography mentioned earlier. Critics have pointed out that the word *informant* carries connotations that make it very similar to the idea of an informer who aids the government or the police. These similarities are troubling both in what they suggest about how research might be used against informants or other members of their communities and in the implication that these individuals are being used by representatives of structures of power as a means to an end that may not be in their best interests. In some instances ethnography has been used by governments and others in positions of power to aid in subjecting people (the informants) to their authority and rule and to exploitation. Such outcomes should not be the goal of ethnography. Because you are dependent on others to learn and carry out research, you have a responsibility to uphold your end of the bargain. This ethical responsibility includes demonstrating respect, offering protections, and providing assistance when appropriate.

To demonstrate this different spirit of responsibility, some ethnographers choose not to use the term *informant*. In some cases, they talk about the people with whom they live and work as *interlocutors*. In other cases, they refer to these individuals as *associates, assistants*, or *coresearchers*. There has also been a move increasingly to publish with these individuals as coauthors to reflect their important role in the whole ethnographic project and the fact that much of the knowledge comes from them. This text will use the term *informants* for the sake of clarity, but it is essential to keep in mind the need for a responsible research relationship that is ethical and respectful of the shared human condition. Throughout the rest of the text, you will find consideration of ethical issues and concerns. Proper attention to these points is absolutely essential in the research process.

Whatever terminology a person chooses to adopt, the larger point concerns the unique research relationships that ethnographers develop as a matter of course. Given the need to learn from others and the accompanying dependence on others, the research process is most effectively understood and conceptualized as a collaborative endeavor. You are ultimately responsible for the research—its design, how it is conducted, and its results—but you must give appropriate respect and credit to the other participants who make the research possible. As a human being studying other human beings, you always have to negotiate and collaborate throughout the research process.

SUMMARY

The early history of ethnography as a research strategy frequently included assumptions that the ethnographer traveled long distances to study isolated groups with relatively static cultures. However, recent critiques and developments have shown that ethnography can be a viable research strategy in a wider set of circumstances, even very close to home, and that the cultures and societies that are the subject of ethnographic study are complex, variable, and contested. In order to study these complex phenomena, you will engage in firsthand research employing yourself as the primary research instrument. Your direct experiences become the lens through which ethnographic data or information is collected, but you are always dependent on your informants to guide you through the research process, and envisioning your work with your informants as collaborative partners will help ensure that your research is productive and ethical.

KEY TERMS

Ethnography

Research strategy

Observer

Research subjects

Informants

Methods

Techniques

Gaining access

Building rapport

Household surveys

Mapping

Kinship charts

Insider's perspective

Participant-observer

Objectivity

Perspective

Bias

"Being there"

Replicability

Ethics

Field sites

Research instrument

Replicability

Validity

Ethnographer's role as student

Informant

DISCUSSION QUESTIONS

1. What are the most important features of "classic" ethnography? What are the lasting influences of early ethnographic work? In what ways was early ethnographic work problematic or flawed?

2. How have ethnographic research and ethnographic writing changed in contemporary work?

3. What does Katherine Frank's ethnographic work represent about the nature of ethnographic research and the way ethnography has evolved over time?

4. What sets ethnography apart from other research strategies in the social sciences? Does this particular approach to research imply specific ethical or practical challenges for the researcher?

5. How does the ethnographer function as research instrument? Should all ethnographers be the same type of research instruments?

6. What is the ideal relationship between ethnographer and informant? What steps should the ethnographer take in order to create or foster such a relationship?

7. Choose an ethnography with which you are familiar. Where does it fall in terms of the categories of classic and contemporary? How did the ethnographer conduct his research in this case? What are the most positive elements of the research and the ethnographic presentation? Are there any problems or potential problems? What sort of relationship does the ethnographer have with his informants?

CHAPTER

2

CHOOSING AN ETHNOGRAPHIC TOPIC

LEARNING OBJECTIVES

- Explain the process of choosing a research topic and developing a research project
- Identify sources for potential ideas related to research topics
- Examine people, places, and events as objects of study for the ethnographer
- Understand the benefit of a relatively specific research focus
- Highlight the importance of studying the nonobvious
- Consider behavior and knowledge as objects of study
- Evaluate practical and ethical concerns related to potential research topics

From the outset, the ethnographer needs to have a central place to collect notes and thoughts for his project. Using either a bound notebook or digital computer files to record your notes and thoughts is best. (Whether you choose a physical notebook or a digital file to collect information, you need to remember that notes in either format can be lost or damaged. You should take precautions to protect your notes by making backup copies periodically and storing them in an alternative location.) As you begin brainstorming about potential topics and questions, you should write down these ideas in the notebook or computer folder that will be dedicated to your research project. You may find it helpful to look back at these initial musings later in the course of the project, and you will also begin to build a habit of writing down ideas about the project in a regular and disciplined way. This collection of notes and thoughts will provide an unvarnished account of the research project from start to finish.

Ethnographic research is a *process* that involves continually writing and rewriting. As the research instrument, the ethnographer will record information and ideas throughout the research project. As you write down notes and ideas, you will almost inevitably evaluate and critique the information you are collecting. This evaluation and critique is an important component of the process and allows you to see missing pieces that you need to address. It also serves to bring ideas and questions to the surface that have not yet come into focus.

CASE STUDY

Rebecca Lester's Choice of a Mexican Convent as a Field Site

In *Jesus in Our Wombs: Embodying Modernity in a Mexican Convent* (Lester 2005), Rebecca Lester provides a rich and nuanced ethnographic treatment of a convent in Puebla de los Ángeles, Mexico, which is associated with a congregation that she refers to as the "Siervas." She describes her time conducting research within the convent and connects her research findings to larger issues associated with historical changes in Mexican culture, politics, and economics and especially to cultural understandings of femininity that fall under the categories of traditional and modern. Using her well-researched ethnographic findings, Lester argues that in the course of becoming nuns in this congregation, these young Mexican women learn and embody an alternative understanding of femininity that exists outside the categories of traditional and modern. She makes a powerful argument that links the experiences of these young Mexican women to the larger historical, political, and economic circumstances in Mexico at the end of the twentieth century.

The student of ethnography should always pay attention to the choices of field site and the origin of research questions. In Lester's case, her choice of field site and her underlying research questions are clearly intertwined. In the introductory chapter of *Jesus in Our Wombs*, Lester describes the "rather circuitous route" (2005, 23) that led her to this particular ethnographic project in a Mexican convent. The path that she describes begins with an interest

The best research topics usually start as "problems" or questions that emerge out of casual or careful observation of the world. A trained ethnographer will begin to see potential research topics just about everywhere he looks. You should try not to go into this project or any other **research project** looking for a topic that just anybody could choose. The project will be much more successful if it comes from a genuine personal interest or purpose. You should aim to choose a topic to which you are personally committed and one to which you envision making an important contribution. You will dedicate a lot of time and energy to this project and will be much more successful if you are fully committed to it. When it comes to choosing a topic, you will benefit from consulting with others—including instructors and colleagues—to benefit from their ideas and experience. You should not, however, expect or ask anybody else to choose your topic. In some cases, the circumstances of a class or a job will dictate specific research topics, but even in those situations you should aim to develop a research program that you are fully committed to carrying out in an engaged manner.

Ethnography offers exciting research opportunities because of the researcher's close involvement in the research process. You will not be stuck in the library stacks or a laboratory (unless you are studying librarians or scientists). If you choose your topic and your field site(s) wisely, the whole research process can be exciting and rewarding. Choosing an appropriate **research topic** involves carefully evaluating the possible topics.

in eating disorders, especially anorexia and its ritualistic dimensions. This interest in anorexia brought her to the historical literature focusing on ascetic nuns during the medieval period. Inspired by the debate about whether these nuns' religiously inspired behaviors related to food could be equated with the contemporary psychiatric categories of eating disorders, Lester decided to undertake ethnographic research in the convent in Puebla.

The convent was a logical choice of field site because it offered her a chance to address the topic of religiously based bodily discipline through firsthand ethnographic research methods. She brought her own expectations to the convent as the field site, based in part on her reading of historical sources and basic cultural assumptions, and quickly discovered that many of these expectations were unfounded. For instance, she found that "with a few notable exceptions, [the nuns] seemed to have remarkably normal relationships to food" (Lester 2005, 25). As an ethnographer, Lester had to work from this essential piece of information. It may have prompted her to reevaluate her approach to the research in some specific ways, but the convent as field site offered a rich location for research related to questions of embodiment, selfhood, gender, and religion.

Lester may not have followed a direct path to the convent as field site, but her description of the route she took offers a good example of the way that clear and deliberate consideration of a general topic—in this case, religion and bodily discipline—can lead to a specific research project and even a specific field site.

WHERE TO LOOK FOR POSSIBLE TOPICS

As the ethnographer, you can begin brainstorming about possible research topics by paying close attention to the human activities going on around you: there may be a particular event or idea that you have often wondered about but never found the opportunity to learn about or investigate. You may have observed or been part of a social or cultural event that seems unique, fascinating, problematic, or inexplicable. Maybe you know of something that has not been studied and needs to be studied—a research gap. The ethnographer may want to contribute to a larger understanding of a particular social or cultural model or contribute to the resolution of a vexing social problem. With your ethnographic research, you can investigate intriguing ideas or events, fill research gaps, and even help to solve social problems.

You should begin writing in your notebook at the outset as a way to keep track of your ideas. Keep it close by so that you can make notes whenever an idea comes to you. Talk to other people whenever you have the chance. Ask them what they find interesting, perplexing, or troubling about the social world of which they are a part. Even people who have no knowledge of ethnography will often be keen observers of the social world. They may remind you of something you have forgotten or draw your attention to something of which you had previously been unaware. Treat these conversations as opportunities to gather information and make notes during or after your conversations.

In addition to these conversational opportunities, you should also read widely to gain a good sense of potential topics. Newspapers and social events calendars can be very helpful resources. The Internet is also an increasingly important place to look for this type of information. These sorts of sources provide a wealth of information about the social and cultural world. You can learn about groups, events, and potential field sites if you pay close attention to these sources.

Without making a concerted effort to find out about events and happenings, you might never become aware of unique research opportunities. For instance, you might never realize that there are gospel aerobics classes in the community every Wednesday night. (This example comes from a former Millsaps College student's ethnographic project, and his choice of topic shows his exceptional resourcefulness in learning about the social world around him.) You need to pay attention to your surroundings and make the most of your opportunities.

If you are invited to an event that might be connected to your research topic or project, you should go. The ethnographer is always looking to learn and experience. Of course, there are practical limits to what you can experience, but you should explore the opportunities whenever possible, especially if you are going to be doing research in a field site where you have limited experience. You have to know what is going on in order to choose a good research topic.

Books and magazine or journal articles are also an important source of inspiration when choosing a research topic. An ethnographic book or article may prompt you to think about your own research topic. You may want to explore a similar topic in a different setting, to update the research findings, or to explore an angle or question that was underdeveloped in the work that you have read. A popular book or magazine article might also be a fruitful source of inspiration. The book or article may describe an interesting situation or phenomenon that you want to explore with an ethnographic approach in order to develop a more complex understanding that is rooted in proper ethnographic research.

You should aim to think broadly and carefully about your research topic. If the situation allows, make a list of possible topics that is as extensive as possible by writing down all the possibilities, even if they seem fanciful or impractical. Once you have this list, you can sit down and evaluate the different possibilities using the criteria laid out in the rest of this chapter. Putting the time and effort into this very first stage of choosing a topic will allow you to proceed with the sort of interest and commitment that makes doing research exciting and relatively easy.

ETHNOGRAPHIC TOPICS: STUDYING PLACES, PEOPLE, OR EVENTS

During the initial stages of evaluating research topics, the ethnographer focuses on what the **object of study** will be. The traditional approach to ethnography assumed that the ethnographer traveled to a place and studied the people residing in that place, but the easy assumption that place is equivalent to people and culture is no longer tenable in most cases. Therefore, you should ask yourself whether your focus will be on a place or places, a particular group of people, or a particular set of events or rituals. These are all potential objects of study. Asking this question allows you to begin moving from the sometimes very abstract level of potential topics (for example, Buddhist religion) to a more concrete level concerning how you will go about studying these topics. You will want to carefully evaluate the place where you plan to conduct research, the group of people you will study (especially what defines or identifies them as a group), and the specific events at which you can conduct participant-observation. You may be able to identify a place and events, but the group of people may be hard to define (for instance, soccer fans) or the defining characteristics of the group of people may be clear (Latino immigrants, for instance), but the place or events for fieldwork may not be immediately obvious. This process of identifying points of focus constitutes an important step in thinking about avenues to research and potential field sites. If the place, people, and events all seem hard to identify, the topic may be too abstract or simply very difficult to research ethnographically.

THE BENEFITS OF A RELATIVELY SPECIFIC FOCUS

In many instances, ideas for potential research topics will be very general. Keep in mind that the power of ethnography as a research strategy stems from its ability to bring the **local** and **specific** into sharp focus. The researcher has the chance to develop detailed knowledge about and from particular places, people, or events. An ethnographic

The Internet and Ethnographic Research

The "place" of Internet-based ethnographic research is cyberspace—a place that is hard to define and conceptualize in many ways because it runs counter to long-held assumptions about social interaction and social groups—but there are groups of people and interactions that exist only in that space. Ethnographic research involving the Internet has to address the very different sense of interaction, community, and space that may characterize the Internet as a field "site." Some ethnographers are reluctant to embrace Internet research.

The Internet and other communication technologies have required ethnographers to reevaluate ways of conducting research. Human beings in many places spend a lot of time on the Internet, where they interact and build social units in fascinating ways that are appropriate for ethnographic study. However, you have to consider a host of issues: How can you be an effective participant-observer in cyberspace? Is it sufficient to do research through the Internet, or should this research be combined with ethnographic research in other field sites? Are there particular possibilities of deception associated with the Internet that may compromise some or all of the information collected? Lastly, if the style of communication characteristic of e-mails and chat rooms is distinct from face-to-face conversation, how does this influence interactions between ethnographers and informants?

The most important thing to remember when contemplating Internet research is that it is not easy. It requires a lot of thought. Plus, the Internet is such a diffuse and vast realm that projects often require particularly extensive research. Some ethnographic projects can usefully combine cyberspace research with research in more traditional field sites. For the most part, the basic principles of ethnographic research outlined here apply to cyberspace research as well.

project will likely not allow the researcher to study large geographic areas, large numbers of people, or an unlimited number of events. Therefore, from an early stage, you must consider the breadth of your initial topic and whether the focus can or should be narrowed. In many cases, you will continue to hone your focus over the course of research. Nevertheless, you will find an inherent tension between this specific focus and a desire to be able to generalize and present findings or recommendations that are applicable to a larger set of circumstances. Choosing the right focus involves evaluating both the knowledge that you hope to gain and the ability to expand that knowledge to speak to other contexts.

An example may help in thinking about how to refine the focus of a research topic. Suppose that the initial idea is to study Orthodox Judaism. This religious tradition is an important topic of research for anybody interested in religion and has a number of important implications for the larger understanding of society and culture. As a topic, however, Orthodox Judaism is very general and not yet focused enough to lend itself to useful ethnographic research.

A number of existing good resources already provide important information on Orthodox Judaism from a doctrinal, practical, historical, or philosophical perspective. What is the project going to add that is not already covered in these sources? Most fundamentally, the study is probably going to provide a local or particular view of the religious tradition that offers a supplement or counterpoint to general treatments and may provide the basis for comparison with other particular ethnographic studies. Your research may help show the connections and disjunctures between ideal descriptions at the general level and real practices at the local or particular level.

Even by narrowing the focus geographically to a plan to work in New York or Los Angeles, the ethnographer is likely to find quickly that Orthodox Judaism in New York City or Los Angeles is still an unmanageable topic from an ethnographic standpoint. At this point, you should consider whether you need to focus on one particular congregation or dimension of Orthodox Judaism in that city and whether you want to examine something specific within Orthodox Judaism—the role of women or ritual symbols, for instance. Asking these sorts of questions will allow you to narrow your topic and arrive at a manageable research focus that helps you draw on your initial interests and commitments while keeping in mind the specific goals that you hope to achieve through your research.

The considerations here are both practical and theoretical. Practically speaking, the ethnographer needs to focus on something that can be researched using the techniques and strategies of ethnography. This usually means that you choose to study something physically close by or a place you can travel to, unless you plan to use alternative avenues like the Internet or memory-based accounts of events and experiences through interviews and oral histories.

You should generally seek a focused topic that involves a field site or sites that you expect to be able to access regularly. You should not choose a physically distant field site if you do not have a reliable form of transportation or know that you will not be able to travel regularly to carry out the research. Some questions or foci are more or less researchable given the practical considerations involved in identifying potential field sites. You can study active women leaders in Orthodox Jewish congregations only if you can identify active leaders in the congregations that you propose to study.

The theoretical considerations have to do with how the research will contribute to a larger body of knowledge and to problem solving in practically oriented research. The ethnographer begins by identifying the unanswered questions in the literature. These questions may not have been posed yet, or they may be vexing questions that many researchers and theorists have tried to answer. If the research can help to answer one or more of these questions, you have a good rationale for conducting the research. You will want to produce a research design that allows you to collect information that speaks to these central questions, whether that is informal economic exchange within the congregation or the experience of adolescent initiates. You will need to do sufficient background research and reading to develop your research topic and to locate it in relationship to the work and thought of others.

A note of caution here: The ethnographer's research focus will likely change and evolve over the course of the project. This shift in focus is to be expected. You should be willing to adapt your plans in the course of your research. You may discover that your initial research questions are unanswerable or less important than you originally thought. Most often these discoveries happen as you learn from informants and pay attention to what is important to them. You will need to decide how to balance your research interests with your informants' interests and needs. The more thought you have given to a specific research topic, the more prepared you will be to adapt and refine your approach over the course of your research. It is helpful to revisit your questions and focus at different intervals in the **research process** to evaluate how well you have achieved your goals and answered your questions and whether you need to shift or redirect your focus. In some cases, you may have steered away from your original focus and might need a reminder to get back onto track.

THINKING ABOUT THE NONOBVIOUS AS DISCOVERABLE

For the new ethnographer, one of the biggest challenges in choosing a topic and designing a **research plan** comes in trying to think and write about that which will be uncovered or discovered during the course of research. You should avoid assuming that you know what your research will reveal. If you truly already *know* what you will find, then the research is unnecessary either because the research has already been done by others or because you have chosen to focus on a topic or question that is patently obvious even to the casual observer. If you *think* you know what you will find, you are likely to fall into the trap of only seeing or reporting information that supports your original ideas and failing to see or report potentially contradictory or complicating information. These sorts of expectations can instill a source of bias from the outset of the project. Developing an appropriate research question is an important early step in the overall process (see Chapter Three). Before you even get to that step, you should make sure that your approach to any given topic is sufficiently open to allow for multiple perspectives and to allow you to design a research plan that will enable you as the research instrument to appreciate and record various types of information, even if they do not support your original ideas or **hypotheses**.

One of the keys to producing a good ethnography is becoming attuned to **the nonobvious**. Participant-observation is a powerful and fundamental part of ethnography as a research strategy because it allows the ethnographer to appreciate multiple perspectives and to engage different types and sources of data. Close **observation** by the ethnographer will reveal things of which the participant is sometimes unaware, and in other cases **participation** is the only way to gain an experiential understanding of fundamental components of cultural and social lived worlds. Along these lines, many anthropologists distinguish between the **etic**, or outsider, perspective and the **emic**, or insider, perspective. Though this distinction can be overdrawn, a good deal of the ethnographer's work is involved in working in the interstices of the emic and etic and sorting through apparent discrepancies between different perspectives, between what people say and what they do, and between what has been reported or described previously and what is encountered in the course of research. Multiple perspectives, apparent contradictions, and the ethnographer's relatively unique position are all part of most good ethnography.

Focusing on the nonobvious allows the ethnographer to engage the complexities that emerge in these multiple perspectives, in society and culture as lived and living phenomena. The power of ethnography is rooted in its ability to get past stereotypes, assumptions, and veneers to the complex inner workings. Building a research project that aims to identify and explore these complexities from the beginning by looking to investigate the nonobvious provides a strong foundation for research.

The ethnographer should avoid choosing topics that can be sufficiently addressed using other research strategies and other perspectives. For instance, you do not need to conduct ethnographic research to learn about the official duties of a health care worker in Tanzania; these duties are clearly laid out in government literature that defines these positions. However, ethnographic research may be absolutely essential in understanding how these health care workers cope with chronic or periodic drug shortages. Similarly, casual observation demonstrates that there continue to be significant gender differences between men and women in the United States today, whether in terms of clothing, educational performance, or professional choices. Clear evidence of these differences comes from a variety of sources (including surveys and reports of test scores), and the researcher does not need to do extensive ethnographic fieldwork to establish their existence. Instead, this situation can serve as the starting point for ethnographic research that examines a number of related questions, including (1) instances of apparent gender equality that run counter to general demonstrable differences; (2) socialization of gender difference; or (3) how these differences are played out in contexts where gender equality is espoused.

These two examples demonstrate the need to avoid topics that are overly obvious in nature and do not require ethnographic research. Focusing on the nonobvious dimensions of a topic will make ethnographic work more interesting and productive. The thoughts, behaviors, and social worlds of human beings are complicated, and the ethnographer studying these things avoids the overly simplistic "facts" or explanations, especially at first.

For many ethnographers, the ultimate goal is to describe and analyze complex social phenomena in relatively simple or finite terms, but the ethnographer cannot simply accept the first explanation offered or even surface appearances. The ethnographer generally assumes that there is more going on underneath the surface than first meets the eye. Therefore, a good ethnographer takes note of explanations, appearances, and experiences and continues to delve deeper by gaining more explanations, different perspectives, and more research experiences.

In the attempt to gain this sort of deep understanding, the ethnographer is best served by choosing a topic and designing a plan that focuses on the nonobvious dimensions of human behavior and interaction. With this focus, you will be able to collect and to analyze information that usually adds to the perspectives of both participants and outside observers. The nonobvious dimensions are often quite complicated, but they are also reflective of the complexity of human cultures and societies. In evaluating potential topics, the ethnographer should consider whether the chosen topics already involve a focus on the nonobvious or how the focus might be narrowed or shifted toward the nonobvious. Including this step in the evaluation process will help you avoid producing a relatively superficial report and concentrate on collecting information that will provide significant new insights and provide the basis for productive analysis.

CULTURAL KNOWLEDGE AND BEHAVIOR IN ACTION AS RESEARCH OBJECTS

The nonobvious dimensions can and should be the objects of ethnographic research. However, the ethnographer should also think in slightly more concrete terms of things that can be observed and recorded during the research process. Thinking about both **knowledge** and **behavior** as objects to be collected can help the ethnographer conceptualize the topic and a strategy for carrying out the research. As you evaluate potential topics, you should consider which forms of knowledge are particularly important to your informants, whether there are different types or sets of knowledge to be considered, and who can grant access to these sets of knowledge. Evaluating potential topics also involves identifying the behaviors that you will need to witness or experience and how these behaviors are open or closed to observation and participation. Addressing these concerns will help you identify the knowledge and behavior that will be your objects of study. This process of evaluation will help you see areas where you may need to do more investigation as well as potential obstacles and likely positive approaches in the research process.

Knowledge is most often accessed through conversations—either informal conversations or more formal interviews—but a lot of knowledge exists in other forms that are nondiscursive, or the knowledge operates outside of direct, verbal communication. As human beings, we possess a lot of implicit or nondiscursive language that we transmit through observation, imitation, and practice. As a result, the ethnographer has to be prepared to acquire knowledge in a variety of ways, both through conversations and through experience and observation.

Behavior, though, seems most amenable to observation. However, simply observing the activities of others provides only one level of information and understanding. Most behavior can be more fully understood by either experiencing that behavior in action or by engaging conversations surrounding that behavior. These sorts of engagements allow the researcher to begin understanding motivations and sentiments that underlie behavior.

For the ethnographer, this discussion carries two important points: (1) while it is often helpful analytically to think in terms of separating knowledge and behavior, in practice they are linked and interwoven, and the ethnographer should not focus exclusively on one at the expense of the other; and (2) ethnographic research that relies solely on observation or conversation and interviews is almost necessarily incomplete. Novice ethnographers sometimes fall into the trap of choosing one or the other instead of looking to combine the two. The ethnographer with a shy, introverted disposition may be inclined to choose a topic that he thinks will allow him to conduct research without having to interject himself into the lives of others. On the other hand, the ethnographer who is a talkative person but nervous about feeling out of place or not knowing how to act in certain situations might lean toward a project full of interviews and conversations that is short on active participation in events and behaviors that are unfamiliar. In order to avoid these sorts of imbalanced approaches, you should aim from the outset to make sure your topic will feasibly allow the unique combination of participant-observation that is the hallmark of ethnographic research. You can ensure this balance by carefully identifying and reviewing both the knowledge and behavior that will become your research objects.

Having identified the people, place, and events that you might study, made sure that the topic is suitably focused on the nonobvious dimensions, and identified knowledge and behavior as research objects, you should be ready to make an informed decision about a research topic. When evaluating a potential topic, if you encounter difficulty during one or more of these steps, that is a warning sign. More background research or a preliminary visit to field site(s) may help to clear up some of these concerns. You do not need to immediately discard a topic that you think has significant potential, but you should aim to achieve as much clarity on these points as possible at this early point in your project. Clarity will help you develop a good research question and research plan and will ensure your research is as effective as possible.

PRACTICAL CONCERNS

To this point, the focus of this chapter has primarily been on the abstract ideas at the heart of a research topic and, in an abstract sense, a given topic's feasibility. In this section, the focus will be on practical feasibility and the researcher's responsibilities. Even the most well-conceptualized research topic in the abstract may face daunting or insurmountable obstacles in the practical arena. For this reason, the ethnographer wants to have a list of multiple potential topics. Political issues, reluctant informants, privacy concerns, finances, and ethical concerns can all be the source of significant challenges in the course of doing research. The ethnographer is wise to try to list and address potential concerns or obstacles from the outset. Doing so will help to avoid wasted research time and frustration.

Issues of Accessibility

The issue of **accessibility** is probably the single most important practical concern. The ethnographer may want to study the *vaqueros* of the Argentinean pampas. However, even if you have been able to address all the points in the first half of this chapter, if you are also living in Chicago or Dallas on a limited budget, you will likely be unable to carry out this fieldwork unless you acquire research funding in the form of a grant and a leave from school or work. Therefore, geographic proximity and financial resources are both determinants of the researcher's degree of access to field site(s). If you are contemplating a local project, you will still need to think about the two variables of location and finances. You will need to have access to the necessary transportation to reach your field site(s). You will also need to be able to cover any significant expenses (gas, tolls, fares, and so on) associated with transportation as well as other related expenses (entrance fees and necessary purchases). You should not choose a field site simply because it is nearby and inexpensive—you need to be interested in the topic and related ideas enough to feel committed to it—but you should also avoid field sites that are so distant or expensive that you will have difficulty carrying out research. Ethnographers seldom acknowledge these practical factors in their ethnographic reports, but these factors often influence the choice of field sites and the course of research.

In some cases, certain individuals are in a position to grant or to deny access to particular field site(s), resources, and people. If you can identify these "gatekeepers" early on, you will be aware of the people with whom you will have to work (or, in a few instances, might want to avoid). You can also perform an initial assessment of your likelihood of being granted access based on whether access is closely guarded and whether there are particular factors that might aid or hinder your attempt to gain access. Some **gatekeepers** occupy formal positions of authority (for instance, government officials and religious leaders) and others function as informal gatekeepers (for instance, family leaders or elders and healers of various sorts). In both cases, their assistance or approval can be invaluable to the ethnographer, and their rejection can be very detrimental to research plans. Sometimes they are able to make research completely impossible either by denying research permits or drawing a curtain of silence in response to research inquiries.

If you know that some or all of the gatekeepers will not be receptive to your research, then you should consider whether you will have enough access to make your project doable. In some instances, you may have to choose between different sets of gatekeepers depending on their relationships and the sites and resources to which they can grant access. In other circumstances, you may be able to avoid or circumvent gatekeepers. You should do this only when necessary and make sure that you evaluate the potential ethical ramifications. It may be ethically defensible to circumvent a gatekeeper who seems to be using her power to oppress or subjugate the informants with whom you want to work, but you also have to think about the potential ramifications for your informants if this gatekeeper finds out about your research activities, and you should design measures to ensure their protection. If circumventing the gatekeeper places potential informants in unusually precarious or dangerous positions, you should forgo this strategy.

Language and Accessibility

Language is one of the fundamental tools for conducting ethnographic research. Conversations and interviews depend on a shared language, and much observation and participation requires that you understand what is being said and even what you are being told to do. Therefore, ideally the ethnographer speaks the language(s) in use in the field site. The ethnographer sometimes learns a language in the course of fieldwork, but this typically involves an extended stay and dedicated effort to learn the language. Working with a translator is sometimes necessary but less than ideal because it makes the ethnographer a less precise research instrument.

Your familiarity with specific languages is another determinant of your access to particular field sites. In the multicultural societies of which we are a part, we often encounter a multiplicity of languages. Consequently, even local ethnographic projects may entail significant questions about language and access. If you are planning to work in field site(s) where English is consistently spoken, you may still find that there is a specialized language or vocabulary—for instance, slang or technical jargon—that you have to master quickly in order to carry out effective research. Therefore, your familiarity and facility with specific languages has a direct influence on the accessibility of a field site to you.

Issues of Privacy

Ethnography as a research strategy asks a lot from its informants. For successful ethnography, informants have to be willing to share their lives and thoughts to a significant extent and to serve as teachers for ethnographers. In many instances, informants share private and personal experiences with ethnographers as part of the research. In some cases, ethnographers actively elicit these experiences as sources of information; in other cases, informants choose to share these experiences and occasionally to include ethnographers in very personal moments and events. Having access to these personal thoughts and experiences is an incredible privilege and can be very informative for the ethnographer, but it also carries significant responsibility for the researcher.

In evaluating potential research topics, the ethnographer needs to think carefully about issues of **privacy** that might emerge in the course of researching a particular topic. Some topics may focus on ideas and behavior that are sufficiently public so that privacy is not a significant concern, but other topics will definitely raise questions about privacy. Any topic that involves illegal or illicit activities, like drug use or covert immigration, will necessitate careful thinking about privacy issues, especially because of the potential negative effects on informants if their identities and activities are made public.

Some standard conventions in ethnographic presentation (including the use of pseudonyms and occasionally composite figures) aim to protect **anonymity** in response to these issues of identity and privacy. Ethnographers often have to take steps to protect notes and even to disguise their research activities to help protect informants' privacy, especially in highly sensitive projects. In some cases, these precautions may not be sufficient, and privacy concerns may make ethnographic work impossible. There are some legal protections of **confidentiality**, especially related to medicine and religion, that the ethnographer cannot breach. Moreover, even in the absence of legal strictures, the ethnographer sometimes must recognize that the potential **benefits** of the project do not outweigh the invasion of privacy that is entailed.

At this early stage in your project, you should try to identify potential concerns related to privacy. If there are significant issues, you will definitely need to consult with experts about the feasibility of proceeding. Evaluating privacy concerns will also allow you to continue to evaluate questions of access. In many cases, exceptionally private arenas present particularly difficult sites to access. For instance, although a number of good ethnographies related to sexuality have been written, sexual behavior remains private and difficult to access in most cases. (Because of the private nature of many activities associated with sexuality, ethnographic research on the subject tends to rely particularly heavily on interview-based data, though ethnographic data on the subject is not limited to interview data.) If your proposed topic raises questions about privacy and access, you will need to think carefully about whether it is ultimately feasible and whether you are prepared to address these questions. Do not hesitate to consult with more experienced ethnographers to get their advice.

CONSIDERING ETHICS FROM THE START: YOUR OBLIGATIONS TO POTENTIAL INFORMANTS

Ethnographers' primary **ethical responsibility** is to their potential and actual informants. Unfortunately, ethnographers cannot provide foolproof protections and guarantees to their informants about what will happen with the ethnographies that they produce, but they should take every reasonable measure possible to protect informants. These protections should begin at the earliest stages of the research process. You should not evaluate potential projects simply on the basis of potential benefit to you, the research community, and its larger audience. You must also evaluate potential benefits and costs to your informants. The goal is for the benefits to significantly outweigh the costs in this ledger as well. These assessments should be fundamental to the decision to pursue a particular topic.

In some cases, the potential negative effects for informants come in presentation and publication, when the informants may be subject to scrutiny and even reprisals. However, in other cases, simply being involved in ethnographic research may place individuals in a disadvantaged situation. Imagine an ethnographer who is clearly studying HIV/AIDS, political rebellion, or transsexual experiences. If the ethnographer is working in a community where there is social stigma associated with the topic under study, a person who is seen conversing or hosting the ethnographer may become the subject of rumor and innuendo and stigmatizing processes. Topics like HIV/AIDS, political rebellion, and transsexual experiences deserve close ethnographic study, but not at the expense of informants' well-being and livelihoods. In choosing a research topic, the researcher should be very careful in considering the ethical concerns or dilemmas that may arise. For a beginning ethnographer, it is a good general practice to avoid topics that involve significant ethical issues. Both beginning and experienced ethnographers should always keep ethical responsibilities to their informants at the fore throughout their research.

TOPICS YOU MIGHT WANT TO AVOID

Each field site requires a unique approach and the flexibility to adapt to different circumstances and opportunities. Therefore, it is difficult to offer definitive dos and don'ts when choosing a topic or field site. However, there are several types of field sites that are frequently difficult to manage, especially when working on an ethnographic project with a relatively limited time frame. This section draws attention to these types of field sites—large-scale retail environments, high-pressure or dangerous environments, and illegal, illicit, and secretive activities—to help you make an informed decision when choosing a topic and prospective field sites.

Economic markets and activities play a dominant role in shaping our everyday lives, and good ethnographic research can help in better understanding the function and effects of different economic activities and systems. Thus, economics can be a fruitful focus for many ethnographic projects. But large-scale retail environments as centers of economic activity are often not amenable to ethnographic fieldwork premised on participant-observation. This stems from the fact that these environments are most frequently premised on impersonal exchanges with limited human interaction. The ethnographer seeking to do participant-observation may very well be frustrated and find it difficult to build relationships with potential informants. Big-box stores like Wal-Mart or Target are generally field sites to avoid, but there may be particular spaces—such as kiosks or food courts—within large-scale environments that are more amenable to ethnography because people interact and create a different sort of social-cultural space.

If the ethnographer has access to particular areas within the larger retail environment—for instance, a break room or training exercises—the site may prove to be much more productive ethnographically. Smaller retail spaces may offer very different sorts of interaction and better environments for ethnographic research. Remember: Not all retail and business environments are the same. For instance, the volume *Golden Arches East* (Watson 2006) highlights the way a space with the same name and markers—McDonald's—can vary dramatically depending on internal and external factors. If your potential topic focuses on business and retail, you need to make sure to evaluate the potential field sites for their suitability for ethnographic fieldwork. Most fundamentally, you should ask how you will practice participant-observation.

High-pressure or dangerous environments may produce potential informants who are too busy to work closely with you or who are reluctant to open themselves to the research process. As a result, field sites like emergency rooms, police departments, and fire departments may be difficult to negotiate for many ethnographers. There are notable instances when ethnographers have gained access to field sites like these by serving as police officers, introducing themselves into the high-pressure, dangerous environment of a firefighter camp (Altork 1995), or doing participant-observation with a search and rescue team (Lois 2003), but the ethnographer may not have the time or resources to adopt these sorts of approaches.

Access designed for the general public—like a police ride-along—is generally not sufficient to sustain ethnographic research, even though it might provide a potential entry into the field site in some cases. Sometimes identifying an alternative field site that allows the ethnographer to learn from the same group of informants and to investigate similar topics can be a helpful way to deal with some of these challenges. For instance, you may be able to study gender or hierarchy among firefighters by working with informants in a softball league or a neighborhood bar if you find that you lack access to the firehouse or it is not a sufficient field site for your project. In fact, you might gain more insight into informal cultural and social relationships in these alternative sites. Generally, you should be careful in selecting topics that require you to study high-intensity or dangerous environments. There may be particular issues of accessibility associated with research on these topics. You should also brainstorm about potential alternative field sites.

Students are often interested in illegal or illicit activities like drug use, prostitution, street racing, and illegal immigration for a variety of reasons, including very important social science questions. In fact, there is a strong history of studying these sorts of activities in the social sciences. Still, pursuing these topics can be problematic for both the researcher and the informants. When contemplating a topic along these lines, you should make sure you know your institution's guidelines and that you consult with your instructor or supervisor about the topic's suitability. You should also think about your own level of comfort with the topic. Ethnographers frequently find themselves in new and uncomfortable positions, and these positions can offer important learning experiences, but you need to be honest with yourself about your preparedness to do research on a given topic and the risks involved. Associating yourself with illegal or illicit activities may place you in a precarious position. The excuse "I was just doing research" is not likely to have a significant impact if you find yourself in a legal jam or other difficulty (see Bourgois 2003 for an enlightening account of his attempt to explain his research to the police). Even if you are prepared to take on the research topic, you must pay careful attention to the potential impact on informants. Human subjects review becomes an especially important step in projects like these to ensure that the research does not involve unnecessary risks for the participants.

Sometimes perfectly legal activities are shrouded in a veil of secrecy that makes it difficult or impossible for the ethnographer to conduct research. You may never be able to access high-level business meetings or confidential medical or legal consultations. You should be honest in evaluating potential topics in terms of issues of access and avoid choosing a topic that requires access to events or field sites that will likely be off limits or out of reach.

SUMMARY

Topics for ethnographic research typically originate in observation of the surrounding social world and a close consideration of key social issues, problems, and questions. In choosing a topic, the ethnographer should carefully consider the fact that the research will require a focus on particular places, people, and events. You will want to make sure that the topic is sufficiently focused and that you have access to the necessary people, places, and events. You may encounter both conceptual and practical obstacles in pursuing a research topic. Ultimately, the ethnographic project should focus on a topic that requires you to investigate the complex, nonobvious dimensions of society and culture by researching both knowledge and behavior.

KEY TERMS

Research project
Research topic
Object of study
Local
Specific
Research process
Research plan
Hypotheses
The nonobvious
Observation
Participation

Etic
Emic
Knowledge
Behavior
Accessibility
Gatekeepers
Privacy
Anonymity
Confidentiality
Benefits
Ethical responsibility

DISCUSSION QUESTIONS

1. Why is it important to think about ethnographic research as a process? What role does writing play in this process?

2. Where can the ethnographer look for ideas about possible research topics? What are the benefits and limitations of different sources of ideas?

3. How do ethnographers identify their objects of study? What practical and theoretical issues should the ethnographer consider when evaluating different potential projects and objects of study?

4. How does the ethnographer go about discovering and studying the nonobvious? What is a good example of an ethnographer who succeeded in studying the non-obvious? How can you tell that this work deals with the nonobvious?

5. What is the difference between cultural knowledge and cultural behavior? Should the ethnographer try to study both at the same time? Does ethnography seem better suited to study one or the other?

6. What are the paramount ethical issues that an ethnographer must consider in designing a research project? Are issues of access and privacy equally important, or does one take precedence over the other?

CHAPTER

3

RESEARCH DESIGN

LEARNING OBJECTIVES

- Develop strategies for turning a research topic into a viable and focused research question
- Discriminate between descriptive and analytical questions
- Explain the link between research questions and research methods
- Identify participant-observation, interviews, and maps and charts as key research methods for the ethnographer
- Examine the ways in which different methods allow ethnographers to collect different types of data and answer different types of questions
- Consider the practical and ethical considerations that determine whether a project is feasible and viable

Once you have chosen a research topic, narrowed the focus a bit, and identified potential field sites with reasonable accessibility, the next step is to formulate a suitable **research question** and to formulate a plan or design that will prepare you to answer that question. Working with a question allows you to direct your research in useful ways and to continually evaluate your success in addressing the central focus. Once you have formulated a working research question, you will then proceed to choose and combine methods in a design that is dedicated to answering the research question. Different types of questions will require different sorts of methods to acquire the necessary ethnographic information and yield productive analysis. This chapter will lay out the process of developing a suitable research question and choosing appropriate methods to answer that question.

TURNING AN IDEA OR TOPIC INTO A RESEARCH QUESTION

Good research is generally oriented around substantive and interesting questions. Sometimes, **exploratory research** is necessary, especially when beginning work on a topic for a field site that has not previously been studied or visited. This sort of exploratory research—a "see what you can find" approach—tends not to work from research questions. The research tends to be more **open-ended**, and the ethnographic presentations that result from this type of research tend to be **descriptive** rather than **analytical**. This text focuses on producing a thoroughly analytical final ethnography. Therefore, the focus here is on developing guiding research questions. The ethnographer may have to do some exploratory research at the early stages—almost all ethnographers do—but these stages should be building toward analytical ethnography.

Generally speaking, developing a research question or set of research questions is a key part of the process of narrowing the focus to a manageable frame. Preliminary topics tend to be rather broad and to include a number of potential questions under their umbrella. For instance, if the chosen topic is campus organizations, a number of questions might develop out of this topic, such as: Do campus organizations depend more heavily on formal or informal leadership models? Do religious and nonreligious organizations have similar understandings of leadership? Are some organizations' leadership models more democratic than others? Are there different leadership structures in place depending on the gender makeup of particular organizations? Do leadership hierarchies in campus organizations replicate the structures of class in larger society? These are just some of the potential questions that might emerge within the framework of social science. An ethnographer planning to study campus organizations probably cannot feasibly expect to answer all of these questions. Therefore, it behooves the ethnographer to focus on a question or a set of related questions that will guide the research process. Choosing the question(s) involves evaluating the general import of the questions and the relative impact on the field and the audience of an informed answer. You want to choose the questions that will make the most significant contribution in terms of building ethnographic knowledge, developing social theory, and solving practical social problems.

In choosing and developing a research question, the ethnographer should avoid overly simplistic or **descriptive questions**. As the ethnographer, you are expected to provide insight and build a productive frame of analysis. If the question can be answered through casual observation or commonsense reasoning, it will not produce insightful analysis. The ethnographer should be wary of yes-or-no questions; these can sometimes be dead ends instead of productive entries into research. The hypothetical questions about campus organizations listed previously all seem to ask for a yes-or-no answer. But they can be productive research questions because they implicitly conjure up a set of analytical questions that center on how and why. The researcher will need to collect data to answer the basic question, but the other essential part of the research process will be to develop a deeper set of understandings or explanations. While yes-or-no questions can usually be expanded by asking questions of the how and why variety, sometimes these expanded questions will involve digging deeper than others. You should aim to provide new descriptive information in your ethnography and to answer the deep questions.

In line with the brainstorming process you used to develop potential topics, your next step involves making a list of all the potential research questions that you can see developing out of your chosen research topic. Once you have a comprehensive list of questions, you can rank them from highest to lowest in terms of import. You will likely find that the most important questions entail the greatest depth of research and analysis. Once you have made your list and ranked the questions, you must decide whether you are satisfied with those guiding questions for your research. If you are, the next step is to refine or to develop the questions. If you are not comfortable with that choice, you will need to revisit your list until you come up with a suitable question that carries sufficient import.

If you are starting with a yes-or-no question, you should write out specific analytical questions that fall underneath or build upon the first question. For example, if your initial question is, Do religious and nonreligious organizations have similar understandings of leadership? then you might come up with associated questions like: Are religious organizations more likely to utilize nonhierarchical or egalitarian structures whereas nonreligious groups tend to be hierarchical? Or is informal leadership (leading by example) more prominent in nonreligious organizations? These two questions both address the larger question of how—how are religious and nonreligious organizations different? Specific information will be required to answer these questions. This process of brainstorming and developing a list of analytical questions may produce a question like: Are religious organizations more prone to egalitarian structures because their belief systems emphasize communal cooperation? Or does the formal structure of most religious organizations mean that there is less room for informal leadership? These sorts of questions involve evaluating *explanations* that answer the *why* questions. Making these how and why questions explicit in specific forms related to your topic is an important step that will benefit the entire research process.

Questions and Hypotheses

Some ethnographers are reluctant to conceptualize their research in terms of the scientific language of testable hypotheses. Because ethnographers do not control the environment and variables under study in the manner of scientific experiments, hypotheses are sometimes difficult to operationalize. Nevertheless, formulating hypotheses can be a helpful way of conceptualizing research in the design stage. Many of the "hypothetical" questions outlined here can be relatively easily translated into hypotheses based on correlation or causation. Try turning research questions into hypotheses in the form of "If *x*, then *y*." This is a useful exercise that may provide some clarity at the outset. If the hypothesis is disproved at the very beginning, you may discover that the how and why questions of your project are harder to answer than you originally thought.

You should also think about your audience. Some audiences want to see testable hypotheses. Hypotheses lend themselves to situations that require definitive answers. Therefore, granting agencies and practically oriented institutions often appreciate this clarity and the outcomes it produces. If your audience is scientific or practically oriented, hypotheses may be a particularly effective way of communicating your questions and ideas.

LINKING QUESTIONS TO METHODS

Once you have developed a productively analytical **research question** or set of research questions, the next step is to choose the **research methods** that best allow you to answer these questions. The types of questions being asked and the type of information needed to answer the questions will determine to a large extent the methods that the ethnographer will employ. If you are interested in uses and perceptions of space or relationships between neighbors or coworkers, mapping may be a particularly appropriate research method for your project. If you are interested in historical recollections or personal perspectives, **interviews** and **conversations** will almost certainly be a key component of your research design. And if your research questions focus on communal events or experiential dimensions, you will definitely want to pursue participant-observation as a primary source of data collection. In almost all cases, a complete ethnographic project will require a combination of methods. It is not a matter of choosing one method at the expense of all others, but a matter of choosing the primary methods that will yield the most pertinent types of information for a particular project.

In order to begin evaluating potential methods, you can brainstorm about the types of information that you would like to obtain and that would be helpful in answering your questions. You can envision the perfect ethnography—what it would look like and what it would include. If this vision for the ethnography includes maps and charts, lengthy interview excerpts, or rich descriptive accounts of events, you can then proceed to consider which methods will produce the necessary ethnographic data.

The point of this brainstorming exercise is to develop a relatively specific list of information to be collected in an ideal situation. Some of the information may not be collectable (due to practical issues of time and access or the imperfect means of accessing people's inner thoughts and direct experiences), but the list will prepare you to choose appropriate research methods. With a complete list, you can use a system of numbers to prioritize the information you would like to collect. You can then prioritize your research methods to maximize collection of the most important types of information. In the end, the primary means of **data collection** (your methods) should match the highest priority in terms of information to be collected.

KEY METHODS TO CONSIDER FOR THE ETHNOGRAPHIC PROJECT

Ethnographers can and do employ a number of different methods and techniques in the course of their research. For instance, a particular project may benefit from the use of focus groups or the collection of extensive life histories. The **key methods** of participant-observation, interviews, and maps and charts are mainstays of the ethnographic research process. You can utilize these methods in a variety of ways and adapt them to your purposes. Exceptions are almost the norm in ethnography, but you should generally plan to employ each of these methods.

Participant-Observation

Participant-observation has been the centerpiece of ethnographic research throughout its history as a research strategy. Participant-observation makes ethnographic research unique and opens avenues to important types of information hard to obtain or access otherwise. You must think carefully about how you can utilize participant-observation in the course of your research. In some cases, your activities as a participant-observer will seem obvious from the very beginning. In other cases, you may have a hard time conceptualizing your role as a **participant-observer**. This early stage is the time to sort through these issues.

For many ethnographers, participant-observation is the way to begin doing research. If there is a public event that you can attend—a festival, a religious service, or a town hall meeting, for instance—this may be the perfect way for you to begin to introduce yourself into your research setting and to begin to collect information. You will likely learn a lot by observing and participating as part of a larger group (an audience, practitioners, or the general public), but you will also probably quickly become aware of things that you need to learn. You may then have to follow up on this initial research experience with direct questions in the course of interviews and conversations. You may also discover that there is a lot going on behind the scenes to which you do not have direct access or that particular types of experiential training or learning (initiations, for example) occur less frequently but are essential to a more complete understanding of the event and the group. Therefore, initial forays into participant-observation are often just the tip of the iceberg and require a willingness to adapt to possibilities and opportunities. These initial stages will likely also involve a higher emphasis on observation, while the dimension of participation will develop during the course of the research as you acquire knowledge and develop working relationships with your informants.

Ideally, you will identify a regular **event** or series of events that you can attend as a participant-observer as a cornerstone of your research plan. This sort of regular, planned participant-observation will help you get started, help structure your research, and help you build relationships with potential informants. You will notice and record different things during the course of your participant-observation and similar events. Some activities and occurrences will become commonplace in your mind, while other variances will be noticeable once you have a sense of the "norm." As you collect information from other sources, you will also find yourself developing new understandings of the things going on around you. If your project lends itself to participant-observation at sporting events, organizational meetings, informal get-togethers, or other sorts of regular events, attendance and participant-observation at these events become part of your research plan as a research method. This will likely not be the only participant-observation that you pursue. One set of experiences with participant-observation may give rise to other opportunities.

If the project does not present an obvious set of regular events, you will have to think more carefully about how you can usefully incorporate the insights of participant-observation into your research plans. Even if you plan to concentrate mainly on firsthand accounts acquired through interviews, doing participant-observation will allow you a different perspective that is based in society and culture *in action.*

Sometimes the ethnographer can do very productive participant-observation by pursuing an apprenticeship. As an **apprentice**, you put yourself in a position to learn from an expert who possesses a great deal of specialized knowledge. Ethnographers have successfully apprenticed themselves to healers and skilled craftspeople, among others. If the project involves working with informants with specific skills and specialized knowledge who may be willing to teach these things to you, you should consider whether an apprenticeship would be a valuable way to conduct participant-observation data for your project.

Too often participant-observation as a research method is equated with "just hanging out." Participant-observation should be planned and purposeful (even though the ethnographer frequently encounters the unexpected in the course of participant-observation). You have to identify good situations and locations for participant-observation. Sometimes spending considerable time in one place is a good approach to participant-observation. Inhabiting space in this way allows you to observe significant numbers of people and behaviors and to participate in numerous interactions. As a result, you are able to create an analytical picture of this cultural space that is more reliable than if it were based on more limited research in the space. If the project focuses on one or two key spaces, this may be a logical approach to participant-observation for the research.

A research topic may focus on an aspect of culture or society that is not easily associated with a single set of events. If that is the case, you should think about places that might offer examples of the larger phenomenon you are studying. Sometimes picking a field site as a case study can be useful in this regard. Even if it is not directly related to the specific topic, you may find a space or event that brings your potential informants together, even if it seems very informal. You may find that conducting participant-observation at a coffee shop or a park or as part of a neighborhood watch group are all ways to establish rapport with informants and to learn more about what they say and do on a regular basis.

In some cases, the ethnographer may want or need to conduct participant-observation in private or secret settings (see, for example, Lester 2005). You will need to plan carefully in order to make this happen. The sooner you can identify this goal and begin to build the foundation for it, the more likely you will be to gain access in order to do research. If you aim to conduct participant-observation in a relatively private or difficult to access setting, you should start by making a list of gatekeepers and issues that you may need to address in order to gain access. You should be frank about your goals, but avoid being too pushy or insisting on access to which you do not have a predetermined right. In many cases, ethnographers have been made privy to the personal, private, and secret sides of things without directly seeking them out. As you build trust-based working relationships, informants may choose to include you in these aspects of their lives. This step often entails a lot of responsibility for the ethnographer who is initiated into a group (Turnbull 1968), becomes an apprentice, or acquires a store of secret knowledge.

You have a number of options for incorporating participant-observation as a method in your research strategy: attending regular events, inhabiting a space over a period of time, seeking an apprenticeship or initiation, and more informal circumstances. You will ultimately have to decide which type(s) of participant-observation and which settings are most likely to yield the information you require. At this early stage, you need to think carefully about whom and what you will be observing and with whom you will be participating. You also need to consider whether this approach will allow you to gather the experiences and perspectives you require. There will be a variety of perspectives and experiences in just about every setting. How you position yourself in terms of participant-observation will determine to a large extent your ability to access these **perspectives** and **experiences**. For example, you can potentially do a lot of participant-observation in hospitals and clinics. How and where you do participant-observation will dictate whether you gain a better understanding of the perspectives and experiences of doctors, nurses, patients, or family members (compare Bluebond-Langner 1978 and Katz 1999).

Interviews

Talking to and *listening to* informants are key parts of the ethnographic process. In these exchanges between ethnographers and informants, the ethnographer has the chance to gain explicit knowledge (that is, to be taught directly) and to ask for clarification or follow up on things observed or explained previously. Through conversation and interviews, you can obtain detailed explanations and rationales as well as background information that help you make sense out of other pieces of information that may lack context. Since one of the primary goals of ethnography is to access insiders' perspectives, interviews and conversations that allow you to record the thoughts and words of informants are absolutely essential. Therefore, you should plan carefully to utilize interviews as a research method to its maximum effect.

Looking back at the list of information that you plan to obtain in your research, you can build a plan for pursuing interviews. These interviews will represent the different sources and types of knowledge that you recognize at the outset. This list should allow you to learn from a range of broadly **representative** informants that will help you see different ideas and perspectives.

Too often the word *interview* prompts thoughts of the formal, rather impersonal encounters associated with a lot of journalism and popular news outlets. The typical ethnographic interview, however, is usually very different from these interviews. Most ethnographic interviews are less formal and are frequently based on some already established rapport or shared experience. The presence of a microphone or recorder and the fact that you are taking notes can be daunting or intimidating for an interviewee. As you build your initial plan for interviews, you will need to think carefully about the degree of formality required and the best time during the process to carry out particular interviews. If you expect potential informants to be wary of your presence and your research agenda, it is usually best to pursue interviews after you have begun other aspects of your research and your informants have gained some understanding of the research goals and some familiarity with the researcher. In many cases, interviews will be better and yield more information if they are rooted in information collected through other methods like participant-observation. Plans for interviews and conversations should include consideration of the people that you plan to interview, the type of interview that will likely be most effective, and whether you plan to conduct interviews at a particular point in the research process.

Maps and Charts

Anthropologists make frequent use of **maps** and **charts** both as a means of collecting and organizing information and as a way of presenting findings. In many instances, the ethnographer attempts to communicate information associated with various senses using written language, but maps and charts allow the ethnographer to make some of this information clearer using visual representation. These visual representations can be the most effective and most efficient way to communicate some ethnographic data. What you choose to represent visually will depend on the specific topic and what you find in the course of your research. At this early stage, you should aim to identify the maps and charts that are most likely to be appropriate and useful for your project.

Early ethnographies were almost incomplete without at least one **kinship chart** and a stylistic map of the local community under study. Kinship charts and stylistic maps are less frequent today as a result of changing foci and changing perceptions of field sites, but they remain effective ways of collecting and presenting information in some contemporary ethnographic work (see Engebrigtsen 2007). Evans-Pritchard's landmark ethnography, *The Nuer* (1940), included two pages of drawings of different types of cattle with captions. This visual aid was an effective way of communicating the importance of cattle in the lives of the Nuer and the classificatory system they applied to cattle. Ethnographers have also experimented with a number of different types of visual mechanisms, including flow charts in corporate settings and drawings by the ethnographer or informants.

In building a research plan and choosing key methods, you need to think about the sorts of visual schema that you might generate or record as a way of collecting information. Do you need two pages of pictures of cattle? Probably not, but some pictorial representations of dogs might be appropriate if you are researching dog shows. Whatever the topic, you will likely find it helpful to work with these visual schema in the process of data collection. Therefore, you need to determine which sorts of schema might be appropriate to your topic and your field site(s). You should make sure you choose an approach that is appropriate for the research topic and questions and not the approach that seems easiest or the most fun. Kinship charts may seem tedious, but in the context of the right project, they can be invaluable. The other techniques can likewise be very useful in certain projects, but not in others.

Maps are most likely to be helpful if you are working with a topic that has a clear spatial dimension. For instance, you may be exploring neighbor relations in the inner city or the suburbs, in which case you will likely want to develop a strong understanding of how **spatial relations** (the distances between residences, orientation of doors and windows, common paths of entry and exit, and so on) are connected to **social interaction**. If the ethnography focuses on the workplace, you may want to make sure you have a clear image of the workplace layout. Such a map can help you understand everything from management-worker relations to the use of break time. In cases such as these, maps can be very helpful. You should include maps if you anticipate that distance or proximity, physical orientation, and physical interaction or isolation might be interesting foci for your research.

Maps can often be drawn early in the research process because they frequently rely mostly on observation. Some ethnographers who have to learn a language or develop research relationships when they begin their research find that drawing maps at the outset helps them to get started with their research in earnest. If you draw maps at the beginning of your ethnographic research, you should expect to add or revise your maps during the course of your research. Your own experiences and learning from informants will almost certainly lead you to see certain aspects or perspectives differently and may even cause you to change your sense of scale or perspective. Remember: maps are representations of physical and imagined spaces that can highlight a variety of different emphases and perspectives.

Kinship charts will be most useful if the project involves examining social relationships among networks of people. You may already know or suspect that kinship plays a role in determining social obligations and defining social boundaries in your field site(s). In this case, developing kinship charts can be very helpful in beginning to identify networks and boundaries and testing working ideas about social relationships. Too often we expect kinship relationships to be most relevant in small-scale communities, but kinship is actually a much more pervasive social phenomenon. As people around the world negotiate the complexities of contemporary societies, many of them continue to draw on kinship in important ways or to rework "traditional" kinship networks and obligations (McCurdy 2008). These networks and obligations should be explored by ethnographers. The ethnographer should also be aware of the possibility of "fictive" kinship ties that can be important and enduring. From churches where members refer to each other as "brother" and "sister" to *hijra* households in India that recreate mother-daughter relationships (Nanda 1999) to organizations like fraternities and sororities that intentionally and explicitly invoke the language of kinship, ethnographers should pay close attention to the role of kinship and consider creating charts that help them to keep track of kinship ties and relationships. Ethnographers have found that seemingly similar kinship relationships often carry very different meanings and obligations depending on the cultural context. Kinship charts can help ethnographers ask important questions about these meanings and obligations in the course of their research. If you know or suspect that kinship plays a role in the social phenomena that you are researching, you should plan to develop one or more kinship charts. You will want to think carefully about whether one kinship chart will be sufficient for your purposes or whether you will need to construct multiple charts to represent different individuals, groups, or networks.

Like mapping, drawing kinship charts can sometimes be a useful way for the novice ethnographer to begin the research process. Informants are often very interested in talking about their families and explaining their importance. Therefore, kinship charts may be a key initial method if you are entering a field site that is new to you. Keep in mind, though, that in some cases both names and kinship relationships can be private and secretive. The ethnographer needs to stay attuned to the appropriateness of inquiries about kinship in a particular situation.

In situations where the ethnographer is researching the flow of information, the distribution of labor, or the exercise of authority, it may be very helpful to represent these flows and the interactions with a diagram or chart. In business environments, these sorts of diagrams are usually flow charts. The ethnographer will often be examining the flows and connections from a different perspective and with different goals, but you can still make use of these sorts of charts and diagrams. In some cases, you may then have the opportunity to compare your version to the ideal version, an exercise that can be very illuminating. Classic anthropological ethnographies often included diagrams of units like "tribes" (Evans-Pritchard's 1940 multiple visual representations of segmentary lineage organization) and "chiefdoms" (typically a pyramid). From state-level bureaucracies to other organizations, the ethnographer must strive to understand the functions and roles associated with different social positions and the practical exercise of power and authority as well as the flow of resources. These different components can often be usefully represented with a diagram. Once you have developed a working diagram and chart, you can then continue to verify how well it represents the continued occurrences within these situations.

One of the most famous diagrams of flows in the history of ethnography comes from Malinowski's *Argonauts of the Western Pacific* (1922). Using a map to show the flow of trade goods in opposite directions through the Trobriand Islands, Malinowski was able to describe the "kula ring" as a process through which local leaders gained prestige by controlling the trade of particular items. The visual organization of the material helped to make Malinowski's discussion a key contribution to early anthropology and the study of politics and economics. In contemplating diagrams or charts that you might develop, you need to consider carefully social structures that might be in play and how you might investigate the flow of goods and services.

Photographs and drawings can also be useful forms of visual data for ethnographers. A skilled photographer may be able to document various aspects of material culture and humans' relationship to the physical world that are related to the research topic. Researchers interested in ethnobotany or technology may rely particularly on this documentation of objects and materials as a centerpiece of their research strategy. These visual records can be used in later presentations and in conversations or interviews where the ethnographer asks for explanations about their production, use, or meaning. A study of floats used in Mardi Gras parades may need to carefully document these floats, the materials used, and the symbols produced. Of course, there are a lot of other topics that would require similarly close attention to the physical or material dimensions of society and culture.

Recently ethnographers have become more interested in collecting the visual representations that their informants produce. In this case, these drawings, pictures, or diagrams become cultural objects that the ethnographer can examine and analyze. Ethnographers have asked their informants to draw pictures reflecting certain ideas or moments, to take pictures, or even to keep journals. These exercises have placed more direct control of the research process in the hands of informants by making them directly responsible for producing the data that are collected. For many, this is an experimental method, but you may want to think about whether you want to explore this option in the course of your work.

WHAT IS PRACTICAL OR FEASIBLE? TIME, AVAILABILITY, AND ETHICS

At this stage in the research, you should be thinking in terms of the ideal research project. As you evaluate different methods, you should consider all possibilities and try not to edit out what seems impractical before you have to do so. Once you have a list of the ideal research questions and the ideal methods for answering those questions, you can then proceed to revise your goals and plans in terms of practicality and feasibility. If an item is high on your priority list in terms of answering your research question, you will want to work hard to make it practical or feasible. If it is low on the list, you may decide to dedicate your efforts to higher priority, and more practical or feasible, research plans.

One key concern is time. If the research is limited by the duration of funding for a project or the school term, you will want to plan to complete your project within those time limits. This may mean you will not be able to observe a full calendar cycle of events or be part of a full agricultural season. You may need to make some practical accommodations based on these limitations. If so, you may turn to indirect research, like written accounts or interviews, so that you can study those events or that part of the season that you will miss. The research plan needs to link specific research methods to the important forms and sources of information in light of the practical circumstances.

Ethnography generally requires a significant time commitment. You cannot be successful without making that commitment, but you probably have other commitments like school and work. You will not be able to conduct participant-observation at events that occur during your calculus class or your shift at work unless you make special arrangements. You need to make sure that (1) you set aside and dedicate enough time to make the ethnographic project successful and (2) that you can navigate and balance your research responsibilities with your other obligations. You want to set your project up to be a success, and time is a crucial element.

With lists of questions and research methods, the ethnographer also needs to think about availability. A lot of the issues related to availability are connected to the issues of access covered previously. Thinking practically, you need to choose field sites and informants that are available to you. If you lack particular language skills, social connections, or personal characteristics, some sites and some informants may not be available to you. Now is the time to carefully evaluate whether you will have access to the sites and informants that you will need to answer your research questions. If not, you may need to revise your research questions in relatively minor or significant ways so that you can use what is available to you in productive ways. For instance, teachers and volunteers may be more available to the ethnographer than students or the homeless as informants, but their perspective will allow the ethnographer to answer only certain research questions. In many instances, certain sites and informants are not immediately available to you, especially the first time you arrive. Working over time to build trust and lay the foundation for research can be a key step that increases availability. In this case, time and availability dovetail. Practically speaking, you will have to balance time and availability with your ideal research project. If time or other constraints do not allow you to pursue all your ideal methods, you may find it helpful to see this project as part of a larger one that you will continue to pursue in the future.

As always, the ethics of the research plan and methods are a paramount concern. In trying to negotiate the concerns of time and availability, you should not detour from an ethical path for your research. You will need to be forthright and honest about your project and your intentions. The ethnographer is not a spy or a mole. The aboveboard approach can sometimes make the process of gaining access time consuming and lengthy. You should make sure you allow time to build trust and for your informants to offer input in the process. If they want you to do things differently or choose not to participate or allow you access to certain things, you will have to adapt in ways that allow you to pursue your research ethically. Hopefully you will find other avenues into your research question and may be able to return to your original plans at another point. Adaptability is the name of the game.

In sensitive cases especially, you should think about whether particular methods pose ethical concerns so that you can avoid problematic methods or institute safeguards. Photographs may represent a particularly delicate issue in some cases; if photography is potentially problematic in some situations, you will have to come up with a careful plan for when, where, and how to shoot photographs. Notes, maps, charts, and interviews all carry potential risks for the participants depending on the circumstances. You need to exercise care, try to foresee potential risks, and take steps as part of the research plan to eliminate or mitigate these risks.

SUMMARY

Research design enables you to ensure that you collect necessary and relevant information in the appropriate ways. The first step in this process involves turning a topic into a research question or set of questions. Good research questions lead from the descriptive to the analytical and address deeper questions of how and why. With guiding research questions, you can identify the types of information you need to collect to answer these questions and decide on your research methods with those ends in mind. Ethnography as a research strategy almost always involves a combination of three key methods: participant-observation, interviewing, and constructing visual representations like maps and charts. Therefore, the research design involves figuring out how best to combine these methods and when to supplement them with additional methods. Both practical and ethical issues are important concerns in determining the feasibility of a given research plan.

KEY TERMS

Research question
Exploratory research
Open-ended
Descriptive
Analytical
Descriptive questions
Research question
Research methods
Interviews
Conversations
Data collection
Key methods

Participant-observer
Event
Apprentice
Perspectives
Experiences
Representative
Maps
Charts
Kinship chart
Spatial relations
Social interaction

DISCUSSION QUESTIONS

1. What are the key steps and considerations in turning a research topic into a research question? What types of questions should the ethnographer seek to develop and build on?

2. As a key method, which sorts of questions is participant-observation best suited to collecting information to answer?

3. What types of data and information is the ethnographer most likely to collect by using interviews as a key method? Are these types of data and information particularly well suited to answering specific types of research questions?

4. Why are maps and charts particularly helpful in studying and analyzing social relationships and interaction? How can different types of maps and charts be used to study different social and cultural phenomena?

5. How concerned should you be with the practical feasibility of your project? How can you determine whether your project is truly feasible?

6. How do ethical concerns influence the viability of a research project designed to answer a specific research question? Are particular ethical concerns associated with particular methods of collecting and recording ethnographic data?

CHAPTER

4

WRITING A PROPOSAL

LEARNING OBJECTIVES

- Enumerate the key components of a research proposal
- Review appropriate literature
- Develop a succinct and effective statement of research problem
- Create a research plan specifically designed to address the research problem
- Connect a specific research plan and question to issues of larger relevance
- Evaluate a research plan in terms of responsibilities to human subjects and prepare for the review process
- Explore the issue of consent in research design and execution

With developed research questions and the key research methods that you can employ to answer those questions, you are prepared to write a formal **proposal**. You may already have consulted with a supervisor or experienced ethnographer in previous stages, but in writing the formal proposal, you are preparing to present your ideas and your plans to a larger audience. Depending on the nature of your project, this audience may include an instructor and classmates, a supervisor, funding agencies, institutional review boards, or the larger public. The point of the proposal is to present a clear explanation of your ideas and rationale as well as your research plans. It offers the opportunity to receive critical feedback that should make your project stronger in the long run.

Proposal writing is a skill that will serve the ethnographer well in a variety of circumstances. Careers in business, the nonprofit service sector, or academics all frequently require the ability to produce a well-reasoned and convincing proposal. You may need to adjust your proposal to a particular audience, but formal research proposals generally follow this standard structure:

1. Summary introduction
2. Literature review
3. Statement of problem or question
4. Research plan and methods
5. Summation of intentions for results and the project's import

This chapter will examine each of these sections in the research proposal in sequence, with a view toward building a complete proposal. The primary goal of any proposal should be to convince the audience (1) that there is strong justification for the project, (2) that you are prepared to conduct the research, and (3) that you have a well-thought-out plan to produce meaningful research results.

Looking at examples of successful research proposals written by other ethnographers can be very helpful in the process of constructing one's own proposal. A straightforward Internet search will turn up abstracts and full proposals for ethnography (or cultural anthropology) submitted to funding agencies like the National Science Foundation, Wenner-Gren, and Fulbright-Hays. These proposals may be more extensive and advanced than your own project, but they can still serve as useful models. In looking to past proposals as models, look carefully at the way the **literature review** section is constructed and referenced and at the specific discussion of methods in the method section. Even if the topic and the research plan in the proposal are completely different, a close reading will provide a good sense of the way a research proposal fits together and the way you can use your proposal to lay out a detailed plan and make a case for the importance of your project.

IDENTIFYING AND REVIEWING APPROPRIATE LITERATURE

You will usually enter a project with some idea about literature related to your topic, especially if your interests or questions emerged from another researcher's previous work. In the literature review, you want to provide the reader with a *summary* of the current state of the field as it relates to your topic. You should provide an introduction to past research, unanswered questions, and significant debates. The literature review serves both to situate the proposed research in a larger context and to provide a rationale for the significant contribution that will help to answer unresolved questions and contribute to important debates.

Obviously, the first step in writing a literature review is to make sure you are conversant with the relevant body of literature. You become conversant with relevant literature by making a concerted effort first to identify and then to familiarize yourself with the available academic literature. You should spend time using research databases and library catalogs and make sure you are using multiple search terms in different combinations to ensure good coverage with your searches. By using the summary description or abstract of an article or book, you can often determine its relevance to your project. As you review sources and identify relevant items, you should keep a summary list of these sources and their relevant points (information, questions, and theories). You can then use this list in constructing your literature review.

In the course of literature searches, you will usually want to concentrate on social science sources. Because ethnography is rooted in a social science perspective, you will generally find the most relevant literature in social science sources. You may have to sort through a lot of interesting, but tangentially related, sources in this winnowing process. For instance, for a project researching the culture of workout gyms, a standard keyword search with the entry "workout <and> gym" may return a large number of articles from the disciplines of physiology and exercise science that reflect good research but do not relate to your interests in social manifestations of race and class in the gym environment. Similarly, if you plan to examine the culture of fast food, you may have to sort through a lot of nutrition sources to identify the ones that are relevant to your project. Sometimes including key words like "social," "culture," "sociology," "anthropology," and "ethnography" can help zero in on the most appropriate results related to ethnographic research. Databases also sometimes have built-in filters that you can use to limit your results to specific disciplines or journals.

You should be careful not to automatically dismiss sources that are not ethnographically based. You may rely less heavily on them but find it helpful or even necessary to cite these other perspectives, especially as a way to demonstrate the utility or value of an ethnographic approach. For instance, you may be able to lead into your ethnography by establishing that exercise science research tends to ignore or downplay the role of race and class in the use and form of workout gyms or that nutrition science too often erases the cultural dimensions of food. If the project is practically oriented, you may also want to offer a sense of current practice or policy, its research foundations (or lack thereof), and its relationship to other research and theories.

All these approaches help to contextualize the project. Ideally, the literature review will explain the current state of affairs and link the proposed research to big questions and debates or holes in current understandings of a given topic. In doing so, the review will draw on the work of others to lead into the proposed research and show your familiarity with the field. The reader of the literature review should gain a sense that you are a good researcher and that you have a firm grounding for your project. In many ways, the literature review is ideally a teleological narrative—that is, it is headed to a clear ending, your project. If the reader finishes the literature review with the sense that the topic or question is the obvious next step in an important trajectory of research, the literature review has done its job.

While you do want to weed out tangential or unrelated sources, remember that you are not necessarily looking for sources that describe the research that you propose to conduct. If you find sources that seem to be very similar to your proposed work, then you need to think carefully about how your research will differ in terms of questions, methods, time period, and so on. You do not simply want to replicate someone else's work unless there is a reason to replicate it, such as dubious results or changes in other variables. For example, you should not become discouraged in your literature search if it does not return any studies of flea markets in Idaho. If you plan to study flea markets in Idaho, you can make the argument that they have yet to be studied adequately and need to be studied. At the same time, you should not assume that a lack of sources about your specific topic means that there is a general dearth of relevant sources. Expanding or tweaking the search parameters will likely yield a plethora of sources. There may be sources examining flea markets elsewhere, but there will also be a lot of sources dealing with the economics of buying and trading and informal economies that will likely be very relevant for the project. Using more general search terms (like "informal economy," in this case) may help you identify relevant sources with important information, questions, and theories.

Cross-cultural examples can often be very fruitful. These examples can provide a comparative basis and help in building a case for the more general importance of the project. For instance, a study of hair salons in Seattle may benefit from comparison with practices and spaces of hair care in other parts of the world. If you have discovered a particular tendency or argued that these practices and spaces fulfill a particular function elsewhere, you may then be able to use your own research to test the general applicability of this argument in a particular cultural setting (Seattle, in this case). Keep in mind that ethnography offers us examples and models from a wide range of settings and can be very illuminating as we build our projects.

Theoretically oriented sources and review articles can also be very helpful sources as you build your literature review. These types of broad-scale perspectives will provide you with a context for the big picture and the more abstract theoretical ideas that emerge in relationship to your topic. You want to build your own sense of how the work of others informs your project, of course, but familiarizing yourself with the ways others conceptualize the state of affairs in the field and how they try to resolve key analytical issues can be very useful.

The quantity of sources will vary widely depending on the context of your project, but you should always aim to identify and review the most important sources that have helped shape the current field. Once you have identified the appropriate literature to review, you are in a position to write your literature review. Taking a look back at your list of sources and their key points, you need to consider whether the sources can be grouped in terms of similar claims or results, competing results or theories, or different foci. Organizing sources in this way can help you determine the key organizing or structuring principles for the literature review.

The length of the literature review should be proportionate to the overall length of the proposal. Within a proposal of three to five pages, assume that the literature review will be between one and two pages long. This length means that the researcher is producing a comprehensive review in a small space. Whereas you may delve deeply into particular sources in other venues, in the literature review you want to bring together a wide range of sources. You should avoid lengthy quotes and expect to reference multiple sources in each paragraph of your literature review. You want to focus on the most important, big-picture points from your sources and build connections and comparisons wherever possible. If the reader encounters an additional source after reading your review, the reader should be able to use your literature review to contextualize that source in terms of the field.

It is often effective to open by stating the problem or question and then delineating different approaches or answers that have been offered. The researcher can often usefully conclude the literature review by clearly laying out what has been answered or resolved and what remains to be studied or resolved. At the end of the literature review, this trajectory or legacy of work described should lead the reader straight into the research topic as an important outcome of that legacy. You can do this even if you are critical of some of the past work and approaches. In this case, the proposed research will fill in research gaps or redirect research and understanding in more productive ways.

STATEMENT OF THE PROBLEM

The framework set up in the literature review should lead directly into a clear statement of the central problem or question(s) at the heart of the project. You should make it as clear as possible that this is a logical or necessary next step in the trajectory of the field that you have just finished surveying. Sometimes you can use the literature review to show how your project will bring together two fields that have been largely separate to this point. Showing how the work will bridge gaps and fill in holes in existing knowledge will help to demonstrate the overall import of the ethnographic research.

Immediately following the literature review section of your proposal, there should be a clear declarative statement of the central research focus or question of the project. This is the heart of the proposal. The literature review leads into it, and the methods section that follows it grows directly out of the research focus or question, as we saw in Chapter Three. You may want to highlight this important section in bold or italics to draw the reader's attention. You need to be particularly confident and assertive in constructing this part of your proposal. You might say something like "This research project will resolve the theoretical debate between x and y" or "Using primary ethnographic data, this research will support or refute the idea that . . ." Alternatively, you may want to state directly or list your questions or hypotheses. This approach may be particularly effective if you have a set of related or nested questions or hypotheses. In this case, a list may show the relationship among the individual items. The researcher may actually outline one or a few major questions or hypotheses and groups of secondary questions or hypotheses that belong underneath the major foci. The schematic outline below represents a project with two main hypotheses and two subhypotheses underneath each of the main hypotheses:

Hypothesis 1
    Subhypothesis 1a
    Subhypothesis 1b

Hypothesis 2
    Subhypothesis 2a
    Subhypothesis 2b

Whatever the format, the main goal of this section is to present a clear set of questions or hypotheses that can be answered or tested using the research methods that follow.

Though this section of your proposal will be relatively short, you should pay close attention to its construction. This section is the chance to grab the reader's attention with an interesting problem or question, show that you have a clear analytical approach, and lay the foundation for the subsequent methods section in which you will describe how to collect the necessary information. There is a tendency to try to include everything in this section. While ethnography will inevitably produce a lot of different types of information, the researcher should avoid the temptation to include every potential direction in this section. At this point, you should have decided on a relatively focused direction for the project, and you want to communicate that specificity and clarity in the proposal. Readers of the proposal will appreciate the clarity and **analytical focus** more than they will appreciate a chaotic list of possible directions or outcomes. The reader will also be able to offer constructive feedback much more easily if the proposal rests on a well-defined list of questions or hypotheses. You may have to revise your focus as the project develops, but you will always want to work to maintain specificity and clarity, even as you adapt and the project evolves. Showing that you can develop and present a clear statement of the research problem at this stage will also demonstrate that you have the skills to adapt and refine your research problem should the need arise as you pursue the research.

A CLEAR RESEARCH PLAN

At this point, the ethnographer has a working list of research questions and the types of information required to answer those questions. Essentially this list functions as an outline of the things that you do not yet know and want to learn, as well as the means to do so. The **research plan** is a clear strategy to find answers to the questions that do not yet have clear or firm answers. The research plan or **methods section** lays out your blueprint for achieving the central goals you have identified.

Constructing the research plan starts with a clear connection among the questions, the types of information, and the methods that the researcher will employ to collect that information. Because you will almost certainly be using a combination of methods in your research strategy, establish this from the beginning. In the opening paragraph of this section, you should identify the length of your project (weeks, months, or a year or more), its location(s), and the primary methods that you plan to employ. In subsequent paragraphs, you can address the specifics of each method that you propose. Therefore, you will have one or more paragraphs on each of the following: participant-observation, interviews, mapping and charts, and any additional methods you intend to use.

In the paragraph or paragraphs on participant-observation, you should be as specific as possible about your research plans involving participant-observation. You need to answer the questions of when, where, and how in as detailed a manner as you can. As to the when, you should be clear about how often (daily? weekly?) you plan to conduct participant-observation and what the occasion or event will be (Friday services, Wednesday dinners, or impromptu gatherings, for instance). Answering the where question should be pretty straightforward; you will want to offer as much detail as you can at the outset. If you will be carrying out research in multiple field sites, you should make sure this is clear. **Comparative data** from multiple sites can be very helpful, but you will want to make sure you are collecting enough information from each site, which connects back to the issue of frequency. Finally, you should address the question of how in relationship to each proposed form of participant-observation. If you are planning to apprentice yourself or become a particularly active participant (for example, as an actor or a team member), you should include this information in this section. If access is a potential issue for a particular site or activity, you should list the steps you have taken or will take to gain access.

At the end of this subsection, you can tie the specifics together by discussing the important contributions of participant-observation to your research endeavor as part of the research plan. You may want to emphasize how this method provides access to empirical data about culture and society in action; participant-observation gives you access to information about behavior, conversations, and perspectives that are not directly solicited by you, and to **experiential data**. You may also want to talk about participant-observation as a necessary precursor to other methods, especially interviews.

In the next subsection, addressing the role of interviews and conversations in the research plan, you should aim for specificity about the types of questions you will be asking, the types of responses you hope to collect, and who the interviewees will be. You can also indicate whether the interviews will be formal or informal and whether they involve asking open-ended questions. The default approach in ethnography is generally informal and open-ended; this approach allows the informant the most chance to guide the interview and to fill the role of teacher. If you are looking to collect lengthy first-person accounts, you will certainly want to adopt this approach, but in some instances a more formal approach or more closed-ended questions are appropriate. Making a decision in this vein goes back to the type of information you need to collect. You may also want to include a sample interview schedule (list of questions) as an appendix to your research proposal.

As part of your research plan, you should include a proposed number of interviews or interviewees, an explanation of how they will be identified (through contacts, participant-observation, random selection, or other means) and what criteria will be used to select them. Remember that good interviews are time consuming; you should be ambitious but realistic about the number of interviews that you intend to pursue as part of your research plan. In choosing interviewees, you will want to think carefully about which individuals might be most knowledgeable or experienced in connection with a particular topic, but you should also think about representativeness. For instance, you will want to decide whether you should interview both men and women along with the question of how age and experience will affect your choice of interviewees.

When it comes to the use of charts, diagrams, or maps, you should explain your approach and rationale for using a specific method or **tool**. You should be as specific as possible in detailing the specific data that will be collected and how they will be used in the project. You will want to include information about particular tools you might be using in association with this method and any assistance or training required to use this method.

If you plan to employ any additional methods, you should provide a clear summary of the techniques and outcomes involved. Then you should conclude the methods section by revisiting the larger picture and the way that this combination of methods will allow you to collect different types of information and combine them productively in an analytical framework designed to answer your central research questions.

IDENTIFYING YOUR PROJECT'S LARGER RELEVANCE

After outlining the existing literature, the central research question, and the intended research plan, the final section of the proposal brings these different components together to highlight the import of the results and the intended audience and usage. With a comprehensive literature review, you will be well positioned to argue for the important contributions this research will make. You should write about it in terms of providing missing information, resolving disputes, and answering key unresolved questions. If your project has a practical application, you should clearly explain how the research can be used to solve a problem and to implement solutions, whether that is a change in policy or a new program.

This section of your proposal should also detail how the findings will be distributed and to whom. Chances are good that you have a particular audience in mind. You should make it clear that you will deliver your important results to the appropriate audience. This step will ensure that the full benefits of the work can be realized. Today it is generally expected that you will share the results of your ethnographic work with your informants. This sharing is a step to ensure that you are not simply extracting information from them in an **exploitative relationship**, and it can offer opportunities for very informative **feedback**. As the ethnographer, you may find that certain important elements are missing or underemphasized in your work or you may uncover

The Proposal Summary

Most proposals typically begin with a very brief, one-paragraph summary or abstract. Usually these summaries are the first exposure that readers have to the project, and in some cases they may be the only part that readers read unless the abstract captures their attention. Imagine a committee member trying to decide which ten projects to fund out of a pool of more than two hundred applications. That reviewer may decide to use the summaries to reduce the stack of proposals to a more manageable number before carefully reading the remaining proposals with an eye to a final funding decision. You want your summary to be an effective advocate for the proposal so that the reader is motivated to read the more in-depth proposal that follows.

Although the summary appears at the beginning of the proposal, writing the summary after you have completed the other sections of the proposal is the best practice. In the summary, you do not need to create new ideas for the proposal. Instead you should pull the biggest, most important elements from the larger proposal. In the space of a sentence or two for each item, you should highlight (1) the general importance of the project in relationship to existing research and theories; (2) the central research problem; (3) the key methods to be utilized; and (4) the significance of the results that will be obtained. A confident, direct tone should be employed for the entire proposal, but this tone is especially important for the summary. In the summary or abstract, you can convey to the reader your commitment, your preparedness, and your conviction that this is an important research project.

significant differences in opinion about what happened, what was said, or how to interpret these things. While it can be difficult to make sense of these differences, these sorts of exchanges can be fruitful extensions of the research relationship between ethnographer and informant that build on the particular dynamic of the student-teacher relationship (see Scheper-Hughes 2001 for a cautionary tale of what can happen when informants and other parties engage ethnographic representations). You may want to include your plan to share the results with your informants as part of the research proposal, especially since it represents a commitment to collaboration and dialogue.

HUMAN SUBJECTS REVIEW AND APPROVAL

Almost all institutions involved in research have an established system for reviewing research that involves the use of human subjects. Unfortunately, there are instances in the history of research in which human participants in research (the people on whom we depend when we do research) have been subject to unnecessary risks, misinformation, and negative outcomes. Some of the most famous examples of research that failed to offer proper protection for human subjects come from the syphilis research at the Tuskegee Institute and Milgram's psychological experiments. Unfortunately, human failings like self-interest, racism, and even greed can find their way into research settings without appropriate reviews and filters.

Human subjects review committees or **institutional review boards (IRBs)** have become a fixture at research institutions like colleges, universities, and hospitals. They have also become increasingly common in other circumstances as groups look to oversee the research conducted involving them or their interests. The committees' or IRBs' principal task is to review research proposals to evaluate relative risks and benefits to participants as well as the measures that will be taken to obtain consent and to protect human subjects who choose to participate in the research. This evaluation includes consideration of processes for explaining the research process to the participants and means for acquiring participants' consent. Generally speaking, human subjects should be able to willingly choose whether or not to participate in the research and have a firm understanding of the goals of the research as well as the benefits and the **risks** associated with participating.

Because ethnography always involves human subjects (that is, informants), it is always a candidate for human subjects review. You should be prepared to present your proposal for review. If you are completing this project as part of a class or a larger project, there may be a procedure in place to review the assignment or project as a whole, and the review will fall under the larger umbrella. Otherwise you will have to submit a proposal to the committee or IRB for review. Depending on the protocol, you may want to include your general proposal and appendixes, such as sample interview schedules. The heart of the human subjects proposal is consideration of the risks and benefits to participants, an explanation of the means for disclosure and obtaining consent, and an explanation of any protections that will be in place to protect participants.

In many cases, the risks to human subjects involved with participation in ethnographic research are relatively negligible. After all, ethnography involves studying the culture and social phenomena that exist prior to the advent of research. The ethnographer is not seeking to control or manipulate subjects the way that an experimenter might. Still, the ethnographer's presence and actions necessarily produce some effect on those associated with research. These effects can be negative if they draw undue attention to something that should remain hidden or discrete or if they prompt others to change their behaviors. In some cases, the risks to participants or informants can be more pronounced, especially if the ethnographer is researching social phenomena that are illegal, illicit, or socially unacceptable. If the research involves experiences of violence or trauma, the act of research may carry risks of exacerbating these experiences or psychological risks associated with revisiting those experiences.

Too often, ethnography involves few tangible benefits for participants. Ethnographers often offer gifts or other forms of remuneration to compensate for the time and energy that informants devote to an ethnographic project, and some informants genuinely enjoy serving the role of teacher in the ethnographic endeavor. Others are probably rightfully skeptical about how their participation will benefit them directly or indirectly. The simple accumulation of knowledge is often only a very indirect benefit to informants. If a research project has a practical application that will benefit participants, you should make sure to explain the benefit in your proposal. Participants may benefit from effective programs and policies, improved working and living environments, or their ability to advocate in their own interests. In some cases, significant benefits can be cited as justification for research that involves some risks, but the researcher must be able to make a compelling argument that the benefits outweigh the risks.

Some of the worst abuses of the research relationship have occurred in instances where the researcher deceived or misinformed research participants. In some instances full disclosure of the research strategy will prejudice the actions or responses of participants, but in these cases there has to be a reasoned plan for preparing the participant prior to participation and debriefing the participant afterward. As a general rule, **deception** or **misinformation** is not a good practice in ethnographic research. There are noteworthy examples of ethnographers who have chosen not to fully disclose their research roles with human subjects approval (see Nathan 2005, for example), but these choices have often also involved significant debate after the fact. Unless you have a very specific and defensible reason not to, you should plan to fully disclose your research intentions to everyone involved. If you are unable to practice full disclosure with everyone (for example, participant-observation in an arena of sixty thousand people), you should still plan to disclose your position as researcher. If someone asks about your work, you should be prepared to explain your research approach and your research goals. Sometimes disclosure can be a healthy entry into a sustained research relationship, especially if you can communicate your own genuine interest and the potential relevance of your work.

Obtaining consent is perhaps the thorniest issue for ethnographers and participant-observers. Whenever feasible, you should plan to explain your project and to obtain consent to observe, participate, and record the words, thoughts, and behavior of individuals. In a very large group, you may not be able to obtain consent for practical reasons, but you should certainly obtain consent in small groups and when working closely with particular informants. Informants should have a reasonable opportunity to approve or disapprove of research activities that involve them. If informants are not willing participants, you should respect their wishes.

Obtaining consent is a bit more straightforward when it comes to interviews. You should include a simple disclosure and consent form or statement with your human subjects proposal. This statement should explain the project briefly and that participation in the interview is voluntary and can be ended at any time. It should also explain any protections that will be used, especially to maintain confidentiality or anonymity. Obtaining consent with a statement like this will allow you to record and utilize the words of your informants with some degree of confidence that you have done so in an ethically responsible way (see Duneier 1999 for a compelling discussion of these issues).

Protections of human subjects can take many forms depending on the circumstances. In most cases, the protections in ethnographic research have to do with protecting anonymity or confidentiality. You should make sure that your research and its products cannot be used against the participants in any foreseeable way. Common steps include using **pseudonyms** or codes to protect the identity of informants in field notes. You may also want to indicate that you will keep notes in a locked drawer or password-protected file as a further protection to ensure that the notes are not used by anyone else without permission. In special cases, you may have to devise more elaborate methods to avoid prompting disputes or confrontations and to protect informants from legal or violent reprisals (Nordstrom and Robben 1995). In extreme cases, ethnographers have chosen not to keep field notes to avoid producing a written record that can be used against informants. Generally speaking, protections to ensure confidentiality are sufficient in most cases. Keep in mind, though, that conversations and research interactions often involve a degree of trust and confidence and that should be respected whenever possible.

SUMMARY

The research proposal lays out a clear rationale and plan for research that connects the specific project to the larger context of research, theory, and practical problem solving. The literature review provides a comprehensive review of the current state of research and thinking related to the topic and shows why the proposed research is relevant and important. The statement of the problem establishes questions or hypotheses that the researcher can directly address with the methods you outline in the following section. The methods section should explain specifically how you plan to employ key research methods to collect relevant data. When constructing a research proposal, you should be prepared for the human subjects review process and make sure you have a plan for pursuing research methods in a manner that respects and protects the interests and wishes of your informants.

KEY TERMS

Proposal
Literature review
Analytical focus
Research plan
Methods section
Comparative data
Experiential data
Tool

Exploitative relationship
Feedback
Human subjects review
Institutional review boards (IRBs)
Risks
Deception
Misinformation
Pseudonyms

DISCUSSION QUESTIONS

1. What are the key components of a research proposal? How should you work to connect these different components as you build your proposal?

2. What sorts of literature should the ethnographer be interested in primarily? How can you determine if a particular piece of literature is relevant to your project?

3. Why does the ethnographer need a succinct and specific research question or problem? Why might the ethnographer have a hard time developing a succinct and specific problem?

4. What sorts of data can you plan to collect with the methods outlined in your research plan? Should all ethnographers try to collect all types of data equally?

5. How can ethnography contribute to larger academic and popular discussions of social issues? What is most likely to make ethnography relevant to wider issues and a larger audience?

6. What are the most important issues to consider in designing an ethical plan for research and preparing for the human subjects review process?

PART

2

ETHNOGRAPHY IN THE FIELD: COLLECTING DATA

CHAPTER

5

A GUIDE TO COLLECTING DATA AND TAKING NOTES

LEARNING OBJECTIVES

- Explain the importance of constructing good field notes
- Appreciate the fleeting nature of much ethnographic data
- Develop strategies for taking effective field notes
- Consider ways to use technology and other sources of data to supplement field notes
- Evaluate the process of transcribing interviews
- Identify and prioritize ethnographic data to be recorded
- Examine the ethics involved in creating field notes and recording data

At this point in the research process, you should have begun to build a habit of writing and recording in your research notebook. This habit is a crucial one for the ethnographer. During the course of the research, you will almost always have notes to take. The more writing and note taking becomes habitual, the easier it will be for you to stay up to date with your project. As the primary research instrument, you will play a vital role in producing, measuring, and recording information or data. Generally speaking, the more information you have to work with in terms of notes, the more likely your project is to be successful, but you want to hone your note-taking skills to

CASE STUDY

Taking Field Notes in Botswana

David N. Suggs has conducted ethnographic research in Botswana since 1984. His ethnography, *A Bagful of Locusts and the Baboon Woman* (Suggs 2001), draws on two primary, year-long periods of research in the town of Mochudi, one in 1984 and the other in 1992. In this work, Suggs examines historical changes and focuses specifically on changes in structures and understandings of age and gender.

Using alcohol, particularly its consumption, as a way to examine these changes, Suggs's research shows that economic changes in Botswana have produced significant shifts with regard to both age and gender. Whereas male elders often used to control alcohol as a social and economic resource, today younger men, who are engaged in wage labor and the cash economy, have increased access to alcohol and are no longer dependent on elders. While Suggs finds that women's public consumption of alcohol is still relatively uncommon in Mochudi, he also explains how their engagement with new economic forms and systems entails newly independent control over resources in many cases. This control over resources has produced changes both in household structures and in women's patterns of consumption of alcohol.

In a very real sense, the previous structures of age and gender have been upended or inverted as a result of a new distribution of resources and different avenues for accessing the dominant economy. Still, Suggs makes a compelling argument for seeing the historical developments in Mochudi and Botswana as a whole in terms of a dialectic of continuity and change. The two seeming opposites coexist in the minds and lives of residents of Mochudi, even if conflicts between old and new cultural models do occur semiregularly. Suggs's work provides an excellent example of an ethnography that addresses cultural change in a direct and meaningful way.

During his first period of fieldwork in 1984, Suggs pursued a research agenda focused primarily on highly structured make the process as efficient and productive as possible. The trick is collecting a broad enough set of information to allow the project to evolve and to develop appropriately without casting such a wide net that you collect a completely haphazard set of information that makes analysis impossible or difficult.

As ethnographer, you should begin taking **field notes** as soon as you can. There will be a learning curve as you refine a system that works for you. You should get used to working regularly with pen and paper or computer and allow your informants to grow accustomed to seeing you taking notes. At times, it may feel funny to write

interviews that specifically sought to collect information about BaKgatla women's socialization and their experience of different stages in their lives as women. This interview-based research, supplemented by informal observation and informal conversations as well as historical evidence, provides the baseline for his consideration of change among the BaKgatla. When he returned to Mochudi in the early 1990s, he "employed a much more open-ended methodology" (2001, 19). During this research stint, he conducted a good deal of informal participant-observation and relied heavily on informal conversations and some formal interviews in collecting ethnographic information. One of the strengths of Suggs's ethnographic work stems from his skill as a storyteller and his ability to weave together information gained through informal observations, interactions, and conversations.

With his focus on alcohol and its consumption, a good deal of the fieldwork that Suggs conducted in the 1990s took place in bars in Mochudi. Because of the specific character of a bar as field site and the relatively informal nature of most of the research that Suggs was conducting, he usually chose not to take notes or to record conversations in bars. Instead, he made a point of taking detailed notes as soon as he left the bar while conducting fieldwork. On some occasions, this practice of note taking involved sitting in his car as soon as he left the bar to write field notes (personal communication with David N. Suggs, 2007). He was able to train himself to remember details for his subsequent writing of notes, but he was very careful to write notes as soon as he left the field site before he lost too much detail in his recollections of events and conversations. Suggs's ethnography is rich in engaging detail, which is a testament to his ability to record detail in his ethnographic record. However, while it includes many rich and descriptive accounts of events and conversations, it includes only a few examples of extended dialogue or conversation. This fact is probably attributable to the way that he chose to take notes as well as his theoretical model and his general writing style.

certain things down, but you are creating an important research record, and the process of writing notes can be an important part of the analytical process as you evaluate what is important and what it might mean. Sometimes you will not recognize the significance of a particular piece of information until you write it down or well after that point. When in doubt, you should write it down.

THE FLEETING NATURE OF ETHNOGRAPHIC DATA

The information that the ethnographer will collect often only exists for short periods of time before it disappears. The words somebody says, along with hand gestures and body language, as well as any number of other facets of human life, happen and disappear rather quickly. If they are to become part of the ethnographic record, they have to be noted and recorded as they happen. There are mechanisms, like cameras, videos, and audio recordings, that ethnographers can use to record and preserve these elements for future study, but these mechanisms have limitations and tend to emphasize some aspects of these events while missing other aspects. The ethnographer is in a position to create the most complete record of these things as they happen. **Ethnographic data** is fleeting, and the ethnographer's job is to record it before it disappears or dissipates.

Firsthand experiences and observations are essential in the collection of ethnographic data and note taking. Recollections after the fact can be interesting sources of information and subjects of analysis, but they are no substitute for notes generated through immediate presence at the moment in question. Human memory is a tricky and complicated phenomenon, and it can complicate the record unnecessarily.

"SHOULD I WRITE IT DOWN IMMEDIATELY?"

Ethnographers employ a number of different strategies when it comes to note taking, especially in more public settings. Some ethnographers travel everywhere with notebook in hand and make notes whenever the occasion calls for note taking. Other ethnographers choose to work with a small notebook to make cursory notes of key points and then to flesh out the notes later in private. Still others choose not to carry a notebook with them and rely on their memory to create notes after leaving the field site. A number of variables can influence the ethnographer's choice. Some environments are much more suitable for immediate note taking. Note taking in private, intimate settings may seem particularly intrusive or distracting. If participant-observation requires frequent movement or use of the hands or if it takes place in a dark place, the practical opportunities for note taking may be limited. Informants' literacy and their general experience with note taking and written records may also influence their response to public note taking by the ethnographer.

Many ethnographers are reluctant to become a spectacle as a public note taker. Because the ethnographer's goal is to learn from others, making oneself the center of attention with a conspicuous pen and notebook may run counter to this goal. Nevertheless, the expectation that the ethnographer will be like a "fly on the wall" is probably unrealistic in most cases, and as informants become accustomed to seeing the ethnographer with notebook in hand, it can become an accepted part of the researcher's persona. For this reason, advocates of public note taking suggest that you begin the practice from the outset so that eventually people will come to see it as normal and it will become less so that less noteworthy (pun intended).

As far as collecting detailed ethnographic data goes, public note taking is probably the best practice in the abstract. Because it involves recording things as they happen, there is less opportunity for distortion or gaps in the record. Practically, though, if someone is constantly asking "What are you writing down now?" that may be more disruptive to the research process than public note taking is productive. You should choose the approach that is best suited to your research circumstances.

The most important thing is to make notes and to create the ethnographic record as soon as possible. The longer the period of time that passes between an event and the note taking about it, the more likely that some elements will be misremembered or not remembered at all. If you plan to make notes after leaving your field site, you need to make sure you budget sufficient time for proper note taking immediately afterward. You should not wait until the next day or even later to make notes.

THE IMPORTANCE OF DETAIL IN THE ETHNOGRAPHIC RECORD

Good detail is an essential part of good ethnography. In writing notes and creating an **ethnographic record**, the ethnographer should try to record as much detail as possible. If you record detail, you have more information with which to work when you return to your notes. You may be very happy when you revisit your notes and discover an important detail that you did not recognize as important at the time. Detail also often helps in the latter stages of composing a final ethnography. Skilled ethnographers can paint vivid pictures and convey the texture of human life in compelling ways. Details—from a person's specific words to the scents wafting through the air or the color of a wrap holding a baby to a mother's back—make an ethnography complete and help you set the context for research and the social phenomena that you are describing and examining. The reader of an ethnography may not always make conscious note of the ethnographer's comment on the shape of a person's face or the size of a sitting room, but you will see the detail as an integral part of most ethnographies if you look closely. Details assist in **narrative storytelling** by placing the reader in the position of researcher or participant as nearly as possible and in documenting the complexity of human lives. Details are the components of society and culture in action.

The details that you notice and record in your ethnographic notes will vary. Your own proclivities and experiences will mean that you bring your own rather idiosyncratic approach to the collection of ethnographic details. That individual approach is to be expected; part of the power of the ethnographic perspective stems from the unique insights that you bring to the project. You will also take note of some details that you might turn away from in other circumstances. This too is okay: you will be recording some details and excluding others. Still, you want to record as much relevant detail as you can, and you want to do so in a relatively systematic manner. Your notes should allow you to identify recurrent details—like food served with every meal or items of clothing always worn at a particular event—and details that occur occasionally or only once. Paying attention to these sorts of details will help you identify the degree to which a particular event or a set of ideas and symbols is part of a regular pattern or a unique occurrence. As you record more detail, you will be able to develop informative pictures of the typical and the atypical that can be the foundation of insightful analysis.

Good field notes include as much of the **sensory experience** of participant-observation as possible. You should pay attention to sights and smells. If you can, you should record the words you hear. Of course, you can never record every detail. There are always more details, and you will come to see note taking as an endeavor destined to failure if you try to record everything. In order to avoid this trap, you should focus on those details that seem most relevant to your research focus. If you are looking at age, language, or ethnicity, you should make sure that you make notes about details related to those topics and prioritiz details in terms of their apparent importance in the given context and their general interest. In deciding which details are essential, you may find it helpful to imagine yourself trying to retell the story of what you are witnessing, hearing, or experiencing. You will want to make sure you record the details that will make the story complete and compelling.

WRITING NOTES VERSUS USING RECORDERS

Most ethnographers use some **instruments** to help them collect data. They rely especially on audio recorders, cameras, and, increasingly, video cameras. These instruments are invaluable aids in the data collection process. They can produce records that the ethnographer (and others) can revisit subsequently. In an ideal situation, you may be able to check for or notice certain aspects or details that you did not make note of originally or use the record to double-check certain aspects of written notes. When possible, you should plan to use these instruments to supplement the ethnographic record created through written notes. Keep in mind, though, that these instruments produce their own partial ethnographic records. Audio recorders record conversations and other sounds only when they are turned on and may not be able to record all sounds in the audio register. More important, these audio recorders do not record any accompanying information about body language, movement, physical interaction, smells, or visual stimuli. Still cameras produce photographs that freeze the record at a particular moment; they do not reflect movement well and may distort the picture of society and culture in action. They do not include information about sounds or smells and reflect a limited viewing angle only from the perspective of the photographer. Video cameras allow the researcher to record visual and audio information and to capture movement, but they also work from a limited viewing angle and fail to capture other important information. When using these recording instruments, you should make sure to use them in concert with written notes in order to produce the most complete ethnographic record.

Cameras and video cameras are probably most effective in collecting information about events and behaviors, while audio recorders are especially helpful in documenting conversations and interviews as well as music. The types of information that you aim to collect will help you decide which instruments you can utilize to best effect. Most projects will consider words and ideas and behavior and events, but many will tend to focus on one or the other. If you are clear about your focus, you are in a position to use these instruments most effectively to collect the data most relevant to your project.

Recording conversations and interviews can be one of the most difficult tasks for the ethnographer. Most people cannot write or type as fast as people can talk, unless they are accomplished at using shorthand. Writing or typing at speed becomes even more difficult if multiple people are speaking and especially if they are speaking at the same time. Therefore, if you anticipate using direct or lengthy quotations from interviews and conversations, recording those conversations can be very important.

For practical reasons, the ethnographer will want to consider carefully the feasibility of using a recorder to record interviews or conversations. Recording informal conversations is not always possible because they happen spontaneously, and the researcher might not have a recorder available or because the use of a recorder would be conspicuous and have an undesirable effect on the conversation. In the case of more planned or formal interviews, you will still want to assess the likely effect of a recorder on the interview. Sometimes a recorder can attract undue attention from passersby, make the interviewee nervous, or change the way that an interviewee responds (for instance, if the interviewee associates the recorder or microphone with stylized radio or television interviews). In other cases, the recorder can be almost completely innocuous. The nature of the response will depend on a number of factors, including the larger political environment, the personal disposition of interviewees, the specific interview environment, and experience with similar technologies. Experimenting with the use of recorders can help the researcher to determine likely reactions in certain circumstances. If informants grow accustomed to your use of a recorder, the recorder's effect may lessen over the course of time. In some cases, though, you may find that you have to forgo the use of a recorder in order to pursue the types of interactions and conversations that you seek for your research.

You can train yourself to record as much as possible in those instances where recording of interviews is not feasible. If you work at concentrating and remembering key components of the interview, you can construct good detailed notes immediately after the interview. Sometimes making quick notes of key phrases, ideas, or moments at the time can help you in constructing the notes after the fact.

Whatever the circumstance, you should always obtain permission before making audio or video recordings, unless you are recording completely public events. You should never do any clandestine or surreptitious recording. Some people may have good reasons for choosing not to be recorded, even if they consent to participate in an interview. Recordings create a different type of record that has to be safeguarded in order to protect participants in the research process.

THE PROSPECTS OF TRANSCRIPTION

If you make recordings of interviews and conversations, the next step is **transcription**. Listening to and typing out the interview, you can create a **transcript** of the interview. Transcription is an important and tedious part of the research process. It allows you to generate a precise record of the words and the overall interaction. As a general rule of thumb, you should allow five to ten hours to transcribe each hour of recorded interview. A tape player or computer program designed for transcription is a very helpful tool since you will have to stop, rewind, and restart many times during the transcription process. How quickly you are able to transcribe will depend on practice, typing skills, the quality of the recording, and the language of the interview, among other things. You need to make sure you include time in your research plan for transcription if you plan to record interviews and conversations. The sooner after an interview you can transcribe it, the better. You will be able to use your recent memories to fill some gaps or interpret some inconclusive parts of the recording. This quick turnaround may also help you connect your notes on the environment and body language to the transcript.

Before you begin to transcribe, you should make a decision about which components of the interview you want to include in the transcript. You should transcribe all of your informants' statements and questions as well as your side of the conversation, including the questions you asked, since responses often make the most sense in the context of the questions in a two-sided interaction. Transcripts can also include information about paralanguage (pauses, stuttering, "aah," and so on). Paralanguage can be an indicator of comfort or discomfort in relationship to a particular topic and can be an important point of analysis, but in a lot of cases it is unimportant. You will need to decide whether you want to include representations of paralanguage and other parts of the audio record (like background noise or interruptions) in your transcript. The transcript of a dedicated linguist will likely look very different from that of a general ethnographer; this difference is perfectly okay. You should aim to produce a transcript that is well suited to your research goals. Selective transcription of particular interviews or particular parts of interviews is acceptable in some cases, but you should plan to transcribe as many interviews as completely as possible. Doing so will help prevent you from having to return after the fact to transcribe an interview that you did not anticipate would be important. Transcribing interviews is also an important part of the early analytical process. Revisiting the interview and paying very close attention can help you see important aspects that you might not have been able to see when you were concentrating on conducting the interview; it can also help you develop new interview questions or new approaches as you continue your research.

The Pragmatics of Using Technology

Technology can be a great ally in the research process, but it can also become a liability if you are not prepared to use it properly. Even when you have planned for seemingly every contingency, things can and will go wrong when technology is involved. Just about every researcher has a story about a time that technology failed during the research process. The trick is to try to limit these instances through preparation and to adapt when failures occur.

It may seem obvious, but remember that all electrical devices, like cameras and recording devices, require a power source. There is nothing worse than finishing the perfect interview only to discover that the batteries in the recorder died during the first five minutes! You should not depend on being able to plug your instruments in everywhere you go. You should be prepared for various contingencies. If you plan to use a rechargeable power source, you need to make sure that you have charged it fully before you begin using it for the day. You should know long a charge usually lasts and carry a backup battery if possible. If you are using nonrechargeable batteries to power your instruments, you should make sure the batteries are fresh and that you have sufficient replacements. Where you are doing research will determine how easy it is to recharge power packs or to obtain good batteries. You will want to make appropriate arrangements if sources of electricity or batteries are hard to obtain.

You want to generate the highest quality recordings possible. High-quality recordings will allow you to examine many different details that may not be available in lower-quality recordings. The interview environment will play a major role in the quality of the recording. You may or may not be able to control things like background noise or possible electrical interference. If you can, you should try to arrange an interview environment that is relatively

(Continued)

(Continued)

quiet and free from technological interference. The quality of the recorder will also determine the quality of your recording. The best recorders produce stereo recordings that offer a more robust set of sounds. Using a microphone attached to a recorder can be very helpful in capturing the most important sounds, like the voice of an interviewee. You should experiment with the recorder and microphone before you begin conducting research. You may also want to test the equipment at the beginning of each interview to make sure that it is working properly. It is very easy to forget to do something like switch on a microphone.

When you use recorders and other technological instruments, you create a valuable part of the ethnographic record. You need to make sure that you protect this part of the record accordingly. You should make sure you cannot accidentally record over or erase interviews by using the tabs on cassette tapes or memory cards. You should create backups of tapes or files. It is a good idea to store backup copies in separate locations. Tapes, memory cards, hard drives, and other storage mechanisms tend to be particularly sensitive to moisture and heat. Common sense in protecting recordings from the elements and other hazards will go a long way in preserving the ethnographic record.

WHAT IS IMPORTANT AND WHAT IS SUPERFLUOUS: "WHAT DO I NEED TO WRITE DOWN?"

One of the hardest decisions for the ethnographer involves distinguishing important information from superfluous or unrelated information. This distinction is a hard one to make for several reasons: (1) you can record many different things in the course of fieldwork; (2) you want to be open to discovery and recording information that you did not originally perceive as important; and (3) information and detail are important both for specific analysis and in constructing an overall ethnographic picture.

Developing a firm rule about what should or should not be recorded in ethnographic notes proves to be impossible because of the breadth of ethnographic projects and the complexity of human life, society, and culture. Yet precisely because of this complexity, the ethnographer can only record a portion of the available ethnographic information. If you are working as part of an ethnographic team, you should be working from firm guidelines or criteria to ensure that you collect similar sets of data, but each researcher will create slightly different sets of notes based on individual differences in perception and perspective. If you are working independently, your unique perspective and your perceptive abilities will be essential to the note-taking process.

The key is to make sure that your notes allow you to address your key research questions and produce the sort of final ethnography that you want to produce. There is a tendency to push ahead with research and to leave review and analysis of the record until the end of the project, but you should plan to regularly review your notes and other parts of the record. You will probably be reminded of key pieces of information that you have forgotten or passed over originally, but you should also evaluate your note taking. Reviewing your notes regularly (about once a week) will allow you to develop your note-taking skills as you continue your research. You should ask yourself if there are things you wish you had included in your notes—specific words or phrases, colors, smells, layouts, sequences, numbers or quantities, or anything else—and make a concerted effort to include these types of details in your future notes.

Though you are working from a research question or hypothesis, you want to avoid creating an ethnographic record that simply affirms what you thought or hypothesized going into the project. You should make sure to note pieces of ethnographic information that may complicate the picture or disprove the hypothesis. In the process, you should look for additional pieces of related information; you may find explanations that support your hypothesis or move your understanding in a different direction. Some of the most important ethnographic insight has emerged out of unexpected findings and situations. Therefore, you want to be alert to unexpected sources of information. Research questions can guide your note taking, but you should not let them blind you to other interesting information. If something seems interesting at the time, you should make note of it, whether it is perplexing or eye-opening. You never know when this piece of information might be the point that takes your research in a new and interesting direction. Yes, this is a tricky balancing act between focused note taking and an openness to new sources and types of information, and it is a skill that you develop over time while doing research.

You are collecting information that will allow you to produce a quality final ethnography. The nature of that ethnography will vary depending on your purpose and your audience, but you want to collect information that will allow you to tell good stories. The ethnographer is always telling stories with a purpose—to set the stage for a particular analytical point or as an illustrative example—but the storytelling depends on contextual detail that adds texture and depth. You can include that kind of texture and depth in your final ethnography only if you include it in your notes. Sometimes it helps to think about your note taking as storytelling. You can imagine that you are writing a letter to somebody to explain what has happened in your fieldwork. Taking this approach will help ensure that you include the information necessary to make the story intelligent and compelling, the same way you would in a letter.

You should make sure you write down anything that seems directly related to your research question. You should also make note of anything that stands out as particularly interesting at the time, even if it does not seem directly related to your research topic. Finally, you should include detail and think about the stories that are being told or waiting to be told.

When seeking to produce good, detailed notes, you should not just write down summary comments like "They had a conversation about religion." The notes need to be much more specific. What religion(s) were they talking about? Who was talking and which individuals were making different points or claims? What prompted this conversation? Where were they at the time? Was the conversation's character amiable or contentious? Was there a recurring theme? The notes should answer as many of these questions as possible. If you are writing notes about a public performance or rite of passage, you should include similar details about who is doing what, their clothing and adornment, their movements, audience reaction, spatial relationships, and other related information.

In much the same way that transcribing an interview can take a lot longer than the interview itself, writing good, detailed field notes based on participant-observation can be a time-consuming process that sometimes takes longer than the original time invested in participant-observation. As a rough rule of thumb, the quantity of notes produced should reflect the amount of time spent doing fieldwork. Sometimes an intense fifteen-minute research experience will produce copious notes, but the longer the research experience, the more notes you should generate. If dedicated participant-observation for an hour or longer produces limited notes (less than a page or two), the field notes are probably not as detailed and conscientious as they need to be. Sharing notes with an experienced ethnographer to get feedback and suggestions can often be very helpful in honing note-taking skills.

Different ethnographers offer different advice about note taking during research. Many ethnographers choose to keep field notes separate from **journals** in an effort to separate personal thoughts and experiences from research activities and data, but others argue that this distinction is somewhat artificial. An increasing number of ethnographers make use of their journals in their final ethnographies. Even if you do not use the journal entries in your analysis and writing, it is important for you to document your personal thoughts and experiences during the research experience. A personal journal allows you to look back on how you have evolved as a researcher and to identify potential biases or particular perspectives that you bring to the material. You can think about three different types of writing or note taking that will take place during ethnographic research: (1) notes on participant-observation; (2) notes associated with interviews; and (3) personal reflections. Each of these types of writing becomes an important part of the ethnographic record. If you can identify these different types of writing in your note-taking practices, you can be relatively confident that you are producing a well-balanced set of field notes. As a rough guide, you should expect your field notes to be at least ten times as long as your final ethnographic project.

THE ETHICS OF COLLECTING INFORMATION

A completely objective stance on data collection would assume that ethnographic data exist in the world as discrete things to be collected by the ethnographer. In many respects, the ethnographer's responsibility is to faithfully document the social and

What Do Good Notes Look Like?

Every ethnographer develops a unique style when it comes to note taking. You may choose to adopt a prose style that uses complete sentences and paragraphs, or you might prefer an outline-style format that uses words and phrases. An outline format is more suitable for notes written on the fly as things are happening, while a prose style is probably more appropriate for notes written after the fact. The key is to ensure that the notes contain the appropriate information and details and that the notes are intelligible after the fact. Notes will not be helpful if they seem random or incomplete when you go back to them a month later. You may find it helpful and efficient to develop shorthand for words and phrases that you use frequently in your research. The notes will be particularly useful if you organize them in such a way that you identify key ideas or events as you create the notes. A system of underlining or stars can prove invaluable once you begin to analyze the information that you have collected. Performing this preliminary step of analysis can also be a productive way to think about what you have accomplished and where your research is headed.

cultural worlds that we inhabit, but, as we have already seen, you have other ethical responsibilities to your informants that are of utmost importance. You should not lose sight of the fact that your "facts" or information are produced through human interaction. As such, these facts and information can have powerful social effects. By taking and collecting other pieces of information, you are creating an ethnographic record that can potentially have negative effects or positive benefits depending on its contents, who has access to it, and how they use it. You should consider these issues as you decide what to record and how to record it, as well as when and how to grant access to the ethnographic record that you produce.

The previous chapter discussed why obtaining consent from research participants is essential. One exception to the requirement for obtaining consent comes in the form of public events. When an event is truly open to the public, there is no expectation of privacy, and the event becomes, in a sense, part of the public record. Therefore, events like a politician's public speech on a national holiday or a parade can be documented by the ethnographer without concerns about obtaining consent from the primary actors.

Things that are written down or recorded through other means often carry a particular power. These sorts of records can be subpoenaed in court and carry more weight than mere word of mouth or "hearsay." In some rare cases, ethnographers have had their records subpoenaed or been called to testify in court cases based on their research. You do not want to create an ethnographic record that can be used against the people that were generous enough to serve as your teachers and participate in your research.

Pseudonyms and codes or shorthand are one way to provide some protection. In some rare cases, you may decide that you cannot record information, as interesting or important as it may be, because the risks of recording it and reporting it outweigh the research objectives. Most ethnographers probably will not encounter a case like this, but they should always be aware of their roles as researchers in creating an ethnographic record.

SUMMARY

A good ethnographer needs to cultivate the habit of regularly writing notes that record details as they emerge in the course of fieldwork. Ethnographic data are rather fleeting and need to be recorded quickly before they disappear or dissipate. You have to determine the most appropriate practice for note taking in your field site. Photographs and recordings can be good supplements to the written record, but they do not replace written notes. Transcribed interviews can supply a wealth of data for use in your analysis and final ethnography. In the end, the ethnographic record is a direct reflection of your activities and experiences in your field site, and ethnographic research involves developing a strategy for recording focused and detailed information while remaining open to other ideas and sources of information.

KEY TERMS

Field notes

Ethnographic data

Ethnographic record

Narrative storytelling

Sensory experience

Instruments

Transcription

Transcript

Journals

DISCUSSION QUESTIONS

1. Why are field notes so important to the ethnographer and successful ethnographic research? How can you make sure that you are taking good field notes? What are the primary challenges that you face in constructing an ethnographic record?

2. Are some types of ethnographic data more temporary or fleeting than others? Can you tell whether the data you are collecting is likely to be fleeting?

3. How did Suggs deal with the fleeting nature of ethnographic data? How did the practical environment in which he conducted research influence his collection of data and the writing of field notes?

4. Should the ethnographer always strive to write notes on events as they are happening? What approach produces the best notes? What approach allows the ethnographer to do the best research overall?

5. Should the ethnographer try to record interviews and conversations? What are the primary considerations in deciding whether to record?

6. When is interview transcription most necessary or rewarding? What sorts of things should you make sure to include in a transcript?

7. Should you choose to leave certain things out of your field notes? Can you tell what is likely to be important in the end?

8. What are some examples of situations where the ethnographer might decide not to record information in order to protect informants from negative ramifications? How might these situations affect your ability to conduct successful research?

CHAPTER

6

PARTICIPANT-OBSERVATION

LEARNING OBJECTIVES

- Discuss and evaluate the apparent paradox of participant-observation
- Develop a reasonable approach to balancing and combining participation and observation
- Evaluate the temporal dimensions of ethnographic fieldwork
- Explain why ethnographers depend on informants as teachers and guides
- Plan to show genuine interest in the research project and avoid deception or misinformation in interactions with informants
- Understand the importance of noting both repetition and variation encountered in the course of participant-observation

Participant-observation is an essential component of ethnographic research. Successful and effective participant-observation requires practice and involves developing a particular research stance and an associated set of skills that allows the ethnographer to make the most out of the unique position of the **participant-observer**. Too often the outsider to ethnographic circles assumes that participant-observation is simple because the researcher is "just hanging out"—having fun and letting things happen. The stereotypical image is the ethnographer who spends every day in a bar or coffee shop chatting with the clientele. Of course, depending on the topic, an ethnographer may have a legitimate reason for conducting participant-observation in a bar or coffee shop. Ethnographers often have fun doing participant-observation, and a good ethnographer generally tries to avoid exerting undue influence on the events involved in participant-observation. Still, participant-observation involves a lot more than just hanging out. As a method, participant-observation is challenging because it can take many different forms and because the **subject position** of the researcher places a lot of responsibility on the researcher. This chapter will lay out the foundation for productive participant-observation and outline the process for developing the appropriate approach and skills for participant-observation on the part of the researcher.

THE APPARENT PARADOX: PARTICIPATION AND OBSERVATION

A skeptic will argue that ethnography as a research strategy cannot reasonably combine participation and observation in a single method because the two activities are antithetical. Underlying assumptions and divergent ways of perceiving the world make

CASE STUDY

Describing Sherpa Rituals

Participant-observation is frequently employed to study the behavior associated with religion and ritual. Sherry Ortner's *Sherpas Through Their Rituals* (1978) provides an excellent example of an ethnography rooted in detailed description based on long-term participant-observation. In her ethnography, she closely examines four different types of ritual or ritualized behavior that she encountered among the Buddhist Sherpa of Nepal. Using detailed description and close analytical examination, she connects each of these rituals to the economy, social organization, and religion of the Sherpa and shows that each of these rituals reflects and produces cultural understandings of the social and the spiritual worlds.

Ortner's participant-observation research at Sherpa parties allows her to investigate the dynamics of hospitality and social interaction at these parties as well as the symbolic meanings of food. She is able to trace the manifestation of concerns about status and authority that occur at these parties and the way the structure of the parties ultimately reinforces a particular social order embedded in the practice of hospitality and the act of sharing food.

the combination of participation and observation hard to fathom for some and hard to practice without a plan and a purpose. Common understandings of the **objective stance** required for scientific research assume that the researcher should be a **detached observer** who does not influence the objects or subjects of study. This equation of research with observation is pervasive in ideas about research and has been a constant source of questions for the ethnographer. While aiming for a *degree* of objectivity is a good thing for most ethnographic projects (with some notable exceptions), the model of ethnographer as an observant researcher wearing a stark white lab coat in an experimental laboratory is ultimately not a fruitful or realistic model. In order to learn about the complex dimensions of society and culture in action, the ethnographer almost necessarily has to become involved on a personal level to one degree or another. Some ethnographers have found that their most important insights have emerged when they have chosen or circumstances have forced them to abandon their practiced, objective stances. The element of personal experience and **social or cultural empathy** can be very powerful for the ethnographer.

On the opposite side, there is a frequent assumption that participants—the insiders—are so absorbed in the event or circumstances that they cannot see the larger picture or perform objective analysis of the events in which they have participated. Intense emotions and sensory experiences can make participatory experiences primary or even overwhelming, and cultural systems often create and inculcate particular ways of seeing and experiencing the world that help to determine what a participant can and cannot perceive or analyze. Still, to assume that every participant is programmed like a droid and wearing blinders to her cultural circumstances is disingenuous. In most

In much the same way, Ortner connects the Sherpa practice of the Buddhist atonement ritual, *nyungne*, with social concerns like family structures and aging. In fact, she argues that the ascetic ritual that seems to run counter to family and social commitments actually is interconnected with the evolution of family structures and the lives of aging adults. Her analysis involves a close examination of both the specific events and stages of the ritual and the symbols and meanings associated with the ritual. The act of fasting as part of the ritual raises the question of the sharing of food as an essentially social act. The central roles of fasting in the nyungne ritual and sharing food in hospitality rituals help Ortner to connect the two analytically.

Ortner's work offers an excellent example of the way committed and detailed participant-observation work can produce an informative and nuanced ethnographic account. Though Ortner offers relatively limited information about the specifics of her research in the text, her analysis clearly depends on an understanding of rituals as key cultural performances that emerged out of her own participant-observation in various settings.

CASE STUDY

The Ethnographer as Musician

In her ethnography of music in Tanzania, *Performing the Nation*, Kelly Askew (2002) offers a detailed and interesting consideration of her role as observer and participant in the course of her fieldwork. She describes different stages in her research during which she was recognized primarily as an observer and stages in which she actively took on the role of participant. Over the course of time, she moved from the role of "official guest" at musical performances to the role of performer in two different Tanzanian musical groups.

As an ethnomusicologist, Askew's research draws directly on the theory of performance in her research. Theories of performance can be applied to various social and cultural situations, but the performative dimensions of music are particularly apparent. During the course of her research, Askew moved from the audience as an observer to the stage as a performer and gained access to multiple perspectives on the cultural politics of Tanzanian music in the process.

Describing this shift in her position as researcher, Askew says that the intense commitment involved in being a performing member of the group meant that her practice of detailed note taking changed owing to time constraints. However, she makes a clear argument for the value of the shared experiences and knowledge to which she had access as a participant performer. As a whole, her research offers an excellent example of the ways that ethnographers negotiate the roles of participant and observer and the benefits of both positions for gaining a full ethnographic understanding of the social and cultural situation.

cases, every participant in an event has a slightly or radically different experience, and participants are often engaged in intricate exchanges of questioning, critique, and analysis. In fact, participants are often uniquely positioned to perceive important connections or contradictions and examine the way their own lived experiences match or conflict with social and cultural expectations. To the extent that the ethnographer's goal is to acquire and to understand the insider's, or **emic perspective**, the ethnographer depends on participation on the part of the ethnographer and the informants. (The analytical distinction between *emic* and *etic* has limitations and should not be overdrawn. If you work from a rigid distinction between insiders and outsiders, you may miss chances for shared experience or the nuances of identity and group membership. In many circumstances, various forms of belonging encompass the ethnographer in various ways.) Participation is a way of obtaining the sort of experiential and embodied knowledge that ethnographers find essential to their projects.

The method of participant-observation seeks to combine the seemingly contradictory stances of participation and observation. By adopting this method, you seek an approach that capitalizes on the positives of each stance and allows you to position yourself so that you can look at the big picture and ask comparative, analytical questions while also drawing on firsthand experience and understanding. Positioning yourself as a participant-observer places you in a powerful research position if you utilize the opportunities properly. The position of participant-observer, however, is not necessarily a natural stance for most ethnographers. They have to seek consciously and intentionally to make the most of opportunities for participant-observation and find an approach that allows them to benefit from the insights of both participation and observation and their juxtaposition.

BALANCING PARTICIPATION AND OBSERVATION

The researcher's individual personality and research plan will likely go a long way in determining which half of the participation-observation equation comes most easily. If you are naturally outgoing and gregarious, you may find it easier to become involved as a participant. On the other hand, if you are more reserved and private in social settings, you may find that you slip more easily into the role of an observer because you feel more comfortable in the background. An honest self-critique helps in preparing for participant-observation. With this self-awareness about level of comfort and personal tendencies, you can develop a strategy to balance the two sides of the equation.

The research topic and the nature of the associated field sites may also lend themselves to an emphasis on either participation or observation. If an event is open to the public and everyone is invited to participate, you will find it easy to take up the role of participant. If participation is enjoyable—including good food or music, a sense of camaraderie, or a hospitable environment—you may also be more inclined to participation. On the other hand, if it is difficult to gain permission to participate actively or involvement carries the prospect of some unpleasant experiences, embarrassment, or unwanted attention, you may be more reluctant to become a participant. Again, you should pay careful attention to these variables as you seek to achieve a balance of participation and observation. You need to be ready to do some things that require some effort and may make you uncomfortable. Participant-observation can often be fun, but it is not necessarily easy or natural in all cases. In many cases, the other participants and observers will be aware of your actions, and they will evaluate your position as participant-observer. They may ask what you have observed as a relative outsider or they may decide to extend invitations, share knowledge, or assume collegiality based on shared experiences. They may even ask whether you experienced the presence of the divine in a particular ritual.

The first step is balancing participation and observation to make sure that you are doing both. You should be clear about exactly what you are participating in, how you are participating, and with whom you are participating. Because it can be easy to become an inactive observer, it is important to check that you are participating and to think specifically about *how* you are participating.

In terms of observation, you want to make sure that you remain observant throughout. Ideally, at the same time that you benefit from the insights and experiences of participation, you want to develop a set of data based on observation. The ethnographer probably always fills the role of observer. Still, examining your notes to make sure they include a perspective based on observation may be particularly helpful at times. Because at least part of the audience for your final ethnography includes nonparticipants, you want to make sure your notes include the information and detail that a newcomer or outsider would find interesting and relevant. A regular participant may or may not take note of specific smells or where people sit during a ceremony, but the observer will. As you write notes and especially as you review your notes, you should make sure the notes include this kind of observational detail (numbers, colors, alignment, and interaction, for instance). Remember that observation is not simply limited to watching and visual data. Good observational research and data make use of all five senses.

True participant-observation, however, involves more than doing one and then the other; it involves doing both participation and observation at the same time in an integrated fashion. You may emphasize one of the dimensions at a given time, but as a good ethnographer you want to maintain a balance of the two. Successfully adopting the stance of the participant-observer allows you to juxtapose two different types of information and to generate insights as well as questions. At times you may find the position of participant-observer is an awkward one; this is to be expected as you grapple with the tension between being a practicing insider and an analytical outsider. You should not, however, let this tension paralyze you as a researcher. In most respects, the more research avenues you can pursue, the better. You should look for opportunities to participate whenever possible and look to train yourself to be an *observant* ethnographer at the same time. Those moments when you observe one thing and experience (or learn that somebody else is experiencing) something different can be eye-opening and incredibly productive. While you may find yourself in an ambivalent position sometimes as a participant-observer, you will find it a rich and rewarding experience at other times. Ethnographers are drawn to the complexities of human lives, and the combined role of participant-observer allows them to explore those complexities from multiple perspectives. Embracing this chance to combine multiple perspectives allows you to make the most of your ethnographic research.

THE IMPORTANCE OF TIME

Like most other ethnographic methods, participant-observation requires considerable time. Spending significant time in the field site(s) allows the ethnographer to develop a deep understanding of the phenomena under study. In almost all cases, the more time you spend doing participant-observation, the more quality information you are going to be able to collect. Therefore, you need to budget sufficient time to collect the appropriate information. Almost all ethnographers have to work within the structure of deadlines or departure dates, but the goal is to make the most of the time within those strictures.

Beginning ethnographers often delay the start of participant-observer fieldwork as a result of apprehension or a lack of confidence. Unfortunately, this act of procrastination inevitably results in reduced research opportunities, even if you subsequently decide to devote a lot of time to the project. *You should begin your participant-observation fieldwork as soon as reasonably possible* in order to get the most out of it. In many cases, opportunities present themselves only after you have made connections and built rapport; this process takes time. Having access to a full cycle of events (shaped perhaps by the calendar year, seasons, or some other unit of time) can be very important to many projects. With a project researching Roman Catholicism, having direct experience with the entire liturgical calendar may help the researcher to understand how periods like Advent and Pentecost shape ritual behaviors as well as personal emotions and social interactions. A study of subsistence farmers in Mozambique that considers the importance of time may discover that family events and celebrations are much more frequent in the dry season following harvest than during the rainy season. A researcher who is not in a position to observe these temporal differences may not fully understand the larger circumstances and might mistakenly assume that one period like Pentecost or the dry season is representative of general behavior and life. Therefore, making the most of your time constraints will allow you to see and experience the most representative range of your field sites.

Whenever you can, you should attend multiple versions of similar events. With more than one experience as a participant-observer at similar events, you can become much more adept at distinguishing unique occurrences, which may be particularly meaningful or meaningless aberrations from regular components of the event. For instance, you may be invited to only one wedding, in which case you will be limited to information about that particular wedding, but if you attend multiple weddings, you can begin to build a composite picture of weddings and compare the elements that differed in the weddings that you attended. As a result, you may be able to examine the ways that social standing and education influence the marriage process through this sort of comparison.

Three dimensions of time are important in terms of fieldwork: (1) total length of time spent in the field; (2) breadth of time spent in the field; and (3) number of times spent in the field. You cannot make up for multiple missed research opportunities with a single lengthy day or afternoon of participant-observation. Nor can you do one really good day of participant-observation and assume that your work is done. You need to spend multiple days or parts of days doing participant-observation. How many days or times will depend on the length of the project, the number of opportunities, and the other research methods that you are employing. If possible, you want to avoid depending too much on a one-time participant-observation event. If it gets cancelled or you get sick, the project may suffer a devastating setback. Still, there are important one-time events that need to be studied ethnographically. If this is the case for the project, you need to plan accordingly and be extra conscientious in taking detailed notes.

DEPENDING ON INFORMANTS AS TEACHERS AND GUIDES

Informants serve an essential role in the ethnographic process as teachers and guides. They fulfill these roles in a variety of ways—answering interview questions, patiently explaining family relations for kinship charts, and showing you around as you map an

Choosing Informants

Ethnographers do not always admit it, but informants choose themselves as often as the ethnographer chooses them. In some instances, a person in a position of authority may assign an individual or individuals to guide the ethnographer through the research process. This may be a form of covert surveillance or an attempt to direct your research in a particular direction, but it may also be a rather simple extension of hospitality. These prearranged relationships can be fruitful if you can develop sufficient rapport and work to mitigate the ways that this person's connections to authority can potentially limit your access to certain dimensions that you want to examine. You always want to evaluate the benefits and limitations of your working relationship with any informant. In most cases, working with multiple informants is a good idea because it allows you to approach similar topics from different angles and develop a more complete picture. Of course, in some cases, as when you apprentice yourself to a specialist, you may decide that the benefits of a single, close working relationship outweigh the prospects of multiple informants. In other cases you have to choose to work with one informant or another because social circumstances (taboos or social antagonism) mean that you cannot work with both of them. These are very difficult situations that you will need to navigate carefully, but you ultimately want to choose the working relationship that is most likely to offer the most informative perspective for your research question.

In informal situations, certain individuals are more likely to approach and befriend the ethnographer as potential informants than other individuals are. Individual personality differences, especially how outgoing or shy a person is, affect the likelihood that they will approach the ethnographer, but social factors can also influence the likelihood that individuals will present themselves. For instance, in gender-segregated or patriarchal settings, women may be unlikely to appear as potential informants because they have been socialized into less public and assertive roles. Similarly, in a gerontocracy, younger members of the community may be less comfortable assuming the roles of teachers and guides. You should be careful to ensure that social structures do not unduly influence your research and limit your ability to access important perspectives. Some structural constraints are easier to overcome than others, and your own social persona will influence your access to some extent, but aiming to gain multiple perspectives through informants who occupy different social positions is an important strategy for ethnographers.

Ethnographers and analysts of their work have noted that socially marginal individuals frequently are among the first to befriend ethnographers as potential informants. Their own marginal positions may mean that they are seeking social companionship and that they can identify with the ethnographers as marginal individuals themselves. Sometimes these individuals are more critical or analytical when it comes to their own societies and communities and can provide the ethnographer with keen insights, but the ethnographer has to be wary of assuming that this perspective from the margins represents the larger whole. As usual, aiming to gain multiple perspectives is a good rule.

area, to name a few—but in the course of participant-observation, you have a chance to develop a unique research relationship with your informants. You may find yourself singing the national anthem alongside your informants or engaging in a dialogue with an informant possessed by ancestral spirits. The participant-observer engages informants directly through shared experiences and physical interaction. The result can be a powerful form of experiential insight that allows you to access to behavior, thought, and emotion. The participant-observer experience is the chance for you to gain perhaps the most direct understanding of the phenomena under study. Informants lead you through this process. Without the informant, the researcher may not know how to behave or respond in a particular situation. But most of this teaching and guidance happens implicitly; the informant may correct the ethnographer or explicitly instruct her on occasion, but in many cases the ethnographer learns through imitation and trial and error. In learning how to function appropriately as a participant, you have to be a skilled observer to learn from the informants and potential informants around you.

As participant-observer, you may be called upon to perform or become the center of attention simply as a result of your presence. As a full participant, you should fulfill these obligations and accept the invitations. In general, though, you want to act like other participants as much as possible. Doing so will give you the best sense of the experiences and perspectives of the other participants. You seek to be open to teaching and guidance from your informants. As a participant-observer, you want to be engaged and interactive, but you should try not to be the primary person responsible for directing activities. Allowing events to unfold as they would in your absence (or as close as possible) provides you with the best ethnographic information.

Ethnographers frequently rely on **key informants.** While they aim to interact with and rely on a number of different informants, certain individuals turn out to be more skilled as guides and teachers. In many instances, ethnographers and their key informants become close friends. Working with one or a few key informants can be very productive because the close relationship allows you to glean deeper levels of information. As you proceed with the research, you should think about the individual informants who might serve as key informants. As always, you will need to be aware of the benefits and limitations of these connections.

GETTING STARTED

The first step in ethnographic research is often the hardest. Many researchers have grown comfortable with the books and journals of library research, and the prospects of field research with living human beings seem daunting. The uncertainty can be exacerbated in ethnography, where the researcher is supposed to cede much of the control over the research situation. If you are arriving anew in a field site where you stand out as physically distinct or a nonnative speaker of the local language, you may be understandably apprehensive about your first steps in the research process. By the same measure, if you are returning "home" to conduct research, you may face the pressure of various expectations and apprehension about your role as researcher. This initial stage can be very important because it sets the tone for the research that follows and creates initial impressions that can be hard to change, but you need not let these concerns paralyze you. If you are prepared with a well-designed research plan, *the most important thing is to get started.* Once you start the research and do your first participant-observation, you will probably find that it gets easier and comes more naturally. In most cases, informants will become increasingly familiar and comfortable with you and your work and they may come to take it for granted. The sooner you can start this process, the better. As you get started, you should remember to show genuine interest and make sure you avoid deception or misinformation.

Showing Interest

If you want **potential informants** to engage your project and assist you with your research, you have to be able to demonstrate and to explain your interests. You do not have to become a cheerleader for ethnography, but potential informants should be able to tell that you are excited and committed to the project. After all, if you are not excited and committed, why should they be? Your goal is to communicate your genuine interest. The sacrifices you are making to pursue the project may help you communicate your interest, but you should remember that you are also asking your informants to make sacrifices in many cases by teaching and spending time with you. You have put a lot of work into this project and begin with an exciting set of ideas. You can make sure you remember and build on this during the first stages.

Informants are generally very perceptive and inquisitive when it comes to ethnographic projects and their purpose. You may receive a number of questions about your project, including inquiries about where the ideas originated, the utility of the project, its audience, and even why you are not studying another topic (that is clearly more interesting or important). You need to be prepared to answer these questions, to *explain* your interest. You probably have relatively long answers to these questions available, but you should also be ready to provide relatively short versions of the answers to these questions. When informants understand the rationale behind the project, they are more likely to see potential benefits that accompany your project and to become supporters within the community or social unit. As you explain your project in different situations, you may find that the explanations give rise to interesting conversations that help shape or even occasionally redirect the project. This exchange is part of the engaged nature of ethnographic research.

Avoiding Deception and Misinformation

We have already learned that deception and misinformation are not acceptable practices. In the course of your ethnographic fieldwork, people will often be curious or wary about your activities. You should be prepared to provide a clear and brief explanation of your project. If individuals want more information, they may ask follow-up questions, but most people will be looking for a succinct explanation. You may want to explain that you are fulfilling your role as a student or an employee, since these are roles that many people will find familiar, but you may also want to provide some perspective on the project and its larger importance. Most of the people you will be talking to and working with will have little to no experience with ethnography. They may find it strange that you can get school credit or get paid for spending time and studying with them. You should be sure to avoid making overly grandiose claims or making promises that you cannot keep.

In some situations, you will have to go through specific channels in order to have your research approved. Many countries have systems in place to review research proposals (especially by foreigners) before they grant clearance or permits. In nonpublic settings, you may have to navigate a process that includes one or more gatekeepers, like owners, managers, elected officials, or self-appointed guardians. Though these obstacles can sometimes be formidable and frustrating, you need to avoid the temptation of misinformation or deception as a way to gain access to your research site. With rare exception, these officers or individuals have a legitimate role to play, and you have to learn how to operate within the existing social system. The most common exception occurs when the system or individuals function to silence certain individuals. In this situation, ethnography can provide an important counterpoint that might generate social criticism or change. Serious situations of oppression and inequality can present real dilemmas for the ethnographer about how to operate within or outside of the system. You should always aim to act ethically as you navigate these situations.

A note of caution: Acting ethically and avoiding misinformation or deception does not mean that you will always agree with your informants or accept everything they say or do as inviolable. It also does not mean that your informants will always accept your analysis and your ethnographic presentation of them. You should be prepared for conflicting views and potential criticism of your work, especially if your work deals with a contentious issue. By being as honest and upfront as possible about your activities and intentions, you can eliminate a potential source of miscommunication and bad feelings.

You may occasionally decide to omit some information in your explanations of your research. This strategy of omission can be important if you think that informants will act differently knowing that you are analyzing a particular topic. If the participants in a town hall meeting know that you are there as an ethnographer studying race relations, they may censor themselves in a way that they would not in your absence. We all tend to put on our best face when we know someone is watching us. One solution in this case might be for you to explain that you are generally interested in social relations in the community without specifically mentioning race. This solution may be most appropriate if you have only one or a few opportunities to do participant-observation in this setting and think that the other participants will be highly cognizant of your presence. On the other hand, you may decide to provide a more specific explanation of your work at the outset and expect that informants and participants will become more comfortable with your presence over time, especially if you are able to do participant-observation over an extended period, during which your presence will probably become less noteworthy. Even if you choose the first option, you are not practicing deception or misinformation; you are omitting some details without misrepresenting your project, and you are doing so because you think a more detailed explanation might unduly influence your topic of study. This strategy should be adopted with caution. When you can, you ought to provide as much information as possible.

Your informants will generally appreciate candor and a willingness to share. Sharing specific interests can also be the starting point of interesting conversations and interactions. Many informants, whether they have been trained as ethnographers or social scientists or not, often have very keen analytical perspectives and will offer their own analyses when they learn what your analytical questions are. You should consider posing your questions with full disclosure to see what kind of response you receive. The topics that constitute your research interest may be things to which your informants have devoted a good deal of thought. If so, it behooves you to initiate these conversations. You need not assume that you are the only person who is thinking, critiquing, and analyzing. You may perceive certain things of which some or all of your informants are unaware, and you may bring to bear a unique version of analysis and comparison, but your job as researcher will be immensely easier if you can draw on the insights and analyses of your informants.

REGULAR VERSUS EXTRAORDINARY BEHAVIOR AND CONVERSATIONS

One of the ethnographer's most challenging tasks comes in sorting through both the extraordinary or unique and the regular or routine. On the one hand, many—if not all of us—have an inclination to direct our attention toward the extraordinary. It grabs our attention and it usually makes for a good story. Much of the "exotic" appeal of classic ethnographies stems from a focus on the extraordinary. Unfortunately, overemphasizing the extraordinary can entail overemphasizing difference and can sometimes be counterproductive if one of the primary goals of ethnography is to build a sense of understanding among humans. On the other hand, focusing on the regular or routine aspects of cultural and social phenomena can cause the ethnographer to miss important variations and produce an account that assumes a degree of regularity and uniformity that usually does not exist in the social lives of human beings.

A good ethnographer recognizes that there are **patterns of behavior, shared sets of symbols,** and **structures** that shape possibilities, but she also recognizes individual interests and idiosyncrasies, the role of creativity and improvisation, conflict, and the ways that social position can produce and reflect significant variety in the group. Therefore, you should plan to deal with both the regular and the extraordinary dimensions of your topic. The topic may entail emphasis on one dimension or the other, but you will find that you need to address both. In conducting participant-observation and writing notes, you should remember both of these rules: (1) pay attention to repetition and (2) pay attention to that which is unique.

Paying Attention to Repetition

You will not be able to confirm that a particular action occurs every time or that certain words or symbols always appear until you have been doing fieldwork long enough to be a part of multiple similar events and numerous conversations, but you want to be aware of signs of repetition from the outset. Paying attention to repetition will help you function more effectively as a participant-observer; the more quickly you are able to learn and adopt shared practices and customs like greetings, hospitality, and polite manners, the more likely you are to find an important degree of acceptance and rapport. Much of this learning occurs through observation of repetitive practices, imitation, and a bit of trial and error. In situations where you come to a field site as an obvious outsider or newcomer, you should try to make your first instinct to observe. You want to give yourself the opportunity to observe and learn appropriate manners of behavior in a particular situation. Developing a default pause to see how others are reacting or responding to a particular situation and then determining whether it is appropriate for you to behave in similar ways can be a very healthy approach. As a student, you learn as a child does, by observing and imitating what others do. Even if you are not a newcomer to the field site and feel comfortable there, you should still pay close attention to these sorts of repeated behaviors and interactions. You may find that some aspects have become so routine that you are no longer consciously aware of them, but you may also find that you were not previously aware of some conventions or that your position as researcher has changed enough to require slightly different behaviors, customs, or responses.

Beyond making you a more effective participant-observer, paying close attention to repetition allows you to examine the central elements of shared culture and social systems. People repeat things for a reason—usually because they are important. Therefore, you can look at repetitive events, behaviors, words, and symbols as an avenue into some of the most important shared social and cultural components. If you notice that houses are routinely divided using the cardinal directions and that women occupy the west side of the house and men the east, this may tell you several things: the cardinal directions, particularly east and west, are especially salient for this group and may have specific meanings; there is a strong emphasis on gender differentiation and at least some degree of separation in this culture; and there are connections between geography and gender in local worldviews. These observations may prompt you to ask follow-up questions, observe to see if similar arrangements apply in other settings outside of the household, or study mythology to see if there are connections to cosmology. If you regularly hear your informants using the same phrase or word, you may discover that this word or phrase has a particularly important meaning or connotation for your informants. You will want to explore when and how these words are used, by whom, and whether they have multiple meanings.

Observing, learning, and documenting repetition allows you to speak with some authority and confidence about key elements of the society or community that you are studying. A good deal of ethnographic knowledge and writing is based on these types of observations. If you can confidently predict that a group, subgroup, or individual will behave or speak in a particular way in a specific context, you have developed a powerful set of information. This information is the way to identity the rules or guidelines that produce social and cultural tendencies. The power of cultures and societies stems from their ability to influence their members and to generate and sustain repetitive behaviors and symbols. You can say, "The x usually do y . . . ," because you have observed this pattern with regularity.

Paying Attention to Variation

Early ethnographers probably paid too much attention to repetition at the expense of variation. This shortcoming stemmed from general notions about cultures and cultural difference, especially assumptions about homogeneity within cultural groups. In their attempt to study and to document different cultural groups, ethnographers too often assumed that they could provide a comprehensive account that explained the thoughts, behaviors, and symbols of everyone in the group. However, even in the smallest social units, we find significant variation that ethnographers increasingly try to study. Awareness of race, ethnicity, age, gender, and other variables of social identity, as well as the role of human volition and creativity has prompted many ethnographers today to focus on conflict and internal divisions. These approaches provide a fuller and more complete picture of the complexity of human social worlds.

A good ethnographer should pay close attention to variation, including things that seem unique or extraordinary. Ironically, in much the same way that repetition can be a signal of importance, events, behaviors, and symbols that vary or seem extraordinary can also be markers of important pieces of information for the ethnographer. For example, sometimes the unique members of a group—shamans, charismatic rebbes, or nonviolent activists—can be key figures for ethnographic purposes. They may be particularly influential in providing direction for the group and resolving conflict. They may also be reservoirs of cultural knowledge that is essential to the group. Their unique attributes may represent the dimension that is considered sacred or spiritual, or they may represent the limits of sociability for the group. Cultivating a relationship with these individuals can provide invaluable insight into the extraordinary aspects of the culture or community. Similarly, extraordinary events—an initiation that happens once a generation, responses to catastrophic natural disasters, and large political demonstrations—can provide an avenue into understanding the flexibility and stability of cultures and social systems and the role of human creativity. If you have the opportunity to include extraordinary events or individuals in your research, it can be a very important opportunity.

Beyond obviously extraordinary or unique elements, you will likely quickly become aware of significant variation in events and conversations. When you expect a particular set of behavior or words because you have observed and recorded it several times before, you may discover a new set. You should take note and immediately begin trying to figure out whether there is an explanation for this variation. Are there different parties involved? If so, how are they different, and how might this influence expectations of behavior and speech? Do the circumstances (whether place, season, or intent) differ from those to which you have previously been privy? Observing variation provides a productive entry into the complexity of social units. It can allow the ethnographer to analyze different subgroups and the significance of social roles and positions and to explore the degree to which conflict and stability characterize the society or culture under study.

SUMMARY

In many ways, participant-observation as a method defines the ethnographic research endeavor. The seemingly paradoxical attempt to balance the subject positions of participant and observer becomes the source of significant insights and important information for the ethnographer, even if the ethnographer's experiences as participant-observer are sometimes disconcerting or challenging. In practicing participant-observation, the ethnographer depends heavily on informants as teachers and guides. These relationships need to be based on honesty and engagement. You need to be open to learn from your informants through participant-observation. Participant-observation yields regular or routine elements as well as information about those occurrences that seem extraordinary or unique. You can learn best by paying close attention to both.

KEY TERMS

Participant-observer
Subject position
Objective stance
Detached observer
Social or cultural empathy
Emic perspective

Key informants
Potential informants
Patterns of behavior
Shared sets of symbols
Structures

DISCUSSION QUESTIONS

1. What are the primary differences between being a participant and being an observer? Can the two approaches or perspectives be reconciled? Why or why not?

2. What is unique about participant-observation as a stance or a method? Why is it indispensable to ethnographic research?

3. How can time and time constraints influence ethnographic research and participant-observation in particular? What steps can you take to make the most of your time while doing research?

4. What is the nature of the relationship between ethnographer and informants? Can the ethnographer be an expert and a student at the same time? How can you cultivate ethical and productive research relationships with your informants?

5. Why is it important for you to show your interest in your research? What might happen if you seem disinterested?

6. Should you share everything with your informants? How can you decide what and when to share with your informants? Is there a general rule of thumb to follow, or do you always have to make situational decisions about when and how to share?

7. What might you miss if you fail to take note of repetition in your fieldwork? What might you miss if you focus on events and behaviors that occur over and over again on a regular basis?

CHAPTER

7

INTERVIEWS

LEARNING OBJECTIVES

- Distinguish between formal and informal interviews and the circumstances where one or the other is most likely to be appropriate and effective

- Understand the importance of approaching the task of interviews as an engaged conversationalist

- Examine the differences between "ideal" and "real" cultures as they relate to interview data

- Explain the importance of listening in the interview context

- Implement a strategy for recording interview data in the most effective manner possible

- Develop an interview schedule and a plan for conducting an interview

- Evaluate potential interview questions in terms of their suitability and effectiveness

In the process of developing a research topic and plan, you developed a host of interesting questions. The method of participant-observation offers you the chance to collect observational, behavioral, and experiential data designed to help answer these questions. You get a strong understanding of how people act and interact in different circumstances. Interviews as a method offer you the chance to ask direct questions and gain access to personal thoughts and experiences. Ethnographers are inherently curious; therefore, asking questions is not usually difficult for them. This chapter aims to provide the tools to ask good questions and conduct effective interviews. Because successful ethnographic research depends less on volume of interviews than on the quality of those interviews, you will want to plan and prepare carefully to make the most out of opportunities for interviews and conversations when they present themselves.

In general, you should aim to design and carry out ethnographic research that combines and balances participant-observation and **interviewing**. However, a firm line between the two methods does not always exist. Sometimes, in the context of participant-observation, chances to ask questions and conduct interviews emerge, and when you are conducting interviews, you want to remain a participant-observer aware of your surroundings and your role in the larger interaction of which you are a part. Sometimes interviews turn into demonstrations or invitations. The ethnographer as researcher wants to make the most of these possibilities. You should think of yourself as both a participant-observer and interviewer, or **engaged conversationalist**, all the time.

CASE STUDY

Kitchen Interviews in Translated Woman

Ruth Behar's *Translated Woman* (2003) is an ethnography that focuses on a single individual named Esperanza in Mexico. Behar set out to study the politics of gender in Mexico generally but ended up writing a book that tells Esperanza's life story and examines the nature of the relationship between Esperanza and Behar as informant and ethnographer, respectively. The bulk of the ethnographic detail is based on lengthy informal interviews that took place in Behar's kitchen when Esperanza would come to visit under the cover of darkness.

Behar has a literary talent for turning these interviews into a compelling ethnographic portrait of Esperanza as an individual and as a member of larger Mexican society. She provides lengthy, uninterrupted passages in Esperanza's words that are detailed and engaging. While Behar readily admits her role as author, editor, and translator, this work provides one of the best examples of the direct power of ethnographic information rooted in interviews and conversations. Behar's close attention to Esperanza's descriptive narratives produces a rich text that pushes the literary boundaries among ethnography, biography, and creative writing.

STARTING WITH INFORMAL INTERVIEWS AND CONVERSATIONS

Lots of people conduct interviews and surveys—marketers in shopping malls and on the telephone, pollsters, journalists, and even the police. As a result, there is a good chance that some or all informants will have some experience being interviewed or surveyed. Those experiences may be positive or negative, and informants may bring certain ideas to the encounter about what an interview should or should not be. The ethnographic interview is different from most of these other interview experiences, and you will want to help your informants see these differences, especially if they have had negative experiences with interviews or they associate interviews with negative situations. *The ethnographic interview should not be an interrogation.* The goal is to learn from interviewees and not to indict them or trick them. You may need to ask difficult questions, but you should avoid deception (see Chapter Six) and try not to place yourself in a position of authority within the context of the interview if you can avoid it.

In some circumstances, an interview complete with microphone and recorder may seem perfectly appropriate. For example, in formal offices associated with bureaucracies, where functionaries are accustomed to interviews and officious encounters, the ethnographer may find interviewees who expect **formal interviews**. In most cases, though, people are understandably wary when the prospect of a formal interview is broached. They may be reluctant to speak "on the record" or wonder why their opinion is important enough to warrant this kind of attention. Because

The ethnographic relationship between Behar and Esperanza originally started with a sense of uneasiness on Behar's part, but evolved to the point where she recognized the importance of Esperanza's stories. She invited Esperanza to tell her stories and eventually asked for permission to record the conversations on tape. These tapes provide the basis of the ethnographic record that gives rise to *Translated Woman*. Behar's skill in presenting these conversations allows us as readers to feel as though we have entered the kitchen with Behar and Esperanza and can hear "the laughter that punctuates all our conversations" (Behar 2003, 7–8).

Behar's decision to focus exclusively on a single individual is relatively unusual, though not unique among ethnographers. She makes the theoretical and stylistic decisions to present Esperanza's stories as directly and completely as possible as a way of communicating the importance of Esperanza as an individual and the importance of her stories. On a more general level, her work with Esperanza is an excellent example of the potential depth and breadth of interview data for the ethnographer. Close attention to detail and careful recording of interviews and conversations are indispensable parts of the practice of ethnographic research.

CASE STUDY

Interviews in the Stairways of Spanish Harlem

In Search of Respect, Philippe Bourgois's study of selling crack in Spanish Harlem, weaves together descriptive accounts, complex theoretical discussions, and direct interview excerpts to present an empathetic and compelling ethnography (Bourgois 2003). Drawing on his own observations and experiences, Bourgois offers the reader a description of the Game Room, an arcade that serves as the headquarters for Ray's crack-selling business on the corner, and he discusses his firsthand encounters with the police and with Ray's aggressive defense of his own position of authority. Through these descriptive accounts, the reader gains a strong understanding of El Barrio as a specific place in Spanish Harlem and of the primary players in the crack economy. However, one of Bourgois's main goals in presenting his findings is to humanize the people who became his informants and friends, who too frequently are demonized in the popular media and other forums.

Excerpts from tape-recorded interviews become the primary means through which Bourgois humanizes his informants. The reader gets to hear

formal interviews tend to be rather impersonal in tenor and character, you may find it helpful to avoid them during the initial stages of your research. Beginning a research relationship in this impersonal way can sometimes preclude more personal research opportunities and invitations to share or experience. You want to be careful not to hide behind the microphone, recorder, or questions while you are doing research.

Unless you encounter a specific set of circumstances indicating that formal interviews are the obvious way to start, you should plan to start with **informal interviews** and conversations. As an inquisitive ethnographer, you should always have questions to ask, but rather than rushing into formal interviews, you can use these questions to glean information from more informal chances for conversation. If you are sharing a meal or drink with potential or actual informants, you can listen carefully to the conversation and look for chances to learn and to ask questions. This approach has two related benefits: first, to the extent that your informants are directing the conversation and talking about topics of interest to them, you can gain a good picture of what is important to them as opposed to determining what is important with a predetermined list of interview questions. You can learn a lot by being *part* of a conversation without completely orchestrating it. Second, you can establish yourself in the eyes of your informants as a person who can comfortably participate in "normal" conversations. The formal interview facilitates the role of an objective observer, but informal directly from individuals like Caesar and Primo in the same way that Bourgois heard and learned from them in the course of his research. The words of Caesar, Primo, and others occupy a primary space in the ethnographic text and enable Bourgois to present detailed analysis and critique of the situations that lead to the selling (and use) of crack without dehumanizing or demonizing individuals like Caesar and Primo. Their words tell us about their experiences with the educational system, their concerns about jobs and respect in the workplace, and even their thoughts on rape and sexual violence.

These interview excerpts become the basis for Bourgois's discussion of social and cultural capital, as well as gender and patriarchy.

Bourgois's work is a testament to the power of interview data. The idea of recording an interview with a crack dealer in the stairwell of a housing project in Spanish Harlem may be a jarring one to many, but his close attention to the specific content of his informal interviews illustrates the importance of interviews and conversations as research strategies and the importance of recording as much detail as possible about those interviews and conversations.

conversations allow you more readily to fill the role of participant-observer. Being willing to be a part of informal, everyday conversation signals your interest in and commitment to fieldwork. It can also open up opportunities for participant-observation when your coconversationalists invite you to see or experience what they are talking about.

If you begin with informal interviews and conversations, you will then later be in a good position to decide which formal interviews you want to pursue. Your formal interviewing will then be more focused and effective. You will be able to ask more informed and pointed questions as a result of the information that you have already collected.

The ethnographer should avoid getting caught in the trap of assuming that only formal interviews can be a good source of information. Instead, you can replace this mindset with an approach that sees a continuum running from formal interviews to the most informal conversations. All these situations can be helpful in terms of ethnographic information as long as you are paying close enough attention to recognize and record important information. When you are waiting at the bus stop or eating a snack in the break room, you should remember that a really enlightening conversation may be just around the corner. You have to be open enough to let it happen and alert to its significance. This awareness fits well with your general need to be open and receptive to opportunities to learn. You simply have to learn how to make the most of situations where the choices, actions, and words can help you understand what is important to your informants and what they think you ought to know or learn.

INFORMAL CONVERSATION AS AN AVENUE TO "REAL" CULTURE

When you record the words of an informant, you may wonder about the degree to which the informant's description matches what happened, what she experienced, or what she thinks. You are essentially raising questions about the reliability and validity of the type of spoken data that you collect through interviews. These questions are valid, since spoken words only allow us to approach thought, behavior, and history indirectly. Interviewees may consciously or unconsciously censor, emphasize, deceive, misremember, or provide a partial account for a variety of reasons.

While a formal interview allows you to ask the questions you want to ask in the order that you want to ask them, this type of interview also tends to occur in environments that are most removed from the rhythm and activities of everyday life. This degree of remove tends to produce situations in which informants are most likely to provide sanitized or idealized answers to questions. For instance, if you are asking questions about gendered divisions of labor, John, a married man, may tell you in the context of a formal interview that he and his wife share domestic responsibilities equally, a response that matches the interviewee's understanding of gender equality as a cultural and social ideal. However, if you have a chance to engage in informal conversation with John and his male peers during which relationships with wives and partners come up, you may learn that John and the other men go to great lengths to shirk their domestic responsibilities. Maybe, for example, you will learn that John "remembers" that they need milk from the store when there are dishes to be washed. If you visited John in his home, you might also observe an apparent disparity between the division of domestic responsibilities.

The circumstances of formal interviews tend to produce idealized answers to questions. If you rely solely on these answers, you will be able to construct a picture of **"ideal" culture or society,** but you will not be able to confidently assert that your information accurately reflects **"real" culture or society**—that is, society and culture in action—which we all know can often differ significantly from the ideal visions of it. Of course, information collected through participant-observation and other sources can provide a counterpoint to these idealized versions, and the comparison can often produce interesting questions as the ethnographer attempts to account for and explain discrepancies. Informal conversations can also be an avenue to more "realistic" accounts by informants. Because the conversations tend to take place in more relaxed circumstances and because they are less orchestrated by the ethnographer, informants can be more candid and less likely to provide idealized versions. The astute ethnographer can make the most of these conversational entries to develop a more rounded ethnographic picture that includes conversations that emerged more "naturally" than a formal interview. Still, the ethnographer's presence almost always has an effect on behavior and conversations, even in the most informal circumstances. Collecting information in a variety of ways is always the best way to collect data that is ultimately reliable and valid.

A GOOD INTERVIEWER IS A GOOD LISTENER

Whether you are conducting formal interviews or learning from informal conversations, in order to be a good interviewer you need to be a good listener. If you are singularly focused on asking *your* questions, you may fail to pick up on important cues offered by the interviewee or speaker. If you are focused on being a good listener, you may very well discover newly emergent questions or see new connections that you had been unaware of previously. If the interviewee keeps talking about religion while you keep asking questions about politics, there is an obvious disconnect leading to miscommunication. As the interviewer, you need to be aware of these situations and adapt to them and learn from them. You may have entered the conversation convinced that religion was completely unrelated to the realm of politics, but your interviewee's responses indicate otherwise. By listening carefully, you may find that you need to begin asking questions about religion or revisit your notes from previous interviews to see whether other interviewees have offered similar responses.

While you are doing interviews, you may feel like the important thing is to complete the interviews and then you can return to analyze them after the fact. You *will* return to analyze them at later stages, but you should not simply conduct the interviews as an automaton and set them aside for later. You need to be an engaged interviewer willing to learn and to adapt. Your interview style and your interview questions are likely to evolve. The goal is to be the most effective interviewer you can be, and listening is the essential skill that allows that evolution into a more effective interviewer. Even perfect questions will yield only a mediocre interview if you are not fully engaged as a good listener.

Being a good interviewer by being a good listener involves three fundamental tenets of the ethnographic research process:

1. You have to be in a position where you are prepared to learn from others.

2. You have to be willing to cede some control of the research process so that your informants can help guide the research.

3. You should always be ready to adapt to circumstances as they present themselves.

When you think of yourself as an interviewer, you should think of yourself as a listener ready to learn and to adapt. Conducting interviews as an active, engaged listener can be a very draining experience because it requires a great deal of effort and concentration. The benefits appear in a rich collection of data produced through interviews and conversations.

HOW TO RECORD INTERVIEW DATA

Recording interview data can be a complicated task. Using an audio (or video) recorder can make the task somewhat easier, even if the job of transcription can be daunting at times (see Chapter Five). When considering how to record interview data—whether you are making primary notes or transcribing a recording—you will want to work from a pretty clear sense of the types of information in which you are interested. There are at least two principal types of information that interviews can yield: direct, discrete pieces of information (like age, religious affiliation, and birthplace) and narrative explanations or accounts. Interviews can also yield information about experience and perception, opinions, thought processes, symbols, and logical or cultural connections, linguistic practices, and social relationships. You will want to pay special attention to the types of information most likely to be related to your research topic and record as much detail as possible.

As I have already noted with respect to ethnographic field notes in general, detail is key when it comes to recording interview data. If an interviewee has told you the story of how he got involved in politics at a very early age, it is not sufficient for you to write a short one-line summary (such as "EJ reports an early interest in politics") in your notes. You should include as much narrative detail as possible. For instance, more helpful and expansive notes might read: "EJ reports that he comes from a political family. His grandfather served two terms as mayor of the town and his dad was elected to the school board before an unsuccessful run for sheriff. So, from an early age, EJ remembers visiting political rallies and speeches and even appearing on stage with his father and grandfather. EJ was always a member of the student council in school and was then student body president in high school. When he finished law school, he saw running for DA as a logical next step." In this more detailed set of notes, you are including a lot more information about family, education, and motivation. You will be able to work with and may be able to compare EJ to other politicians who "report an early interest in politics." You may want to include even more information. Did EJ smile or become emotional when talking about his father and grandfather? Did he seem proud of his involvement with student council or did he look back on this as a rather immature way of imitating adult politics? Some of this information might be included in a complete audio transcript. Other pieces can be provided only by the ethnographer's accompanying notes. You should make sure to note elements like impressions, setting and surroundings, body language, and important moments during the interview. If you are not able to record the interview, you will want to be able to recreate key responses or exchanges as closely as you can as soon as possible after the fact. If you plan close analysis of words, phrases, or other linguistic dimensions, you will want to keep close track of these elements as well.

You will find interviews most rewarding if you can avoid thinking about them as simply a way to collect straightforward information (like age and whether someone has ever been initiated into the Elks). These discrete pieces of information can be important pieces of the ethnographic puzzle, but they are usually most illuminating in concert with the other types of information that can be collected through interviews. Pointed questions are necessary at times, but interviews offer a time to encourage interviewees to tell stories and provide deep explanations. The ethnographer's job is to elicit and record the wealth of information that comes in those stories and explanations. It is okay if your interviewee "goes off on a tangent." In fact, what seems at first like a tangent to the researcher may ultimately be most illuminating. Chances are good that the connections may make perfect sense from the interviewee's perspective.

USING AN INTERVIEW SCHEDULE

An **interview schedule** is a list of interview questions. It is generally organized in a particular order to guide the interview from start to finish. The ethnographer should avoid asking questions in a random or haphazard fashion. A good interview will evolve with a good conversational flow that allows both the interviewer and the interviewee to become comfortable. For this reason, an interview schedule can be an important tool to ensure that the researcher has a good set of questions and an appropriate plan for asking those questions in the course of an interview. Still, you may find that using an interview schedule is tricky at times because interviews often do not go entirely according to plan. What might have "flowed" when you went through the interview schedule may not flow in practice, and your interviewee may have her own ideas about what the interview ought to include and how to proceed.

In some relatively rare circumstances, ethnographers stick to a strict interview schedule, asking the same questions of each interviewee in the same order. Doing so ensures that the circumstances of the interview (for example, order and wording of the question) do not affect the responses collected and that comparable sets of data come out of each interview. Still, this strict use of an interview schedule can produce rather formal exchanges and close the door to potential research avenues that emerge during the course of research. Therefore, many ethnographers choose to follow an interview schedule more loosely or not at all. Most ethnographers will benefit by using an interview schedule and also allowing for some variation and change in the process.

Before your first interview, you should come up with a list of questions that you would like to have answered. The questions should cover the major topics and include prompts that will elicit stories and lengthy explanations. Once you have a list of questions, you organize the list as best you can in a logical order by placing connected or follow-up questions together with related questions and so forth. You now have a preliminary interview schedule. Once you have the schedule, you should study it so that you are comfortable with it going into the interview. You can take a copy with you for reference, but it is preferable to devote most of your attention to the interviewee and her responses without having to constantly consult your schedule. Even though you are working from the schedule, you should feel free to ask additional questions that seem relevant during the interview. You may also find that some questions are unnecessary because they have been answered in the course of other questions. By working loosely with the interview schedule and listening closely to the interviewee's responses, you can respond to the specific opportunities of a particular interview and constantly revise the schedule based on your interview experiences. By the end, you will have a much more effective schedule with improved questions and probably a new order.

HOW TO START AN INTERVIEW

Starting an interview can be one of the most challenging parts of the interview process. The first few minutes frequently set the tone for the rest of the interview. As quickly as possible, you want to establish an environment in which the interviewee/informant is comfortable offering honest and expansive answers. You want to avoid establishing an antagonistic interview relationship. The interviewee will frequently pick up on cues from the interviewer. Whether consciously or unconsciously, he will be analyzing you and your questions and developing ideas about your questions and your research project. With your opening questions, you want to set the tone by showing genuine interest, but you also want to avoid coming across as naive or completely uninformed or overly confident in your knowledge. Your informants probably do not want to spend their time telling or explaining things that you should already know, but they may also wonder about the point of the interview if you already seem to know everything. Walking this line as the interviewer is one of the many challenges you face. In interviews and conversations, you should be as open as possible about what you do and do not know and aim to demonstrate your desire to learn from your interviewee.

One of the first steps in planning for the initial moments of an interview is to determine whether it is a good idea to ask personal questions of the interviewee from the outset. In many instances, people are most comfortable talking about themselves, and many people like to talk about themselves. We all know a few people who like to talk about themselves a little too much! In these situations, asking questions about personal histories and personal experiences can be an effective way to begin an interview. These personal questions should not be invasive or ask about sensitive personal issues; they should simply ask about personal experiences instead of abstract ideas. For instance, you may decide to ask an interviewee to tell you about her first memories of school or the family farm. Vivid memories may prompt extensive stories and recollections. If so, the interviewee has already shown a willingness to talk and explain, and it is your responsibility to build on that willingness.

In some circumstances, interviewees may be especially wary of personal questions, especially if they know that the researcher is interested in a topic that touches on private dimensions or socially unacceptable behavior. In these instances, interviewees may be understandably reluctant to respond to questions asking where they are from, where they live, or even who they are. If you start out asking these questions, interviewees may become reticent from the start. If they get in the habit of not answering questions or simply answering with as short an answer as possible, this habit is likely to continue during the rest of the interview. If you can anticipate this reluctance to talk in personal terms, you can plan to begin with impersonal or abstract questions that the interviewee may be more comfortable answering. Instead of asking about the interviewee's first experiences with school, you might ask her to tell you about the educational system itself and how it works or does not work. This approach allows the interviewee the opportunity to speak more generally but also offers a space for the interviewee to connect to personal experiences; it probably will not feel as threatening, and you have the chance to listen and to ask follow-up questions.

You should try to start the interview by asking "easy" questions. They should be easy in the sense that the interviewee is comfortable with them (that is, confident in his answers). Personal questions are good because the interviewee usually is the expert on these matters. Asking factual questions about names, places, and dates can also be an easy way to help the interviewee build confidence in providing information. But you should avoid asking too many questions like these that can be answered with a single word or phrase or even a nod or shake of the head at the beginning. You want to establish a pattern for the interview from the outset, and that pattern should include room for the interviewee to provide lengthy explanations and interpretations if at all possible. Asking questions that encourage the interviewee to tell a story can be a great way to establish this sort of pattern and to create a congenial interview environment. If you respond in appropriate ways with laughter and expressions of surprise, sympathy, and even horror to that first story, the interviewee will be more likely to respond with more stories and lengthy expositions. You are asking questions and guiding the interview. You are an active participant in the conversation, but the more space you can provide for the interviewee to expand on important points or direct the conversation in a particular way, the better the interview will be. Remember, you are conducting the interview to learn and hear what your interviewee thinks. Sometimes, if you can create the appropriate environment, an interviewee will take an interview in an unexpected direction and open up a whole new avenue of insight and analysis. The job of the ethnographer as interviewer is to create opportunities for this. The predominant character of an interview often emerges very early in the encounter, and it can be very hard to change the pattern of an interview once it is established.

GOOD VERSUS BAD INTERVIEW QUESTIONS

There are no firm rules about what makes a good or bad interview question because interview questions tend to be unique to a specific ethnographic project. Occasionally you may be able to adapt interview questions from another project, especially if your project involves revisiting a similar site or topic. In this case, the adapted questions can be good because they have presumably already gone through a test process of trial and error in the previous project and because they will produce comparative data that will allow you to connect your work to the work of others. Still, in most cases, you are going to be developing your own interview questions to suit the needs of your project. Following are some rough guidelines to help you in coming up with good questions and avoiding bad ones.

1. *Ask more open-ended questions than closed-ended questions.* The ethnographer can collect a lot of good, specific information with closed-ended questions. However, **open-ended questions** will provide the sort of expansive and deep data that are at the heart of most good ethnographic work. Open-ended questions are harder to

create, but the effort to do so will help ensure that you are asking good questions that yield the appropriate information for your project.

2. *Avoid questions that suggest an answer or imply that you already know the answer.* The goal of any interview question is to learn about the perspective of the interviewee. Interviewees can be very susceptible to suggestion from the interviewer. Whenever possible, you want to avoid putting words in the mouths of interviewees or unnecessarily influencing their responses. Avoiding this sort of influence means avoiding questions that include components like "Isn't it true that . . . ?" or "Right?" at the end. If the questions are worded in either of these ways, you have already suggested to the interviewee what you think the answer is or should be. The interviewee may or may not be willing to disagree with you even if she is inclined to offer a different response. Asking questions in these ways can also come across as condescending if the interviewee thinks you are asking a question to which you already know the answer.

3. *It is okay to ask follow-up questions and to double-check answers.* If something comes up that you do not completely understand or if you simply want further explanation, your job as ethnographer is to ask one or more follow-up questions. Asking follow-up questions is one of the many situations where the ethnographer adopts the position of a student looking to learn. If you ask a question like "It is very interesting to learn that the group makes masks on the first day of the celebration, but how are they used?" or "If I understand correctly, the application is first reviewed by the floor manager, but what happens after that?" you communicate interest and that you are trying to learn while asking for additional information or explanation. Interviewees are likely to respond positively and helpfully if you show that you are paying attention and learning from them. Double-checking a seemingly clear response can be delicate at times, but you should do it, especially if that is a particularly important point in your research. Sometimes an interviewee will contradict himself or appear to do so. If you ask him about it directly, you may or may not resolve that contradiction, but the more information you can gain about the interviewee's thoughts and opinions on the topic, the more information you have to work with and analyze. Sometimes these contradictions are at the heart of ethnographic research. In the case of particularly complex or controversial topics, you may want to ask a series of different questions that approach the topic from slightly different angles. This approach can be very illuminating. You just need to make sure you do not unnecessarily tire your interviewee with questions that you perceive to be overly repetitive.

4. *Hypothetical questions can be good interview questions.* A well-crafted "What if . . . ?" question can help you learn about a wider range of situations than you may have a chance to observe or your interviewee has directly experienced. It can also allow you to explore larger thought processes and decision-making steps to see if certain thoughts and behaviors apply in other circumstances. You may want to ask your interviewee whether you think her relationship with her boss would be better if the boss were a woman instead of a man. Asking a question like this will allow the researcher to learn more about the interviewee's thoughts on gender and relations

between workers and management. In most cases, you will want to keep your hypothetical questions well within the range of the plausible. You should not waste your interviewee's time with what she perceives to be "silly" questions.

5. *Avoid "simple" questions.* If you think a question is simple, chances are good that your interviewee will too. You should steer away from these simple questions whenever possible. They are probably not going to yield very helpful information. If you can see or discover something for yourself, you should try to do so. If you attended the soccer match, you do not need to ask what the score was. You should focus on the things that your interviewee can tell you that you do not have direct access to—the interviewee's perspective, experience, and opinions. You may want to use your interviews to confirm some pieces of information that you have collected through participant-observation or other interviews or conversations. If you recorded an observation that about 75 percent of the crowd at the soccer stadium was male, you may want to check to see if your informant noticed this. Or if another informant told you he thought everybody in town was supporting one of the two soccer teams, you may want to check to see if your other informants agree with this assessment.

Questions That the Ethnographer Can't or Shouldn't Ask

The interviewee always has the right to refuse to answer a question or stop an interview. You cannot and should not force the interviewee to answer if she does not want to answer. In most cases, however, once she agrees to an interview, the interviewee will answer almost all questions. An inappropriate question, though, can disrupt the flow or even bring an interview to an abrupt end. Obviously, you want to avoid these sorts of inappropriate questions for both practical and ethical reasons.

The initial explanation of the interview and the research goals should prepare the interviewee for the types of questions you will be asking. Imagine an interviewee who thinks she is being interviewed about religion and all of a sudden is asked about her sexual activities or personal finances. Either type of question is likely to surprise her and even make her uncomfortable or suspicious. She may be much more reluctant to proceed with the interview or answer the rest of the questions openly. The interviewee may find the approach to particular questions novel or counterintuitive, but you should strive to make sure interviewees are prepared for the general topics that will be covered in the course of the interview. This initial explanation is particularly important if the interview will touch on potentially touchy or explosive subjects such as sexuality, religion, politics, health, money, or illegal activities.

(Continued)

(Continued)

If the interviewee knows you are going to ask about one of these topics, he is much more likely to be prepared to answer questions along these lines.

You should not ask questions designed to elicit private information unless the questions are directly related to your research. You should always aim to respect conventions of privacy and your informants' right to control (that is, to choose to share or not to share) information about their personal lives. In some cases, it may help for you to clarify that you intend to use pseudonyms or take other steps to protect confidentiality so that the interviewee knows how her personal information and identity will be used and protected.

Ethnographers ask a lot from their informants—from sharing their time and expertise to housing and hosting ethnographers in many cases—but sometimes there are things and questions that the ethnographer cannot ask. It is best to build a relationship and trust before asking someone to share something very personal, and even then some things remain too personal or private to share—especially if it will eventually be shared with a wider audience in a report or presentation.

The ethnographer should respect these boundaries. Sometimes informants will *choose* to share information that seems very personal or private. This is the best way to collect such information. You may want to try asking indirect questions, which offer interviewees the opportunity to share personal information if they choose to do so. For instance, in many contexts, asking a person whether he is infected with the HIV virus is simply too invasive of a question. But you might be able to ask your interviewee how serious he thinks the HIV problem is in the local community or whether he thinks it is common for people to go for HIV testing at the hospital. The interviewee may answer by telling of his own experiences with HIV testing or his own HIV status (a lot of people tend to use personal examples to answer questions) or he may elect to keep his own counsel.

One of the benefits of long-term ethnographic fieldwork is that informants tend to become more willing to share information with you as they become more familiar with you and your work. Sometimes letting time run its course is the only way to gain access to certain types of information. Of course, if you act in a way that betrays trust or fails to inspire confidence, a long-term research presence can have the opposite effect on informants' willingness to share. If you suspect you might be asking some touchy questions, you should consult with your instructor or supervisor and others to get their thoughts on what is appropriate or inappropriate. You should also keep in mind that learning private information—about an informant's health status or illegal activities, for instance—places tremendous responsibility on you to protect her confidentiality and prevent negative consequences for your informants.

WHEN TO CONDUCT FORMAL INTERVIEWS

Ethnographers tend to conduct relatively informal interviews, but there are situations in which formal interviews are more appropriate. When the circumstances entail a significant degree of formality in the interaction generally, a formal interview may be expected and may be most effective. For example, if you have arranged to interview a high-ranking government official by scheduling an appointment with her administrative assistant and you find yourself seated in a well-appointed office decorated with the trappings of governmental hierarchy and bureaucracy, a formal interview may be the only realistic option. If you adopt an overly casual approach, your interviewee may feel you are wasting her time or not respecting her position.

Formal interviews that follow a strict interview schedule can produce especially uniform sets of data that lend themselves to direct comparison because the researcher is collecting and comparing responses across an identical set of questions. If this type of direct and careful comparison will benefit the project, you should consider doing relatively formal interviews using a strict interview schedule. Think about conducting these sorts of interviews during the latter stages of your research, after you have conducted several informal interviews and engaged in informal conversations. In this way, you can benefit from the opportunities that the informal approach offers for the informant to direct the conversation and explore unforeseen angles and directions. The formal interviews that follow will undoubtedly benefit from the knowledge you have gained in these earlier stages. You will likely find you ask different questions and in different ways than you would have at the outset. The interview schedule rooted in ethnographic work will almost certainly be better and more effective.

SUMMARY

Interviews allow the ethnographer to hear from and learn from informants directly. You should be prepared with thoughtful questions whenever the opportunity for conversation with informants arises, but more than anything else being a good interviewer involves being a good listener. Context determines to a large extent whether a formal or informal approach to interviewing is appropriate, but most ethnographers will benefit if they begin with a commitment to relatively informal conversations and interviews. Working with an interview schedule and a strong sense of what makes questions good or bad, the ethnographer can gain a great deal of information through interviews.

KEY TERMS

Interviewing

Engaged conversationalist

Formal interviews

Informal interviews

"Ideal" culture or society

"Real" culture or society

Interview schedule

Open-ended questions

DISCUSSION QUESTIONS

1. What are the respective benefits and limitations of formal and informal interviews? Is there any difference between an informal interview and a regular conversation? Why is it a good idea to start your research with relatively informal interviews? In what sort of situation does this not hold true?

2. What does the ethnographer need to do in order to be an engaged conversationalist? How is this approach different from some of the common ways interviewing is practiced and perceived?

3. Why are interview data indispensable to the work of Behar and Bourgois as well as others? What sorts of information or perspectives do ethnographers gain through interviewing that they would have a hard time accessing otherwise?

4. Why is "real" culture important to the ethnographer? What is the best way for ethnographers to use interviewing as a research method to examine real culture? Can you think of an ethnography that you have read that does this particularly effectively?

5. What does the ethnographer need to consider in recording interview data? Does the purpose or context of the research influence the interview notes produced?

6. How heavily should you rely on your interview schedule? Are there situations where schedules are unnecessary or potentially hinder the course of research?

7. How can the ethnographer work to establish a positive and productive interaction at the outset of the interview? Why is establishing this sort of interaction a particularly important goal for the ethnographer as interviewer?

8. What distinguishes a good interview question from a bad interview question? Can you always tell one from the other before you conduct an interview? What types of information or knowledge will help you distinguish between good and bad questions?

CHAPTER

8

ANALYZING ALONG THE WAY

LEARNING OBJECTIVES

- Identify key themes and questions that emerge during the course of research
- Develop and implement a strategy for organizing field notes
- Make a list of things learned to this point in field research
- Make a list of things that still need to be investigated as research proceeds
- Consider whether the central research question needs to be revised
- Evaluate and revise the ongoing research strategy in order to collect the necessary information and answer evolving research questions
- Plan to get feedback from informants about information collected and analytical ideas
- Begin writing preliminary pieces of the final ethnography based on research to this point

In the midst of the ethnographic project, the ethnographer has begun to collect a lot of information and create an ethnographic record. This record will eventually include field notes on participant-observation experiences, interview notes, and probably transcripts, maps, and charts. Each event or conversation related to the research project should be producing multiple pages in the ethnographic record. At this pace, the record can become quite voluminous and a bit unwieldy. With this sort of large and varied ethnographic record, analyzing the findings along the way helps you organize your thoughts and notes in a way that allows you to make the most use out of the information you are collecting.

Without analyzing along the way, you may find that when you return to your notes and other parts of the ethnographic record, they seem like a jumbled mess. Therefore, organization and efficient use of the record are two good reasons to analyze along the way, but the most important reason for analyzing in the midst of the ethnographic research is to make sure you make the most of your research opportunities as you move forward. You want to avoid reaching the end of your research period only to discover you did not really understand what people were talking about when they referred to "the big test" on a regular basis or you realized too late that when you were asking about gender relations, everybody kept bringing up economics and the local price of fuel. If you had become aware of these things earlier, when you were still conducting research, you could have asked questions and taken other steps to find out what "the big test" was or what the connection was between gender, economics, and the price of fuel. Analyzing the information that you have collected in a continual fashion as the project proceeds will allow you to begin to see connections, test analytical ideas, and identify gaps in the ethnographic record that you are producing.

IDENTIFYING KEY THEMES AND QUESTIONS: PAYING ATTENTION TO YOUR DATA

As you analyze the information or data that you have collected to this point, one of your goals should be to identify **key themes** or questions *as they emerge from the data*. Indications of key themes appear in stories, phrases, symbols, or ideas that reappear multiple times in the record you have collected. This recurrence offers a good indicator of their significance. The more frequently a symbol or idea recurs, the more evidence you have that it is shared and may be important to the group represented. You should make a list of these items as potential key themes and symbols and add to it as you become aware of additional stories, phrases, symbols, or ideas that occur in the ethnographic record. Making this list is one of the first important steps in ethnographic analysis. The list constitutes one of the ethnographer's first efforts to separate salient points and themes from the rather messy ethnographic record. It is the beginning of an analytical framework that you can refine and build as you move forward.

At the same time that you are identifying key themes, you are probably struggling with key questions or problems. Taking the time to analyze the data you have collected while you are in the midst of your research will allow you to see these questions and problems more clearly and take steps to address them as you continue your research. Looking back at the ethnographic record, you should make a list of the points or moments you still find perplexing or confusing. The list can include apparent contra- dictions—where two or more people contradicted each others' accounts or where what was said did not correspond with what was done or what you expected—in the ethno- graphic record. If your informants keep asking questions of you or asking you to find answers to certain questions, you should take note of these too. This list of questions can be a fruitful guide as you proceed with your research. The questions represent one way informants can offer feedback and shape the ethnographic project. Without step- ping back to think about the types of information you have collected to this point, you might leave these questions and problems unaddressed in the course of your research.

Identifying key themes and questions in the midst of the ethnographic project will make you a more effective researcher from that point forward. You will be tuned in to key analytical categories and the questions that you want answered. The most impor- tant point about this process of ongoing analysis is to play close attention to the ethno- graphic record—to the information you have collected to this point. The analysis will only be valuable if you can connect it to substantiating evidence from the ethnographic record. You should take this opportunity to read through notes and revisit recordings carefully. You should not assume that you know what was said or what you wrote. Sometimes going back to old notes while you are still in the midst of the ethnographic research seems like a hard thing to do, but it is an essential part of a commitment to ongoing analysis and making the most out of your research time and opportunities.

HOW TO ORGANIZE YOUR NOTES

Field notes can seem like an overwhelming mess. The ethnographer must figure out how to manage them in a way that leads to productive analysis in the end. The most important first step is to devise a plan for organizing the notes. Organizing the notes will help you identify key themes and gaps in the research and make it much easier at any stage to find the pieces of information you are seeking. This first step in organization involves evalu- ating the nature of the ethnographic record that you have produced to this point. Along these lines, you can compare the volume of interview notes and participant-observation notes to see if you have the appropriate balance for your project. If you discover that you have a lot of participant-observation notes, but your interview notes are sparse, you may come to the conclusion that you need to devote more attention to interviews as a research approach or that you need to take more detailed notes about your interviews. On the other hand, evaluation of your notes might suggest that you have produced only limited participant-observation data to this point and need to redirect your research activities in that direction to produce a more balanced ethnographic record.

The next step in organizing your notes involves identifying key **categories** and linking related parts of your notes to these categories. In the process of identifying categories, you will be performing the first level of analysis as you look to identify the most important variables or ideas to constitute the categories. Ideally, the categories will crosscut the types of research techniques used so that you can connect information collected through participant-observation to information gleaned through informal interviews. You might, for instance, be able to use the category "mother-child relationships" to connect an interesting interview segment about Alice's relationship with her mother to observations that you made in the day care center.

You should start by making a list of possible categories and not edit too much as you make your initial list. Some of the categories may end up not being helpful for organizing and making sense out of your ethnographic record, but you can decide that at a later stage. You can begin by thinking about the categories and ideas that you thought would be most important when you started your project. The next step requires you to consider the research you have done to this point. You need to identify the most salient or recurrent points and themes that seem to have emerged from the research and add them to the list. You will also want to identify moments in your research experiences that stand out to you as most important or revealing and write those down. Adding them to the list means you will seek to figure out what you think they represent in terms of themes or categories. Some moments are important because they seem to contradict general trends or belie common understandings. These outliers or exceptions to the rule can help you evaluate the categories you are working with and consider their possible limitations. Once you have a list of categories, you should review it for any overlap or redundancy. If some categories work better as subcategories of larger categories, you will want to organize your list along these lines.

You now have a working list of categories that you can use to organize your notes. You should not be afraid to revise this list as you move forward. You can treat it like an organic part of the research process that will grow and evolve as the research continues. Some parts may ultimately produce analytic dead ends, and new categories may emerge that could prove particularly fruitful.

One of the popular, old-fashioned ways to categorize notes included punching holes in note cards in certain places to correspond with particular categories. The ethnographer today can try this technique, but it is no longer necessary. Today, computer databases will allow you to be much more sophisticated in your sorting techniques, but often a combination of sticky notes, basic codes, and highlighters works equally well. The goal is to be able to identify easily those parts of the ethnographic record that relate to a particular topic. Whenever you want to analyze this topic more closely, you can collect the different parts of the record related to the topic and begin with a close analysis of your data.

WHAT HAVE YOU LEARNED?

Now is the time to take stock and figure out what you have learned or discovered. In this process, you should focus on things you have learned since the beginning of your ethnographic research. The knowledge you have gained may take the form of confirmed

Using Computer Databases

There is a handful of databases designed specifically for use with ethnography (such as NUDIST). If you have access to or can afford one of these options, they are worth investigating. Because they are designed for use in ethnography, some of the steps may be easier or more logical than in a generic database program. However, more general databases can be used successfully to organize your ethnographic records. Databases may also allow you to link audio or video files with written notes and transcripts, and computers offer a powerful way to search large records. Databases will not, however, do the work of analyzing, sorting, and categorizing for you. Setting up a database for use with your project will take some time and effort. A relatively small ethnographic project may not merit the time and effort required to set up a database. If you are comfortable with computers and expect to use these sorts of database skills on this and other future projects, setting up a database may be very beneficial.

hypotheses, insight into unanticipated behaviors or speech, and answers to previously unanswered questions, among other things. Making a list of the things you have learned to this point in your research will assist you in examining your progress to this point. The list helps you see the accomplishments you have achieved already in the research process. You have undoubtedly learned a number of interesting things. You may be struggling to find answers or to gain access to certain things, but you will find you have learned a great deal in the process and that much of what you have learned was unanticipated. In these unanticipated pieces of information, you may find an exciting new direction for your research or the next project for the future. Once you have this list, you can add items to it as often as it is appropriate. Setting aside some time to review your research and revise this list on a regular basis will be helpful.

Making a list of the things you have learned to this point also allows you to evaluate your research in relationship to your original research goals. You can go back to your original list of research questions and your research plan to see how many of the questions you have answered and how much of the research plan you have accomplished. Chances are good that there are still a good number of unanswered questions from that original list, but you hope to have begun to make inroads in terms of collecting information and answering some key questions that helped to inspire the project in the first place.

WHAT DO YOU STILL NEED TO DO?

By checking off the questions to which you think you have found answers—"think" because you may often find the answer is not as easy or as obvious as you thought it would be!—you are also creating a list of questions still to be answered. Now that you are in the middle of your research, you should have a better sense both of which questions are answerable in the course of your research and which questions seem most important and pressing. As you review the list of things you have learned and your original research questions, you can work toward developing a new, revised list of questions that you want to answer as you proceed with your research. Putting these questions in order according to their relative importance for your project as it stands now ensures that you prioritize your research plans as you proceed. Your fieldwork experiences may have taken you in a direction that pulled you away from your primary research question; this step will be a chance to remind yourself of key research questions that deserve your renewed attention. On the other hand, the fieldwork experiences may have helped you perceive a situation or set of parameters different from what you expected to find when you began the project. If this is the case, the relative importance of your research questions may have changed significantly. What was low or absent on your original list of questions may now be at the top of your list of "Things to Figure Out" and, conversely, what seemed most important at the outset may now be low on your list of priorities.

Evaluating your research in terms of modified goals will help you direct your endeavors toward the most important research questions with a renewed and revised sense of importance. As you move forward, you want to seek answers to as many of these questions as possible, starting at the top. Keeping this list close at hand and consulting it regularly will help you make effective research plans. However, as you make research plans, you should be prepared to revise the list as your research experiences help you continuously review and revise your achievements and objectives.

HAS THE RESEARCH QUESTION CHANGED?

At this point, you have produced a revised list of research questions. The bigger issue is whether your central research question needs to be changed or revised. In a significant number of cases, you will find that you need to develop a new central research question that matches your primary interests now that you are fully engaged in the research. For instance, you may have begun your study focusing on the effectiveness of local efforts designed to reduce infant malnutrition, but you may now be convinced that the competition between children and adults for food resources is a more appropriate and interesting topic. (Depending on circumstances and factors like supervision and funding, you may or may not have the leeway to change your research question as much as you would like.)

The most important thing at this stage is to revisit the central research question to make sure that the ongoing work is based on a solid foundation that will produce the desired results. If your original research question is fixed and unchangeable, you may need to redirect your research efforts in order to get back on point. If the research question can be modified and you decide such revision is desirable, you can then proceed with research specifically dedicated to that new research question.

TWEAKING THE RESEARCH DESIGN

As you pause to review your findings to this point, now is also the time for you to evaluate your research design, its effectiveness thus far, and its appropriateness for the rest of your research. You can start by reviewing what you have done and how it compares to what you proposed to do in your research design. You should consider whether you have done more or less participant-observation than you planned and whether you have conducted as many interviews as the research design called for. You should also consider whether you have undertaken avenues of research that the research design did not anticipate.

Next you will need to compare the data you have collected to the type of data you thought this research design would yield. You may or may not have been able to collect detailed information along the lines that you envisioned. This process of evaluation in the middle of the research process allows you to decide whether you need to devise new plans for accessing those pieces of information. Chances are good that you have found it easier to access and collect certain types of data than others. This discrepancy can occur for a variety of reasons. Among other things, certain topics or areas are more private or sensitive than others; you find it easier to ask about some things than others; you may have encountered a general reluctance to share with an outsider researcher; and pure happenstance in the course of research may have led to inevitable shifts in plans and focus. Thinking carefully about the data you have been able to collect along with the data that have been elusive will allow you to ensure that you collect as much pertinent information as possible.

In order to gain this information, you may need to revisit and tweak the research plan. You may need to rethink the balance of participant-observation and interviews that will yield optimal results. You may have discovered that you need to emphasize one method over the other in order to collect relevant data. You may need to plan to interview different people or ask different interview questions designed to elicit different types of responses that will give you access to different types of information. Now is the time to revise your research plan to match what you have learned in the course of this plan to this point. You do not have to conduct twenty formal interviews simply because that is what the original plan said. Nor do you have to attend twenty Sabbath services if you have already attended ten and you think your time will be better spent attending religious education classes held in women's homes.

You may have designed the perfect research plan at the beginning of your project, in which case you should stick with your plan (and pat yourself on the back). This perfect situation is pretty unusual, though. Most ethnographers will have to adapt their research plan to the contingencies of research in the field. This is normal. You should be ready to come up with a new, revised plan for the rest of your research time and focus on collecting the most important types of information that you have yet to collect sufficiently. In developing a revised research design, consultation with a mentor, instructor, or supervisor is always advisable.

GETTING FEEDBACK FROM YOUR INFORMANTS

The best ethnography is rooted in a strong engagement with informants that allows them to teach you and direct the research in interesting and important ways. As you have been conducting participant-observation and interviews, ideally you have found ways to learn from your informants and have tried to make the most of opportunities when they seemed to be pushing the research in a particular direction. As you look to begin concerted analysis at this midpoint in the research process, you have the chance to share your analytical ideas with your informants. Informants often bring an interesting and keen analytical perspective to bear on your work. You should not assume that they are incapable of understanding analytical ideas or theoretical frameworks. They probably do not share the same background and training that you have and may therefore have a different perspective, but they are informants because they are real experts on the subject. Sometimes this different perspective allows them to see connections and flaws in the analysis that you cannot see.

Once you have developed a list of things you have learned, you can make plans to share all or part of this list with one or more of your informants. However, you do not have to share it as a list. You may find it most helpful to share the ideas contained in the list in the course of casual conversation. However you choose to share it, the purpose is twofold. First, this is a mechanism to test your developing knowledge. Your informant(s) may confirm or contest the information you have collected. If they confirm it, you gain confidence that these are valid pieces of information upon which to build your ethnography. If they contest one or more things, you may need to reevaluate your list of things you know. Perhaps this is a point of debate among your informants or there is a good reason why your informant denies or doubts something that you are confident is true. By sharing your knowledge with informants and getting their feedback, you are performing a test of validity on the information that you are collecting.

Second, your informants have a chance to add to or augment your analysis. When you say, "It seems that young people routinely defer to their elders when food is served at weddings," your informant may respond by saying, "That's right, this happens because weddings are an extension of family ties, and the elders are most closely linked to the continuation of the family" or "Yes, that happens at weddings, but at funerals the youth are served first and the elders receive the leftovers." The question becomes whether you had already collected these pieces of information and whether you had made the connection(s) that the informant is making implicitly or explicitly. You may have attended several weddings but no funerals. You may now look for an opportunity to attend a funeral (even if this seems like a morbid research strategy) to gain better insight into the relationship between age and food at communal events.

When you are seeking feedback from informants, getting different perspectives from different informants can be very helpful. Remember that each informant will have a different perspective on things. The differences may be slight or radical. Examining these differences helps the ethnographer gain a better understanding of the complexities that characterize all social groups and make ethnography so challenging.

You will probably find that some of your informants are more curious and analytical when it comes to your research. Seeking feedback from these individuals may be particularly beneficial. They are likely to ask penetrating questions and to offer hypothetical explanations for things they have heard, observed, and experienced. You may even want to ask questions like "Why do you think that . . . ?" These sorts of questions will encourage them to think analytically in order to come up with explanations. You can then evaluate their interpretations and explanations to see which ones are most relevant or illuminating and how they help you build your own analytical framework.

Many early ethnographers made the mistake of assuming that their informants were incapable of critical analysis of their own social and cultural situations. The argument was that as insiders they lacked the distance or perspective to see the larger picture. A closer and more realistic examination shows that people in all sorts of different circumstances routinely analyze and critically examine the social and cultural worlds of which they are a part. If the ethnographer can tap into that analysis and criticism, the ethnography will be much stronger than it would otherwise be. Ethnographers envision this sort of **collaborative critical analysis** when they talk about their informants as coresearchers. There are a lot of exciting opportunities and models for collaborative research in ethnography today. Still, in most cases the ethnographer will have to make the ultimate decisions about how to resolve (or not) discrepancies and what to do when accounts or perspectives seem contradictory. In some instances, your familiarity with other research, theoretical models, and comparative data will allow you to perceive comparisons and analytical approaches that may not be accessible to most or all of your informants. In this case, you will have to decide whether the analytical approach is appropriate and furthers ethnographic understanding. Informants may insist that social reality is one way, while the ethnographer's observations and experiences clearly suggest that it is different. You should take note of these differences and seek explanations. These experiences may offer important avenues into understanding the perception of reality that is part of a culturally lived world. That culturally and socially lived world is ultimately the ethnographer's object of study.

WRITING AT THE MIDWAY POINT

Whether you realize it or not, you have undoubtedly been doing a lot of writing throughout the research you have already done. *Ethnography is about writing*. From research proposals to field notes and interview notes, all the way through to the final ethnographic product, ethnography is a writing-intensive process. Like most other types of writing, ethnography involves revision at all stages. It may seem like every time you get ready to write something down with authority or confidence, you see or hear something that makes you question that very thing. This experience is an all-too-frequent occurrence for the ethnographer. (Clifford's 1983 analysis and critique of ethnographic authority highlights the precarious nature of the ethnographer's authority. You should be very careful about claiming an authority that you do not have a right to claim.) Still, the more information you can get down on paper, the more you have to work with as you proceed.

You have probably already created a large number of pages or files with your notes and brainstorming lists. These notes should remain mostly unedited. As you create the ethnographic record, your focus should be on taking what you observe, hear, and experience and putting it down on paper as directly as possible. Even the seemingly obscure details can become an important part of the ethnographic record.

Too many ethnographers make the mistake of leaving the rest of the writing and all the editing and analysis to the very end. Beginning the process of analytical writing and revising while you are in the midst of your research can be incredibly productive. It gives you the opportunity to develop your analytical ideas more fully, to produce a document or documents to which someone else can respond, and to begin developing sections of what will eventually become the final ethnographic report or paper. Following are two ways you can approach this type of writing while in the midst of your research.

1. *Write pieces of the final report.* You are probably better prepared to write about some parts of your research than others at this point. You can begin writing the pieces with which you are most comfortable. Starting with a high comfort level will help you get started putting something on paper or screen. This can be the hardest stage of all in writing. If you are confident in what you are writing and do not come across something that calls into question what you have written, you may be able to slide this piece into the final ethnography with relatively little revision. Writing these pieces now has the advantage of allowing you to write about these things when they are fresh in your mind. These sections may actually be harder to write if you leave them until later. Your focus will probably turn elsewhere. If so, you will have to work harder to recall and revisit the associated research.

2. *Write about particular moments.* The ethnographer often has a good sense of the most important or revealing **moments** as they happen ethnographically. These moments—key events, exceptional interviews, and unexpected occurrences—should occupy a central place in the ethnographic record. They will play a key role in shaping your ethnographic understanding and can serve as good illustrative examples when you present your findings. Therefore, there is a good chance that some version of an account of these moments will find its way into the final ethnography. You can go ahead and begin writing up an account of one or more of these moments. This writing will likely be very descriptive in the beginning. You should already have a largely descriptive account in your notes. You can take that account and look to turn it into a version that will be accessible to a wider audience. You may need to provide additional context and extra explanations for it to make sense as a stand-alone narrative. A good ethnographic description will include a lot of detail. You want to paint a picture, so to speak. But even so, your notes may include details that can be edited out to make a more readable and accessible account. These moments stick out in the ethnographic experiences because they carry particular meaning. Once you have constructed a good

descriptive account, you can continue writing about this research moment by explaining the ethnographic significance of the moment or event. By focusing on what it means and what it is connected to in the ethnographic record, you move from the descriptive to the analytical and start to lay the foundation for a larger **analytical framework** for the final ethnography.

SUMMARY

Analyzing and organizing the ethnographic record while still in the midst of the research allows you to make the most out of your fieldwork. Looking back on what you have collected and produced to this point, you can evaluate the relative success of your research plan, what you have learned at this stage, and what you still need to accomplish in the course of your research. This sort of evaluation of the ongoing research means you can revisit your original research question and research design to see whether one or the other needs revision to match the realities of the research context or changing priorities for research. You can use key themes to begin to organize the ethnographic record with an eye toward the final analytical picture that will connect disparate pieces from your experiences and notes. At this stage, you should begin writing pieces of the final ethnography that relate to key moments or experiences and areas of the ethnographic record with which you are particularly comfortable.

KEY TERMS

Key themes
Categories
Collaborative critical analysis

Moments
Descriptive account
Analytical framework

DISCUSSION QUESTIONS

1. How do you benefit by analyzing in the midst of your research? Does it make sense to analyze and write before you have all of the information that you need?

2. What is a key question or theme, and how does the ethnographer identify them? How do these questions and themes help you organize your notes? What can you accomplish by organizing your notes at this point in the research process?

3. How can lists of things learned and things that still need to be investigated help you in deciding whether you need to rework your central research question?

4. Should you even contemplate changing your research design halfway through the research project? What circumstances warrant a revised research plan? What

is the relationship between questions asked, types of data sought, and ethnographic methods employed?

5. Why is it important for you to seek feedback from your informants throughout your research? How can informants help you see your data in new or different ways?

6. Which pieces of the final ethnography are you most likely to be able to draft at the midpoint of the research project? How does writing pieces for the final product help your ongoing research?

CHAPTER

9

ETHNOGRAPHIC MAPS

LEARNING OBJECTIVES

- Understand and explain the importance of space and movement in ethnographic research
- Distinguish between different types of ethnographic maps and identify the appropriate circumstances for employing each type of map
- Consider the role of scale in conceptualizing and drawing ethnographic maps
- Use maps to represent and analyze dimensions of space, shape, and distance
- Apply mapping techniques to represent geography and geopolitics as well as domestic spaces
- Decide whether cognitive or conceptual maps are appropriate for a particular ethnographic project
- Employ maps to represent movement and behavior

Many, if not most, ethnographies include maps of some sort. The scope and purpose of **ethnographic maps** vary a great deal. Maps can serve as a representation of the physical and geographic layout of space, large or small, or as a representation of how individuals conceptualize space, or both. Contemplating whether you want or need to draw maps in the course of your ethnographic research will require you to think carefully about the role of space in the social and cultural phenomena you are studying. With some notable exceptions, ethnography involves both studying *in* specific places and studying the actual places and spaces that informants inhabit. (Ethnographers are increasingly pursuing multisited fieldwork, working in multiple

CASE STUDY

Space Among the Gabra of East Africa
John Wood's study of the Gabra, pastoralists who reside in northern Kenya, indicates that the Gabra understand their social world and the environment they inhabit in terms of a binary structure that separates men from women and male from female (Wood 1999). However, Wood's ethnographic research also suggests that Gabra culture also includes ways to disrupt or overcome those gendered structures. The primary example of ways in which the culture inverts or breaks down these structures appears in the figure of the *d'abella*—older males in the group who are understood to become like women. They are still men, but they also take on the characteristics of women in clothing and activities and they embody a particularly powerful, but ambivalent, social and spiritual position within the larger community. Wood argues that both structuralist and poststructuralist models of culture must be applied to understand the Gabra and their gendered structures.

These gendered structures are closely connected to the Gabra's perception and use of space. As a result, Wood

uses a number of maps as supplements to his textual analysis in *When Men are Women* (1999). Starting at the level of the household, he offers a map of a typical Gabra home, which is divided into male and female spaces (see Figure 9.1). At the level of the community, Wood uses maps to show how Gabra notions of the inside and outside are linked to underlying understandings of masculinity and femininity (see Figure 9.2). The life cycle for Gabra men involves leaving the inside of the community and moving to the outside, especially in tending to herds of cattle that must move across the landscape, depending on seasonal variations in rainfall and other factors. The movement of groups of Gabra during the course of the year and the movement of Gabra males from the inside to the outside and back to the inside over the course of their lifetimes are all essential pieces of information in the larger ethnographic understanding of Gabra culture and the way it links ideas about gender and space.

The maps in Wood's ethnography are very schematic representations that convey a lot of information and provide visual locations, sometimes quite distant from each other. The exciting studies that have emerged from multisited fieldwork help raise important questions about how ethnography deals with issues of place and space.) You should begin by identifying the space(s) you are studying. If the layout of that space plays a role in what you will be describing and analyzing, you probably should consider including one or more maps in your ethnography. You may also want to include a map as a descriptive way of setting the scene for your ethnography. You can start by trying your hand at drawing some maps in your field notes or journal. You can never be sure when these maps might help spark a memory of a particular moment in research, inspire specific analysis, or fit right into the final ethnographic product.

FIGURE 9.1. *Map of Gabra Household Highlighting Cardinal Directions and Male-Female Separation of Space*

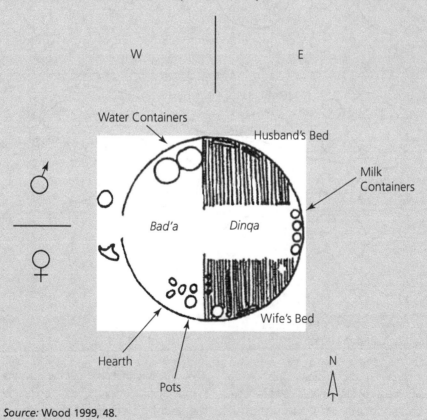

Source: Wood 1999, 48.

FIGURE 9.2. *Map of Bride's and Groom's Camps and Movement of Marital Procession Among Gabra*

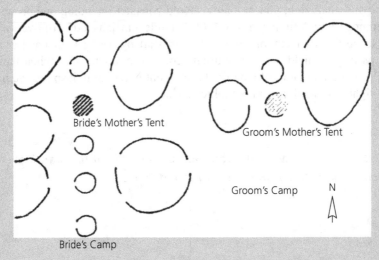

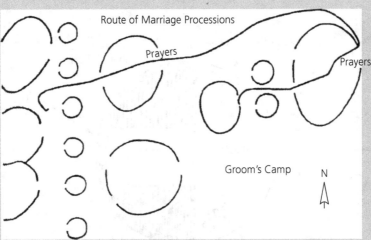

Source: Wood 1999, 133.

support and confirmation for his analytical argument about the presence of gendered structures and the limits of these structures as a defining principle for Gabra culture.

They offer information about the ways the Gabra organize their domestic space and the spatial movements of the Gabra in relationship to pastoralism as a way of life.

SPACE AND MOVEMENT AS KEY COMPONENTS OF CULTURE

Almost all ethnographers will discover that **space** and **movement** are crucial components of their studies. In some cases, the particular characteristics of a space will allow culture and society to take particular forms that would be impossible elsewhere. For instance, one might argue that the culture of Venice is made possible only by the unique spatial characteristics of Venice as a city—the network of canals, specific modes of transportation, and other aspects. On the flip side, space can also limit the possibilities for culture. Quality of soils can determine possible agricultural activities and building techniques, and the relative availability of land can determine the likelihood of finding low or high population densities and, as a consequence, urban sprawl or urban high-rises. From the very outset, space helps us to understand why particular cultural and social phenomena are present or absent.

Movement is also a key aspect of culture generally. The scope of human movements can be highly variable, but most human beings move through space in ways that are culturally influenced and, as a result, important for the ethnographer. Whether it is visiting kin; traveling back and forth between the house, gardens, and fields; seeking a religious specialist; or forced movement; ethnographers should pay close attention to the ways their informants move through space. This may involve examining daily routines within a household or community or larger-scale experiences with an important historical dimension associated with moving households or lengthy migrations. Movement, on both micro and macro scales, is an important part of human life.

Maps are one tool ethnographers can use to capture and analyze the importance of space and movement. Maps are not a substitute for detailed field notes or interview transcripts, but the visual style of presentation can be a powerful addition to the ethnographic record. Maps are most likely to be helpful additions to the ethnographic record and the final ethnographic product when one or more of the following situations appears in ethnographic research: the physical or social environment seems to play a significant role in shaping culture and society; there are significant flows of people or goods like trade goods; and space or physical dimensions serve to divide groups of people—for instance, men and women, old and young, initiated and uninitiated, rich and poor, or specialists and laity.

THE IMPORTANCE OF SPACE, SHAPE, AND DISTANCE

Shapes and **scales** of distance constitute two key features of good maps. You can use these features to communicate important pieces of information and set up your analysis of ideas, behavior, and spatial dimensions in your ethnography. Distinctions between circles, triangles, squares, and other shapes may seem incredibly simplistic for ethnography, but in many cases close examination of shapes and their meaning can be informative. In many ways, basic shapes are the starting point for maps. In order to be able to carry out this sort of analysis, you have to be careful to record this type of data appropriately. This may include notations about the shape of a building or room or about the configuration of interactional spaces. Shapes can be overanalyzed, but thinking about how shapes reflect modes of interaction (dyadic or communal) and how the physical layout reflects underlying cosmological and practical ideas can lead to productive insights in many cases. You should not assume that the significance of shapes will always be patently obvious. You may not come to recognize the circle as a key metaphoric shape in your field site until you have been conducting fieldwork for a considerable period of time. Therefore, in your field notes you need to make sure you are taking note of spatial relationships and shapes whenever possible. Making it a habit to sketch a quick diagrammatic map when you visit a new site or notice significant differences in spaces you have visited before can help you produce a rich ethnographic record.

Like shape, **distance** is a key component of much ethnographic analysis. From studies that explain health care decisions in terms of the distance to hospitals and medical clinics and the relative proximity of folk healers to studies that examine how distance mirrors social distinctions and maps inequality, ethnographers frequently examine the role of physical distance and proximity between individuals, households, resources, infrastructure, and a number of other things. A map is often the easiest way to present information about distance and proximity. A map can clearly show the relative distances a patient would have to travel to visit a biomedical doctor and a folk healer. It can also represent how the physical arrangement of a community reflects social groups, social distinctions, and relative privilege or poverty. Sometimes *distance* in the social and cultural sense is not just a matter of physical distance. Distance can be created by both physical-natural features and social boundaries or impediments, and good maps covering these topics will include these sorts of boundaries and impediments. In a sense, ethnographic maps can show both physical and social distance and proximity.

Pared down to their basic features, maps are visual representations made up of shapes, markers of distance, and indicators of boundaries or edges. In choosing how to construct your maps using these different components, you make analytical decisions about how best to present the lived and conceptual spaces of culture. Start by thinking about how you can use maps to create a more complete ethnographic record, and then proceed to consider which sorts of maps might be important additions to your final ethnography.

LARGE- AND SMALL-SCALE GEOGRAPHIC MAPS

Because ethnography has frequently focused on far-flung and relatively isolated communities, **geographic maps** and **geopolitical maps** have been a common feature of the genre. When the reading audience is likely to be unfamiliar with locations, distances, geographic features, and political units and boundaries, these maps can provide invaluable signposts for the reader. Typically these maps appear at or near the beginning of the ethnography, and the reader can consult the map whenever references are made to geography in the text.

Mapping Tools and Ethnography

Technological innovations offer new and interesting options for the maps in ethnography. Satellite images available on the Internet through services like Google Earth can be incredibly powerful tools, especially since they allow the ethnographer to adopt the bird's-eye view that is often difficult to achieve otherwise. Ethnographers and others often draw maps from this perspective, but they seldom actually see things from this perspective, unless they are able to climb to a particular altitude. You may find that seeing the geography directly from this perspective allows you to understand spatial dimensions in new and productive ways. You may also find that the resolution of images for the areas you want to look at is of variable quality. The level of resolution may simply be a product of chance coverage, or it may reflect the relative geopolitical significance of the area. Remember that these satellite images were or are generally being produced for specific political purposes that are distinct from the researcher's ethnographic goals. Without the resources and connections to generate new images, the ethnographer will probably have to work with the images that already exist in the public domain.

You can also use tools like global positioning systems (GPS) and geographic information systems (GIS) to generate your own maps. Using these tools effectively will probably require some special training, but researchers in disciplines like archaeology and geology have found numerous uses for this technology, and ethnographers are utilizing it increasingly in the course of their research. Tools and software allow the ethnographer to create sophisticated spatial models that may be helpful in tracking movement or migration over time, the movement of resources, and a number of other things. Geographic modeling is most likely to be useful in relatively large projects where a lot of data can be entered into the model. If you think this sort of modeling might be helpful for your project, you should consult an expert to find out what sort of training and equipment you might need and whether using GIS modeling would be an efficient use of your time. Even if you do not use mapping technologies for this project, you may want to keep in mind the possibilities for future ethnographic research.

Geographic maps are most useful in situations where certain features of the environment such as lakes, mountains, rivers, valleys, coasts, and islands feature prominently in the larger ethnography. If altitude is of particular importance, a topographic map may be useful, but in most cases a general geographic map that indicates proximity and distance between key features is most appropriate. Imagine an ethnography of traditional fishing practices among indigenous groups in the Amazon River basin. You may want to show the reader how far the village is from tributaries and streams as well as the river itself. You may also want to show how natural and human-made features within the river system permit or make impossible certain fishing practices. Alternatively, you may find that a river or stream effectively divides the population under study. In all of these cases, a geographic map is likely to be a useful aid for the reader.

While geographic maps focus mostly on the physical features of the landscape, geopolitical maps represent the myriad ways that humans impose political and social units and boundaries on the landscapes they inhabit. Sometimes these units and boundaries match physical features (as when rivers mark a national border), but these units and boundaries often reflect relatively arbitrary divisions of the physical landscape that are imbued with historical and political significance. Whether doing a study of cross-border trade on the United States–Mexico border or the local politics related to the proposed incorporation of a particular area into a metropolitan area, a geopolitical map can be an invaluable tool in presenting a complete picture of the ethnographic situation. In at least some cases, geopolitical boundaries (and their crossing) become a fundamental part of the ethnographic topic.

Both geographic and geopolitical maps can be used at a variety of different levels. If the ethnography addresses international connections and exchanges or historical migrations, a large-scale map covering an international region may be most appropriate. If the ethnography focuses on a much more local setting, the map may represent anything from a city block to twenty square miles. The geographic scope of the map depends entirely on the description and analytical scope of the rest of your ethnography. The map should match the content of the text as closely as possible in order to be as useful as possible.

Maps of this type can often be borrowed or adapted from other sources. If you choose to do this, you must make sure you have the appropriate permissions to reproduce and adapt the maps to your ethnographic needs. If you are adapting a map, you may want to highlight certain features and eliminate other references in order to make your conceptual points as effectively as possible. Maps can and do include a lot of information. Therefore, you should make sure your map includes the necessary information and this information is clearly discernible. Generally these maps should have an indicator for geographic north, a scale for distance, and a key for all notations and symbols that appear on the map.

The use of geopolitical maps in particular is the subject of some debate. Too often the inclusion of these maps seems to assume, and even to excuse, the general reader's lack of familiarity with international geography. Residents of the United States, in particular, are too frequently unfamiliar with the geographic features of other continents and of the geopolitical units of the international world (particularly locations of countries and names of capitals and large cities). Maps placed at the beginning of ethnographic texts can support this lack of geographic knowledge and even reinforce the notion that ethnography is the study of the exotic and geographically distant. You can forgo using a map to indicate where a country or community is located. You can assume your audience has some basic geographic knowledge, but you must recognize that there are limits to that knowledge, and you ultimately want your reader to work from a clear sense of the geography at the heart of the ethnography.

MAPPING INTERIOR SPACES

Taken as a whole, ethnographies probably incorporate nearly as many maps of **internal spaces** as geographic and geopolitical maps. These maps reflect ethnographers' attention to the local and the specific and a particular fascination with domestic and ritual spaces. This mapping of internal spaces can be applied to a variety of research settings, from the workplace to interview contexts.

Mapping of homes and **domestic spaces** is an important feature of many ethnographic projects. From Bourdieu to Wood, ethnographers have frequently found very productive focal points of analysis in households and compounds (or *kraals*). Drawing and analyzing maps of domestic spaces can reveal and represent many facets of society and culture, including gendered behaviors and divisions, separations of sacred and profane or clean and dirty, separations of public and private spheres, relationships between generations, extended kinship ties, and domestic economic activities. In some cases, a close examination of these domestic spaces, spatial relationships, and axes of orientation can help the ethnographer detect underlying understandings of the world that link daily activity to larger cosmologies and mythologies (for example, Wood 1999).

If a significant portion of the ethnographic research takes place in domestic spaces, you should try to draw maps to supplement the notes you are taking. You may want to draw a single map that represents the typical or "ideal" organization of domestic space. In this case, you might choose one home or household as your primary example, or you might choose to construct a composite that represents the "ideal" by combining common features from several different examples. Alternatively, you might choose to draw multiple maps representing different spaces. This choice may be most appropriate if you notice significant differences between the spaces under consideration, especially if you can group or categorize the different types of spaces and your analysis suggests that the different layouts may be linked to other components of your analysis. For example, a strict separation of public and private spaces in the home may be linked to gender segregation, whereas a less rigid distinction between public and private spaces may be linked to less gender differentiation.

Ethnographers also frequently choose to map ritual spaces in similar ways. These ritual spaces are frequently replete with powerful symbols, and the layout and organization of these spaces are important symbols to be analyzed by the ethnographer. As with domestic spaces, mapping and analysis can highlight gender roles and separations of sacred and profane, among other things. Examining the layout of ritual spaces can sometimes help in examining and analyzing the relationships between religious leaders and followers and participants. If the organization of space helps separate them and keep them separated, the ethnographer may ask if this feature is representative of hierarchical organizational structures, a cosmology that suggests that ordinary people are unable to contact or connect with the sacred, or a highly specialized division of labor. If the space

CASE STUDY

Mapping Apartments in Cairo

In *Remaking the Modern*, Farha Ghannam (2002) addresses the idea of modernity in a relocated housing block on the outskirts of the city of Cairo. The residents in this apartment complex have been subject to a series of modernizing efforts and policies from the Egyptian government and find themselves relocated to apartments that seem to offer them predetermined domestic spaces over which they have relatively little control. However, Ghannam's careful examination of these apartments as cultural spaces to be examined ethnographically shows that her informants actually control and modify these spaces in interesting and culturally relevant ways. For instance, apartment residents sometimes add to their apartment spaces by closing in external balcony spaces and adding or removing other structural elements (see Figures 9.3 and 9.4).

These moves by residents to control and modify the space represent their ability to act as agents in the force of modernizing forces that might otherwise control or marginalize them. By modifying the apartments, the residents assert

FIGURE 9.3. *Map of Cairo Apartment Showing Modifications of Original Layout*

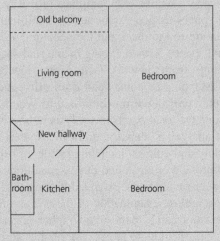

Source: Ghannam 2002, 97.

some control over their experiences of modernity in Cairo. The modernity that they experience is not monolithic or entirely overpowering. The residents' actions and their spatial and architectural initiatives allow them to enter larger cultural processes as actors. In a sense, they are debating the meanings of modernity by acting inside and outside the space of their apartments.

itself takes the form of a circle, a cross, or a subdivided rectangle, this tells you and your audience a great deal about social organization and overarching cultural symbols.

If your research involves participant-observation in rituals or ritualistic behavior, you may want to consider mapping the space(s) that host these events. In drawing your maps, you should think about the boundaries for the space (walls and doors or other features that mark the space as ritual or sacred), internal organization (location of

FIGURE 9.4. *Map of Modified Apartment Including New Balcony*

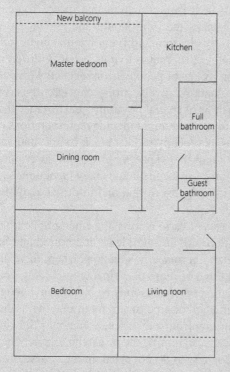

Source: Ghannam 2002, 156.

In order to effectively communicate the role of space and spatial modifica-tions in her research and her under-standing of her informants' experiences of modernity, Ghannam frequently includes maps of the apartments to show both how her informants use their space and how they have modi-fied the apartments in ways that escape the direct control of the government or housing authority. She utilizes maps of interior spaces to great effect in her eth-nography examining the use of space in Cairo. The maps themselves are rela-tively simple schematic renderings, but they offer a powerful representation of the ways that residents of apartments organize and modify their spaces in an effort to control and modernize their residences.

The maps become a representa-tion of people's actions and behaviors as well as their ideas about their lives and experiences with modernity. Maps of bedrooms, kitchens, living rooms, bathrooms, and balconies may seem rather mundane in the abstract, but in this context they contain a lot of impor-tant ethnographic information that supports Ghannam's overall analysis of the relationship between modernity and space.

chairs, benches, or mats, and altars or centers of ritual activity), the spatial distribution and division of participants, and the location of key ritual objects. You can imagine that you are drawing a map for someone entering that space for the first time. In essence, this is the ethnographer's task. Along with the textual descriptions and expla-nations, the map should ideally allow readers to make sense of the space even if they have no previous experience with this particular set of ritual behaviors.

If the research does not involve participant-observation in domestic or ritual spaces, you still should not bypass the idea of mapping internal spaces too quickly. You should evaluate your research site(s) and think about the types of internal spaces you encounter in the course of your fieldwork. Whether that internal space is an office cubicle, a warehouse, a Harley-Davidson dealership, or a livestock barn, there is a pretty good chance that your notes would benefit from a map of this space. You can apply the same general principles to these maps that you would apply to maps of domestic and ritual spaces. You should start by clearly identifying internal and external boundaries. You can then consider whether different activities occur in different spaces and whether particular individuals or groups of people are associated with particular spaces. You might also want to evaluate relatively strong or weak divisions reflected in social organization and relationships of spatial proximity and distance that seem most relevant. A map of a corporate office space might include representations of spaces like offices, cubicles, meeting rooms, photocopy rooms, break rooms, and any other relevant features. A visual representation of these spaces can support description and analysis that links hierarchy to allocation of space, examines how layout encourages or discourages regular dialogue, and investigates formal and informal activities in the workplace.

In addition to maps of internal ritual spaces of various sorts, the ethnographer may find it helpful to map out the spatial relationships in interviews and conversations. This sort of mapping is likely to be particularly germane in situations where there are multiple participants in the dialogue. With three or more participants (including you, the ethnographer), the physical location of the participants may be significant enough to merit analysis. An individual who sits in another area of the room may be a relatively marginal participant or may be monitoring from a distance. Sometimes drawing a schematic map of the interview situation can also remind the researcher of silent participants in conversations or interviews. People who do not speak in the course of an interview or conversation may not appear in transcripts or interview notes, but their presence may have had a significant impact on the conversation in terms of comfort and willingness to discuss certain topics. Interviewees may "perform" for an audience, or they may be reluctant to speak candidly in the company of certain individuals. For these and other reasons, drawing a schematic map of the interview context in each set of interview notes is good practice. This map helps complete the ethnographic record and may aid in subsequent analysis of the interaction at the heart of the interview. Sometimes knowing whether the interviewer and interviewee were facing each other directly, how far apart they were, and the physical context can be important components in deep analysis.

COGNITIVE OR CONCEPTUAL MAPS

Whether you are constructing maps of geographic, geopolitical, or interior spaces, these maps are mostly focused on the physical dimensions of space. The maps should reflect physical objects and features as well as dimensions like spatial distance. In some cases, though, the ethnographer may discover that senses of space and place are important but have less to do with the physical layout of space and more to do with how individuals and groups conceptualize space and, ultimately, the relationships between concepts or ideas. In a case like this, you may find it very helpful to construct cognitive or **conceptual maps** that represent the way your informants understand the lived worlds of which they are a part. These types of maps become a reflection of conceptual "landscapes." They attempt to represent how informants perceive the world around them. You have to be careful not to assume that informants see and understand things in the same way that you do. While you may perceive the same basic physical features, you may be operating from very different mental models for understanding those features. In at least some cases, you will encounter significant variety when you examine those features that different individuals (both ethnographer and different informants) perceive as primary, secondary, or unimportant. Understanding how different people organize and conceptualize these features offers an important window into the larger sets of ideas at work in the ethnographic research.

Imagine, for instance, doing research in a village community surrounded by a primary rainforest. A geographic map can clearly show how space is divided between the village and the rainforest. It can also show distances between communities, access to specific resources like clean water, and a number of other things. If the ethnographic mapping stops there, however, it probably does not offer much insight into how village residents understand the relationship with the rainforest that surrounds their community. They may perceive the rainforest as a dangerous or wild space that encroaches upon or threatens the space under human control in the village. In this case, a map can help show the clear conceptual boundaries between the village and the forest that reflect dichotomies like safety-danger and human-animal. Alternate conceptual models may exist, though. Perhaps the villagers see the boundaries between the village and the forest as much more permeable and flexible. Their gardens may extend into the forest in ways that belie ideas of a strict boundary. They may actually spend a good bit of their time on a daily basis outside the village in the forest, and they may divide the forest into different areas (such as for ritual purposes, hunting, harvesting honey, or disposal of waste). Here internal divisions may or may not be linked to physical features. (This hypothetical example comes in part from Colin Turnbull's 1968 *The Forest People*. This example does not follow exactly Turnbull's description of the BaMbuti worldview, but it does draw on his comparison of the way the BaMbuti perceive their surroundings differently from their villager neighbors.) Paying close attention to informants' actions and explanations offers the best way to gain a full understanding of how conceptual models related to various aspects of life come into play. A conceptual map may help you demonstrate the powerful ways cultural models operate to shape human understandings and use of space above and beyond physical dimensions.

Generally speaking, maps of physical spaces will allow you to address and analyze the relationship between behavior and space most directly, whereas conceptual and cognitive maps will allow you to examine the relationships between ideas and space. As we have already seen, both behavior and ideas can be important areas of study for the ethnographer. You should think carefully about whether your research focuses on behavior or ideas or both—as this question of focus is linked to your overall research questions and your methodology—and how maps can supplement the information you are collecting in other forms within the ethnographic record. You will almost certainly draw more maps as part of the ethnographic record than you decide to include in the final ethnography. This surplus of maps in your field notes is to be expected; you are documenting the ethnographic research experience. Some of the maps will be most helpful in sparking your recollections and furthering your analysis. In some cases, you will decide that a version of a particular map will help readers as they proceed through the ethnography. *Sometimes*, a picture (in the form of a map) really is worth a thousand words, but you should not assume that a map can completely replace textual description and analysis. Most maps need detailed explication in order to be useful.

Completely Cognitive Models

Because ethnographers are especially interested in questions of motivation and the relationship between behavior and thought, there is a strong history of ethnographies that concentrate on the role of ideas and thought. For at least some ethnographers, the ultimate goal of ethnography is to discover and understand the thought processes that lie behind social and cultural behavior. From this perspective, the ethnographer is trying to present the insiders' perspective. If done properly, this sort of ethnography can provide a complete conceptual framework or "map" representing the internal thought processes and categories of a member of a given culture or society. Ethnographers working from a theoretical perspective inspired by structuralism, ethnoscience, cognitive anthropology, or hermeneutics are most likely to produce these sorts of ethnographic models. In their strictest form, these maps or models may be completely divorced from the physical dimensions of space. In a sense, the physical space of culture or society is relatively or completely unimportant from these perspectives. What matters is what is happening in the mind and perhaps in speech.

Good ethnographies of this sort demonstrate the power and central importance of ideas and cognitive frameworks. The most powerful dimensions of culture frequently appear in culture's influence on our perception of the world. Still, most ethnographers want to deal with both thought and behavior (and their connections or intersections). In these cases, a cognitive or conceptual map that links mental models to the physical world can often be particularly effective.

REPRESENTING MOVEMENT AND BEHAVIOR ON A MAP

A map is like a photograph in the sense that it represents a particular moment in time. Therefore, the map from one moment in time may be subtly or significantly different from that representing another moment, even if the space under consideration is defined in the same way. Over the long term, rivers may move, roads may be built, and geopolitical boundaries can change. Therefore, almost by definition, a map is a relatively static means of representation. There is some apparent irony in using this static form of representation as a way of understanding human behavior, which is usually anything but static. Most often, maps represent categories and locations linked to behavior: a map may indicate areas of craft production or political meetings. Using maps in this way means representing behavior indirectly—referring to areas where activities take place rather than the activities themselves. Such a representation is often sufficient, especially if the ethnographic text offers details about the behaviors and activities.

In other circumstances, however, the ethnography will benefit if the ethnographer constructs a map that attempts to incorporate some other dynamic elements—such as physical movement and change over time. Maps that trace human migrations and trade goods are probably the best examples of maps that incorporate representations of physical movements. Arrows showing paths and directions of movement can be invaluable symbols within these maps. The size, color, and boldness of the arrows can help differentiate between the movement of different people and objects and indicate the frequency and intensity of movement. If your work involves looking at the movement of people and objects, you can draw maps to reflect these movements. Trying to reduce these movements to symbols and a schematic visual representation can sometimes be an important analytic step as you work to identify the most important and prevalent characteristics of the movement you have encountered in the course of your research.

If the course of research leads you to analyze change (be it cyclical or directional), you should consider the potential for using maps to reflect these changes. Because maps are like still photographs, you can use a series of maps like a series of still photographs to represent different stages in the dynamic process of change. You might draw maps that show the community before and after the construction of the new highway through town, or you may want to represent the changes in the organization of space according to climate and seasonal variation. In that case, maps representing summer and winter may offer good illustration of the changes you observe. You can pair different sets and types of maps together to show anything from long-range change (years, decades, or centuries) to short-range change (seasonal or daily). You should think creatively about how you can use maps to reflect change, especially if your project includes a historical component. Sometimes even more sophisticated combinations of maps, including layering, can be especially effective in demonstrating the dimensions and effects of change.

SUMMARY

Ethnographers make frequent use of maps both in recording information and presenting their findings. The maps they produce and use range from geographic and geopolitical maps to maps of interior spaces and the conceptualization of space. In each case, the ethnographer uses maps to examine the perception and use of space as they relate to other interrelated dimensions of society and culture. Maps can become powerful visual symbols of various social and cultural dynamics. They can also facilitate your attempts to make sense out of movement and change.

KEY TERMS

Ethnographic maps
Space
Movement
Shapes
Scales
Distance

Geographic maps
Geopolitical maps
Internal spaces
Domestic spaces
Conceptual maps

DISCUSSION QUESTIONS

1. Why do ethnographers rely on mapping as a key research method in so many different circumstances? What aspects of human society or culture are most amenable to representation and analysis through maps?

2. How can an examination of space and shape contribute to ethnographic study? Are there instances where interviews and other methods will not allow you to study space and shape appropriately?

3. What sorts of information can the ethnographer collect by drawing small-scale maps and maps of domestic or interior spaces? Besides the examples provided in the case studies, are there other examples of good ethnographies that build on these types of maps? What would those ethnographies be like without the maps?

4. Are there ways in which human beings experience the spaces they inhabit and the world around them as something other than physical or material? Can ethnographers use maps to represent these experiences of space and the larger world?

5. Should you try to record and analyze movement and change in relationship to culture or society? If so, how can you use maps to represent the movement and change you encounter in the course of your fieldwork?

6. Compare and contrast the ways Wood and Ghannam use maps in their ethnographies. Do they seem to be using maps for similar purposes? Can these two ethnographies be used to demonstrate the range of uses for ethnographic maps?

CHAPTER

10

TABLES AND CHARTS

LEARNING OBJECTIVES

- Represent human interactions and relationships using charts and tables
- Use tables to represent important social and cultural categories
- Examine interpersonal relationships as a manifestation of culture
- Utilize charts to represent key organizing social principles
- Identify the potential significance of kinship in a particular fieldwork setting
- Draw a kinship chart
- Evaluate the potential for other charts, especially organizational charts, in ethnographic research

In addition to maps, ethnographies frequently utilize various types of **charts** and **tables** as key forms of visual presentation. The ethnographer can use tables to convey information about important mechanisms of classification and conceptual categories, as well as more statistical information about percentages and rates of occurrence. Charts offer the ethnographer a clear way to represent **relationships** and **interactions**, as well as **directional flows**, as key parts of the ethnographic situation. Charts generally highlight the various dimensions of interpersonal relationships at the heart of culture and society. The type of chart or charts you choose to use will depend on the overall structural and organizing principles you uncover during the course of your ethnographic research. If you can identify the primary bases for social interaction—kinship, economics, politics, ritual, religion, or something else—and the general character of the social unit—hierarchical, bureaucratic, egalitarian, or otherwise—you will be in a good position to decide what types of charts might be most appropriate and applicable in your ethnographic work.

ETHNOGRAPHIC TABLES

Because ethnographers often need to document various social and cultural categories as well as associations within or between those categories, tables are a regular feature of many ethnographies. Tables can include information about everything from foods and household items to mythic themes. As a form of presentation, tables offer a concise way of organizing information and building associations. They lend themselves in particular to models of culture or society that assume relatively clear boundaries between categories, though tables can also be constructed to show the crossing or blurring of the categories represented.

Some of the best examples of tables that represent social and cultural categories come from the work of ethnographers rooted in the theoretical schools of structuralism and ethnoscience. Because these theoretical schools focus on mental structures and categories, much of their ethnographic work utilizes tables as tools for delineating and illustrating conceptual categories that operate in the context of their ethnographic research. In their analyses of kinship and myth, Claude Lévi-Strauss and Edmund Leach, both structuralists, utilized tables regularly. Similarly, ethnographers employing an ethnoscience model are interested in discovering insider or local categories of knowledge (see McCurdy et al. 2005). As these categories are discovered, they can be translated into tables that show how categories and labels fit together to create larger structures and systems of knowledge. A well-developed table of cognitive categories can offer a powerful tool for understanding ways of thinking and ways of acting in the world.

INTERPERSONAL RELATIONSHIPS AS A MANIFESTATION OF CULTURE

Absent continuous human interaction, "culture" and "society" may exist in enduring mental models and accepted standards of behavior, but culture and society really acquire substance and significance as subjects of study when the ethnographer can

CASE STUDY

Categories in Tanzanian Health and Illness

In the course of my own ethnographic research investigating the intersections of religion and healing in southern Tanzania, I discovered that Tanzanians frequently make a distinction between *homa za mungu* (godly illnesses) and *homa za binadamu* (human illnesses). Understanding this distinction between categories of illness is essential for understanding the decisions that Tanzanians make when they or a family member falls ill. Whether they perceive the illness to be a godly or human illness influences whether they will go to the biomedical hospital or to a traditional healer for treatment and indicates what type of diagnostic processes they think can determine effectively the causes and appropriate treatments of the illness. These conceptual categories can be linked to different sets of symptoms, but there is not a one-to-one correlation between symptoms and the two categories. In fact, the same set of symptoms may be classified as either human or godly based on a number of other factors, especially effective diagnosis. Therefore, a table representing these therapeutic categories might include the following characteristics that aid in defining the two categories:

Illness categories

Symptoms or diseases

Diagnostic tools or processes

Causes

Effective treatment

study the way interactive interpersonal relationships give rise to structures, habits, ideas, conflicts, and the rest of the things that make culture and society complex and interesting. In other words, the cultural and social phenomena that are the subject matter of ethnographic study depend on interpersonal relationships and human interaction. In **interpersonal relationships** and the **interactions** that they influence or give rise to, ethnographers have the opportunity to study culture and society in action.

One of the ethnographer's primary tasks involves documenting and analyzing the manner in which interpersonal relationships and associated expectations shape human interaction. Organizing structures are present in almost all situations, but many participants come to take the structures for granted. If you are observant, you can bring these structures to the fore by using charts in the course of your ethnography. Obviously, each human being with whom you come into contact has unique motivations, experiences, and personality. You cannot assume that society or culture completely *determines* the nature of interpersonal relationships. You need to recognize and leave room for individual variation, but over the course of the research project you should be looking to identify key factors that play a role in *shaping* interpersonal relationships. In the end, you will likely be able to identify certain relationships between individuals, who represent specific categories of people, that are particularly important for understanding the larger whole. Particular expectations and styles of interactions or behaviors will characterize these relationships. For instance, your ethnographic research may show that workers are clearly expected to show deference to their boss in the factory or that children in the United States generally expect their parents to provide for them until the age of eighteen.

Understanding important interpersonal relationships will allow you to develop a strong sense of the underlying principles at work. In some cases, you may find that **kinship** is the basis for the most fundamental social units and relationships. In other cases, you may find that **hierarchical relationships** based on different ascribed or achieved statuses related to gender, age, education, election, selection, or a number of other factors shape most interactions that you observe and in which you participate. Identifying the organizing social principles, be they kinship, hierarchy, egalitarianism, economic exchange, or something else, will allow you to evaluate how individual research experiences and specific ideas and experiences recounted by informants fit into the larger whole that you are studying. You may be able to explain gift giving at weddings with reference to familial expectations of reciprocity or an individual's markedly distinct behavior in two different situations by the presence or absence of a hierarchical "superior" to whom the individual is supposed to act with considerable reserve and respect. Charts can help the ethnographer represent the key **organizing social principles** that you see at work in your research. Kinship and hierarchical charts or models are probably the most common forms found in ethnographies, but you should aim to produce charts that are most representative of the social and cultural realities that emerge in the course of your research.

KINSHIP AS AN ORGANIZING PRINCIPLE

Kinship was a staple of anthropological ethnography from the very beginning. Especially because these early ethnographers tended to work in relatively small communities, they found that kinship was an important factor in the organization of the societies they were studying. In the absence of formal political structures, kinship often appeared to be the most important factor tying the communities together. Kinship can determine how resources are shared. The kin group is also often a powerful site of socialization. As a result, kinship can influence or regulate everything from marriage to religious activities in a community structured by kinship. Ethnographers discovered that in these sorts of circumstances knowing who was related to whom and what that relationship meant was absolutely essential. Kinship ties shape reciprocal obligations, dispute resolution and the management of conflict, the form of marriage and families, and many other facets of culture. For example, in situations such as these, knowing that George is more closely related to his father's brother's son, Frank, than he is to his mother's brother's son, Charles, may help the ethnographer understand why George is more likely to turn to Frank than to Charles when his child is sick with malarial fever.

The example above may seem rather abstract, but "mother's brother's son" and "father's brother's son" is the classic stuff of ethnographic kinship. When early ethnographers began identifying kinship as an important organizing principle in the communities they were studying, they also quickly realized that people determined and classified kinship ties in highly variable ways. In the United States today, the most common means of reckoning kinship involves **bilateral descent**, which suggests that individuals are equally related to both their mother's and their father's sides of the family. Following this line of logic, the kinship system suggests that an individual's mother's brother's son or father's brother's son would be equally related in terms of kinship classification. In the United States, both the mother's brother's son and the father's brother's son would usually be considered first cousins. Bilateral descent is, however, a relatively rare way of tracing kinship if we look across the world and throughout human history. **Unilineal descent**—tracing kinship through either the mother's side (**matrilineal**) or the father's side (**patrilineal**), but not both—is actually much more common if we take a big-picture view.

Drawing a Kinship Chart

An anthropological kinship chart uses a limited number of basic symbols to represent various kinship relationships from the perspective of a particular individual. That individual is referred to as "ego" and an e (for ego) indicates the position of that individual at the center of the kinship chart. Ideally, a kinship chart should include as many related individuals as possible. In practice, the ethnographer wants to make sure the kinship chart encompasses the individuals for whom kinship helps create or shape interpersonal relationships with ego. The extent of coverage will depend on the scope of effective kinship.

Basic Kinship Symbols

- ▲ Male
- ● Female
- ■ Person of indeterminate sex
- = Marriage
- ≠ Divorce
- | Descent
- / Deceased individual
- e Ego

With these essential symbols, the ethnographer can construct most basic kinship charts. You start with a circle or triangle for ego. From ego, you draw a vertical line up to the equal sign that connects ego's parents represented by a circle or triangle respectively. If ego's parents are divorced, you will have to place a diagonal line through the sign for marriage to indicate divorce. If they were never formally married, you may want to use a wavy equal sign to show

(Continued)

(Continued)

a sexual or procreative relationship that was not a formalized marital relationship. If ego has any siblings by these two parents, you draw a horizontal line through the vertical line of descent and add vertical lines of descent downward from the horizontal line to triangles or circles that represent siblings, who will be on the same horizontal level of the chart as ego. You can follow these same basic steps to trace kinship relations back another generation to ego's grandparents or to add siblings for ego's parents. You can also use similar principles to add children for ego and others depicted in the chart. Each time you add a generation or extend the chart horizontally, it gets exponentially more complicated. You need to make sure you start with a big sheet of paper and turn it so that the long side runs horizontally. The charts will usually get messy very quickly. With each chart you construct, you will gain some familiarity with the process and develop strategies for incorporating a range of possible relationships, including multiple marriages and adoption. Your main goal should be to represent the key relationships for ego that are shaped by kinship ties.

Because kinship charts are based on biological models of kinship, they have to be revised constantly to deal with various cultural possibilities. To represent kinship events ranging from adoption to reproductive technologies, ethnographers have to find ways to improvise. The point of a kinship chart is to diagram all individuals who have a demonstrable kinship relationship with ego; this includes people who may or may not be directly related through biological descent or marriage. In some cases, ethnographers find that "fictive kinship" relationships—where there is no assumed biological or marriage relationship, but kinship-based terms of address like *brother, sister, auntie,* or *uncle* are used on a regular basis—play an important role. The ethnographer has to find a way to chart or describe that variation on kinship as an organizing principle. Be prepared to be creative in drawing a kinship chart, and be prepared to work through multiple versions. The basic symbols give you a sort of code that is intelligible to all ethnographers. You should try to make it your own and remember that kinship systems are seldom as perfectly logical as they might appear at first glance.

The original example with George, Frank, and Charles presented earlier probably comes from a patrilineal descent system. In a patrilineal descent system, the father and the father's brother are both going to trace their ancestry back to their shared father, George's grandfather, and their children are going to be members of the same descent group. The mother's brother, however, almost certainly traces his descent back to a different ancestor and a different descent group since it probably would have been considered incestuous and therefore taboo for two members of the same descent group to marry. Because his children trace their descent group through him, the children of the mother's brother, like Charles, will be members of a different descent group from George's. Among patrilineal groups in Tanzania, people will refer to the children of a father's brother in the same way they refer to children of their own biological parents—*dada* (sister) and *kaka* (brother). Children of a mother's brother will be referred to as *binamu* (roughly equivalent to cousin). These differences in terms of address mark clear differences in degrees of relatedness and are reflected in the closeness of emotional ties, support networks, and the provision of bridewealth.

This text is not the place for an extended discussion of kinship from an anthropological perspective. There are many possible variations on kinship principles, and the ethnographer who finds kinship as a key variable in the course of research should aim to identify the underlying principles at work. Kinship charts are a key tool in this process. By drawing a kinship chart, the ethnographer can trace and better understand relatedness. The basic outline for a kinship chart is rooted in biology, but the ethnographer's main task involves figuring out how these biological relationships get translated into social and cultural realities. There is almost nothing that is "natural" about a particular kinship system. Each system is a cultural model for how individuals are related and what those relationships imply socially and culturally. Using a kinship chart, the ethnographer works to understand the kinship terms that a person would apply to specific individuals and to categories of relatives like mother's sister or father's brother's daughter and the nature of relationship implied by that term. Kinship terminology can help the ethnographer understand whether two or more people are socially close or distant and what social functions they might perform for each other.

As ethnographers increasingly conduct research in urban and industrialized, even postmodern, conditions, many of their ethnographies have moved away from kinship as an organizing principle. As a result, kinship charts are a less an essential part of ethnography as a genre than they once were. In many ethnographic research contexts, kinship may not be the dominant organizing principle; it may not seem to play an important role at all. Kinship may not even be a key organizing principle in small-scale societies, and the ethnographer should avoid assuming that it is. You should not feel that you have to draw kinship charts just because you are doing ethnography. Nevertheless, you should remain cognizant of the ways that kinship might appear as an organizing principle, even in novel or unexpected circumstances. The work of McCurdy (2008) and others shows us that kinship can sometimes be an enduring organizing principle well beyond small-scale communities.

OTHER ORGANIZATIONAL CHARTS

Ethnographers can use kinship charts as one way of representing social organization and relationships. However, kinship is only one of many possible organizing principles that you may uncover in the course of your research. Therefore, you should be ready to utilize alternative types of charts that represent other organizing structures or principles.

CASE STUDY

Connecting the Yanomamo Through Kinship

Perhaps the most ambitious attempt to use kinship charts as a foundation for ethnographic research can be seen in Napoleon Chagnon's research among the Yanomamo, who live in the rainforest in Brazil and Venezuela. Chagnon has a primary interest in Yanomami violence and its connection to reproduction and marriage. Building on anthropology's longstanding interests in kinship and marriage, Chagnon set out to construct overlapping kinship charts that would allow him to link different Yanomami communities, particularly in terms of the "exchange" of wives as reproductive partners.

From *The Ax Fight*, a documentary film that Chagnon produced in collaboration with filmmaker Tim Asch, to the most recent editions of Chagnon's well-known, and oft-revised, ethnography of the Yanomamo (Chagnon 1997), kinship charts have been a staple of Chagnon's ethnographic work. He uses the kinship charts to show intermarrying between different lineages and villages (see Figure 10.1) and uses kinship ties to explain the development of hostilities and potential lines of cleavage and alignment within Yanomamo communities (see Figure 10.2).

FIGURE 10.1. *Kinship Chart with Matakuwa as Ego, Showing Direct Descendants and Excluding Spouses*

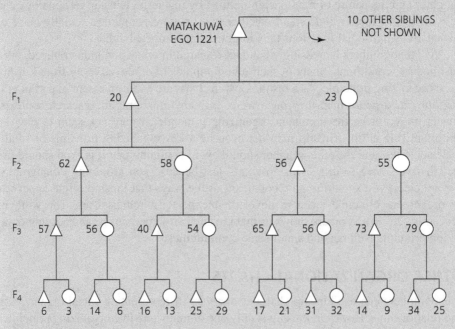

Source: Chagnon 1997, 151.

FIGURE 10.2. *The Role of Kinship in Village Fission Among Yanomamo*

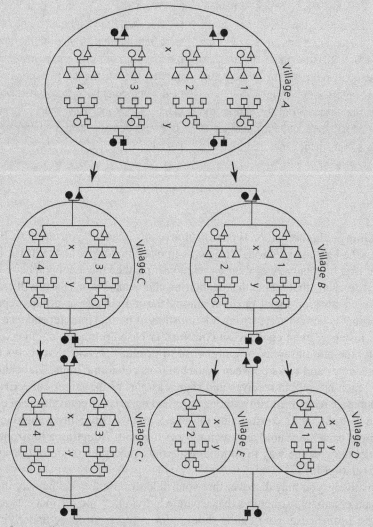

Source: Chagnon 1997, 143.

Chagnon aims to link instances of violence to competition among men over women. His approach provides a good example of the way ethnographers sometimes rely heavily on kinship charts as a form of data collection and ethnographic representation. He has collected voluminous data on kinship and marriage among the Yanomamo with the aim of being able to track and explain relationships above and

(Continued)

(Continued)

beyond the village level. Though Chagnon's interpretation of the Yanomamo and his claims about their fierce or violent tendencies and behaviors have been heavily critiqued, the kinship charts provide him with a powerful set of ethnographic information to draw upon in building his ethnography of the Yanomamo. Chagnon's ethnographic understanding of the Yanomamo depends on the structuring principles of kinship and marriage. These principles lie at the foundation of his larger analytical framework. In a very real sense, his work builds on the assumption that in order to understand the Yanomamo one has to start with kinship. Many ethnographers use kinship charts on a more limited basis, but they can still be important components of the ethnographic picture when kinship plays a significant role in shaping relationships and behavior in the ethnographer's field site.

In determining whether other types of charts are needed, you need to begin by identifying the key organizational structures in place in your field site. If the field site is characterized by relatively egalitarian relationships, then the ethnographer will likely need to utilize charts that reflect that egalitarian character. These charts will emphasize the relative equality of social position among the individuals or groups represented and will probably demonstrate strong relationships of mutual interdependence in many cases. For instance, in an **egalitarian community** based primarily on an economy of reciprocity, the ethnographer might choose to produce a chart that shows the flow of food resources and tasks between households as economic units. The chart would show how each household receives and shares as part of the larger collective unit. It would emphasize relative equality among units and the relative equivalence of exchange among the households. In constructing this chart, you will probably want to make sure you represent each household as structurally equivalent. Adopting a horizontally oriented model may be one way to communicate the egalitarian nature of the social and economic relationships.

Alternatively, you may discover that your field experiences are heavily influenced by dominant organizing structures that separate individuals into distinct categories and social roles. In this case, your charts should aim to represent those underlying structures of distinction as they apply to the research question at hand. In ethnographic research contexts where there are high degrees of specialization and stratification, the ethnographer's charts should reflect these social characteristics. Whether doing research in a law firm or a hospital, the ethnographer will likely find that specialization of tasks, along with different levels of social status that imply differing levels of power and responsibility, shape the nature of regular activities and social interactions. You can use a chart to help present to the reader the relationships between partners, associates, paralegals, and secretaries in the law firm or doctors, nurses, orderlies, and patients in the hospital. Similarly, the ethnographer whose research project includes examining the government and informants' interactions with the government (or some other large institution) may find it helpful to create a chart or diagram that maps out different offices and individuals that are part of the bureaucratic governmental system. This sort of diagram can help the ethnographer identify gates and gatekeepers in the system and dimensions of the system that may influence issues of accessibility and communication, among other things. Paired with a detailed examination of events and interviews related to the system, these schematic representations can be a powerful way to understand the ethnographic situation and present it to the audience.

Organizational charts can represent various types of relationships or flows. A chart can help show how physical goods or resources are collected and distributed. A chart can also reflect structures of decision making. Whether the ethnographer encounters a top-down decision-making structure or a system of nested hierarchies with most ordinary decisions made below the top level of the hierarchy, you can demonstrate these processes in the form of a carefully constructed chart. Charts can represent the nature of social positions and social relationships as well as the flow of resources, decisions, and information. In some cases, the ethnographer may find that the chart represents a complex system of flows, with movement in multiple directions at the same time. For instance, decisions might be disseminated from the top down at the same time that information is collected from the bottom up. Examining the directions of these flows and their confluence can lead to illuminating analysis of the existence and exertion of power or authority, sources of antagonism or potential sites of breakdown, as well as opportunities to build on shared interests.

Using Charts Produced by Others

Occasionally the ethnographer will have access to charts produced by others. For instance, an ethnographer working in a corporate environment may be privy to flow charts produced for specific purposes within the corporation. Like other documents and artifacts (see Chapter Eleven), these charts can be invaluable resources for the ethnographer. They offer an insider perspective on organizational structures, authority and decision making, and flows of resources and information. With this information, the ethnographer may be able to discern structures and processes that would otherwise have been opaque or hidden, at least at first. Still, you need to be careful about how you use these charts. The charts are not necessarily transparent representations of the organization and its structures; they are almost certainly idealized representations of the way the organization *should* function. The ethnographer may find that the actual functioning of the organization or system is very different. You should keep in mind the distinctions between ideal and real

(Continued)

Continued)*

culture and look to construct your own charts based on participant-observation and conversations or interviews. Placing these charts alongside those produced by others can potentially be very illuminating.

Depending on the circumstances, the ethnographer may be able to do similar comparisons with kinship charts or tables. You may find occasion to compare the charts and tables you have produced for ethnographic purposes to charts and tables produced for other purposes. For instance, you might compare your kinship chart to an informant's family tree or you might compare your table of categories to an organizational table that an informant consults on a regular basis. This sort of comparison can highlight the various perspectives and purposes informing the production of these visual representations. It can also lead to productive conversations with informants when you ask for feedback about the charts and tables you have produced.

SUMMARY

Ethnographers use tables and charts primarily to represent categories and relationships. Tables allow the ethnographer to present information about conceptual and social systems of classification as well as underlying patterns among groups of people. Charts constitute a primary tool as you look to identify and examine the organizing principles that characterize a social group or social interactions. Kinship charts are a staple of ethnographies concerning groups and situations where kinship is a key organizing principle, but you can utilize other types of charts to reflect alternative organizing principles that you encounter.

KEY TERMS

Charts
Tables
Relationships
Directional flows
Interpersonal relationships
Interactions
Kinship
Hierarchical relationships

Organizing social principles
Bilateral descent
Unilineal descent
Matrilineal
Patrilineal
Egalitarian community
Organizational charts

DISCUSSION QUESTIONS

1. Which sorts of information can be most easily and effectively conveyed with tables or charts, respectively? What are the best examples of ethnographies that utilize tables, charts, or both to particular effect?

2. When should the ethnographer consider using tables to represent cultural and social categories? Are there instances in which these categories are particularly important for ethnographic presentation and understanding?

3. How are kinship and organizational charts similar to or different from each other? How do these particular types of charts help the ethnographer represent particular organizing principles in society?

4. Why have so many ethnographies included kinship charts? Are kinship charts a thing of the past, or should ethnographies still feature kinship charts on a regular basis? What do kinship charts help highlight about social relationships and interactions?

5. Can the ethnographer find use in charts and tables drawn by others without an ethnographic goal? Why or why not? Do these sorts of charts raise particular questions or concerns for the ethnographer?

6. Why was Chagnon so committed to the use of kinship charts in his ethnographic work? Can you think of other ethnographic projects that would lend themselves to extensive use of kinship charts? Can the ethnographer rely too heavily on kinship charts?

CHAPTER

11

ARCHIVES AND SECONDARY DATA

LEARNING OBJECTIVES

- Evaluate cultural artifacts as potential sources of ethnographic information
- Link artifacts to historical, social, and cultural circumstances of production
- Integrate use of historical archives into an ethnographic research plan
- Recognize the benefits and limitations of archives and documents as ethnographic sources
- Identify and analyze contemporary cultural artifacts
- Explain the importance of authorship, context, audience, and purpose in considering cultural artifacts ethnographically
- Combine usefully analytical or academic sources with primary cultural artifacts

As a general rule, ethnographers depend largely on the ethnographic record they create in the course of primary data collection. This ethnographic record should be expansive and detailed and should offer a wealth of information upon which to draw in the course of constructing an ethnography for presentation. You are intimately familiar and integrally connected with reservoirs of information that you construct. A good ethnography will build directly on your notes and be rooted in primary data. The ethnographic record, however, has its own limitations. It is generally limited to those things to which the ethnographer has direct access, though the ethnographer can attempt to access some things that are only available indirectly. For example, you may decide to ask interview questions that ask informants to draw on individual or collective memories of the past. The ethnographic record is typically limited by both time and space or distance.

Because you conduct fieldwork for a discrete period of time and your notes generally cover that specific period of time, the ethnographic record typically lacks historical time depth. Similarly, you face practical limitations in terms of both geographic area and the number of people you can include in your research. Ethnographers can and do choose varying degrees or lenses of focus, but the ethnographic perspective tends to be localized, even in multisited projects that engage various different localities as field sites. Long-term studies involving ongoing research endeavors in a particular field site and **ethnographic teams** that allow for larger numbers and areas of coverage are two ways to expand the ethnographic record. Ethnography as a whole, however, is best suited to relatively localized studies of specific time periods.

While the ethnographic record is always limited in some ways by issues of **coverage** and **perspective**, the ethnographer can take intentional steps in research design and data collection to address these issues. In response to these characteristics of the ethnographic record and ethnography as a research strategy more generally, ethnographers frequently turn to other sources of information that help by providing historical context as well as a larger frame of reference. These sources of information include **archives** plus contemporary **cultural products**. The ethnographer should be ready to delve into historical documents and be cognizant of **cultural artifacts** as well as specialized sources of information and documents. Close examination of these sources of information will reveal comparative and contextualizing information that can help raise as well as answer key ethnographic questions.

CULTURAL ARTIFACTS AS SOURCES OF INFORMATION

In a very real sense, all the resources upon which the ethnographer draws are cultural products; the main distinction between direct ethnographic sources and indirect cultural artifacts has to do with the ethnographer's presence or absence in the processes of production as interviewer or participant-observer. When you are part of the process of production, you are able to draw directly on ethnographic resources. Even so, you should remain aware of how the contexts of the research—location, time frame, and participants, especially—influence what is being produced in terms of an ethnographic record. When you are not actively engaged in producing the objects of analysis, you

CASE STUDY

The Cultural Artifacts of
Christianity in Ghana

In his recent work on new Pentecostal churches in Ghana, Paul Gifford engaged in ethnographic research that sought to make the most out of a wide range of cultural artifacts that were available to him and supported or furthered his analysis of the rapid growth of these churches. Gifford (2004) chooses particular churches and particular leaders to focus on in *Ghana's New Christianity*, but his overall goal is to speak to the popularity and development of new Pentecostal churches at the national level in Ghana. He connects the emergence of these forms of Christianity with the recent economic and political history of Ghana as a nation. He suggests that "all charismatic churches highlight success, victory, and wealth" (2004, 195) and that the growth of these churches stems from Ghanaians' economic and political marginalization and the threat of additional marginalization that globalizing processes carry. Because the scope of his research is decidedly broad, he turns to

cultural artifacts as a way to access some of the forms of Pentecostalism that he examines in his work.

During the course of his fieldwork in Ghana shortly after the turn of the millennium, he explains that he tried to attend as many religious events as he could, but he acknowledges that "not even a large team of researchers could attend them all, such is the richness of the phenomenon" (2004, x). Therefore, he turned to cultural artifacts in the form of print and audiovisual media produced by religious groups in Ghana. In these media forms, Gifford had ready-made access to the broad phenomenon of Pentecostalism and was able to use these sources to complement his ethnographic data based on participant-observation and interviews.

In trying to address the big picture of religion in Ghana, Gifford is willing to consider a wide range of sources of information. His analysis includes reference to popular bumper stickers and advertising slogans. These cultural artifacts serve as representations of Ghanaian culture at the beginning of the twenty-first century.

have even less control over the circumstances of production. As a result, you mainly have to address issues of coverage, representativeness, and perspective after production in the analysis phase.

Material culture—the physical objects used and produced by a culture—constitutes perhaps the most obvious group of cultural products and offers an interesting analytical entry into ethnographic study. Many classic ethnographies offered detailed lists or discussions of material culture. While these sorts of lists and discussions are less common in contemporary ethnography, there is still tremendous value in paying close attention to material culture. Ethnographic methods that highlight behavior are particularly likely to produce a focus on material culture, but even research focused primarily on ideas and symbols can involve investigations of material culture in productive ways. You should not lose sight of the "things" that surround and connect you and your informants in the course of your research. If you are able to handle a musical instrument or put on the clothes associated with a performance or ritual, you may gain direct or indirect insight into the events and conversations that you document in the ethnographic record. You can also pay close attention to particular items that informants present or suggest as particularly meaningful or important. If informants keep referring to specific items in the course of conversations and interviews, or if you observe that a particular object appears frequently and plays a prominent role in specific events, these indicators suggest that a particular part of material culture deserves ethnographic attention. Some very effective ethnographic descriptions and analyses take material culture—clothing or ritual objects, for instance—as the starting point.

Archaeologists and art historians are most known for the study of material culture or **artifacts**, but ethnographers should make sure they consider artifacts as sources of information. While the range of artifacts can be highly varied, humans in all cultural and social contexts produce objects that can be examined as dense representations of society and culture. A hand-woven basket used to collect tomatoes in a garden may represent gender relations and economic pursuits, among other things. A mass-produced skateboard probably represents industrial relations of production and corporate advertising as well as symbols of nonconformity, teenage angst, and socioeconomic class. Almost everything that humans produce has meaning and purpose, and the ethnographer should consider these dimensions of artifacts as cultural and social products.

Artifacts as social and cultural products include documents, photographs, and publications. While one might be inclined to think about these items as distinct from other forms of material culture such as a hammer or an MP3 player, analyzing these kinds of documents as cultural artifacts helps the ethnographer determine how to utilize these resources in the course of ethnography. The ethnographer must consider purpose and meaning when evaluating and analyzing cultural artifacts. When working with documents and photographs, you should pay particular attention to the producer (author or photographer) and to the contexts of production, including purpose or message and intended audience. Given the necessary technology and knowledge, individuals and groups produce and use documents, photographs, and publications in numerous ways. The meaning and purpose of similar items may vary significantly depending on context. While a photograph of a single individual in the United States may be a form of artistic representation found on the walls of a gallery, a photograph of a single individual in Tanzania is often an important item for securing government and bank documents.

The ethnographer must recognize that these cultural artifacts are produced for specific purposes, including personal communication and record keeping, institutional record keeping, affairs of business and government, and various other purposes. In order to use and analyze these artifacts, you must be prepared to think about how they are similar to and different from other sources of information on which you rely. You are actively involved in the research activities that produce the ethnographic record, but the cultural artifacts typically exist independent of you and your research. Thinking carefully about what was and was not preserved, which perspectives are highlighted, and how context influenced what is written or recorded is an absolutely essential step for the ethnographer. Critical analysis allows the ethnographer to decide what the artifacts suggest and what they do not suggest and how you can or cannot use the artifacts to build an argument or ethnographic description.

Archives almost always reflect the interests of the archivists, and collections may underrepresent or completely ignore individuals, events, opinions, and perspectives, especially in cases of conflict or strong power differentials. There are a number of good works examining the history of missions in southern Africa (including Landau 1995 and Comaroff and Comaroff 1991) that rely heavily on historical archives. However, these archival sources offer only a partial picture of these historical events and experience—in part because many of the indigenous Africans who were the targets of missionary efforts did not produce the accounts and documents that were preserved. The European missionaries were the principal producers of most documents, in the form of records and letters, that were eventually preserved and archived. Therefore, European perspectives tend to be overrepresented in the archival documents, and African perspectives tend to be underrepresented on the whole. As a result, reconstructing indigenous responses to missionization is particularly difficult and may even be impossible. Combining these documents with oral history sources is one strategy that could balance the accounts and perspectives, and these sorts of questions about balance and perspective recur frequently in work with archived sources.

In the same way that you must think carefully and critically about what your informants do and do not represent, you must consider the strengths and limitations of the cultural artifacts to which you have access. Approaching documents (and photographs) as cultural artifacts ensures that you remember that these items are produced for specific reasons, as are more material artifacts such as shovels or cooking vessels. The ethnographer is ultimately interested in the processes and circumstances that produced these artifacts—these processes and circumstances are the ethnographer's subject matter. Appropriately careful and critical analysis of these products can tell you and your audience about ideas, language, gender relations, economics, and demographics, among other things.

MAKING ETHNOGRAPHIC USE OF ARCHIVES

In contemporary society, many institutions and organizations actively engage in recording their own histories by collecting **documents** (and artifacts) in archives. Governments, educational institutions, religious institutions, and many others frequently archive documents. If you know where to look, you can potentially identify multiple archives that can be of use in the course of your research. Archives exist at various levels (local, regional, national, and international), they may be centralized or

CASE STUDY

The History of the Maasai

The Maasai, pastoralists living near the Kenya–Tanzania border in East Africa, frequently appear as figures representing "tradition" and the enduring power of culture, both in regional and international discussions and venues. Dorothy Hodgson's work among the Maasai interrogates the assumptions and stereotypes that color perceptions of the Maasai and investigates the ways Maasai practices, ideas, and symbols have evolved as a result of historical factors and processes. She has conducted extensive ethnographic fieldwork among the Maasai and connects those ethnographic data sources with her work in oral and archival history.

In *Once Intrepid Warriors*, Hodgson's (2004) book that examines ideas of gender and ethnicity in relationship to development, she begins her treatment of the Maasai in the 1890s at the advent of European colonialism in East Africa. Using a combination of archival documents and oral histories that she collected, she then proceeds to trace the history of the Maasai all the way to the contemporary period. In doing so, she shows how Maasai culture has changed and adapted to a variety of different circumstances. By turning to history, she is able to demonstrate that the image of the Maasai as an unchanging, patriarchal group of pastoralists that is so common in many circles is both a historical product and not necessarily representative of the Maasai as a whole at any point.

Hodgson's work is an excellent example of the way ethnographers can draw on historical sources to understand current manifestations of culture and build a bigger picture that addresses changes over the course of time. The historical perspective that Hodgson employs provides a necessary corrective to overly static depictions of Maasai culture and opens the way to consider competing definitions of what it means to be Maasai, which vary according to social position and historical time period.

decentralized, and they may or may not be well organized and catalogued. Investigating the availability and accessibility of archives related to your field site is an important step for you. You should keep in mind that archives may be physical or virtual or a combination of the two, and there may be versions of informal archives (like personal collections or institutional files) that can be very helpful in the research process. However, some relevant archival sources may not be located at or near the field site. For instance, documents related to missionary activity in East Africa may be located in church archives in Europe instead of local churches in East Africa.

When archives are available, the primary documents provide a rich sense of history. The ethnographer can use the documents to answer questions about how long social and cultural phenomena have been in existence and to build a larger picture that considers historical antecedents and the course of social and cultural change. Because the time frame of ethnographic research tends to be rather limited, it is sometimes difficult to use ethnographic data in isolation to address issues related to change. If you can compare interview data with archival letters and speeches or information gained through participant-observation with firsthand accounts of the past, you are able to introduce a comparative dimension to your work that allows you to address more fully issues of continuity and change.

Contemporary ethnographies frequently include historical sections that set the stage for the presentation of ethnographic findings. This sort of historical context can be absolutely invaluable, especially if the ethnographic record suggests significant historical continuity or change. A historical perspective may help the ethnographer explain labor relations on a citrus farm or current ideas about race and ethnicity in New York City (see, for instance, Bourgois 2003). In this way, historical sources can make sources of ethnographic information even more revealing and meaningful. These sources are most effective if they offer effective parallels and contrasts to the ethnographic data and if they offer insight into historical processes, links, and causes.

Issues of Access

In much the same way that you must negotiate access to various field sites, you must also frequently negotiate access to archived resources. Sometimes gaining access involves solving practical issues and meeting formal or bureaucratic requirements. For instance, language can pose a practical barrier, especially if the documents to be accessed are recorded in a different language from the primary research language. An ethnographer utilizing Zulu and Xhosa to conduct ethnographic research in South Africa may find that archived documents are written in Dutch and Afrikaans. In addition to practical language issues, the bureaucratic dimension of archives can also produce various practical limitations on access. For instance, if the archives are maintained by the government, you may need a specific permit or clearance to work in the archives.

Beyond the practical and formal questions of access, ethnographers often also face more informal questions in negotiating access to particular archives. Each institution, organization, or individual that maintains an archive does so for a specific purpose or set of purposes and may be wary of an "outside" researcher who does not necessarily share the same goals or intentions. As you do when you ask permission to work with informants, you should be as honest as possible in presenting the purpose and scope of your research. While you may not ultimately gain access to all archived documents, you should still inquire about all relevant sources of information. In many cases, working to establish a sense of trust often goes a long way in terms of gaining access, as it does with participant-observation and interviewing.

CONTEMPORARY CULTURAL ARTIFACTS

In addition to the sorts of historical cultural artifacts found in formal archives and personal collections, ethnographers often work with contemporary cultural artifacts. Ethnographic research takes place within living societies and cultures that are also its object, and the individuals and groups with whom the ethnographer comes into contact continue to produce artifacts as they pursue livelihoods, enact rituals, and exchange ideas. In your field site, you will almost always encounter cultural artifacts like newspapers and magazines, movies and music videos, as well as clothing and advertisements. These cultural artifacts are part of complex processes in which culture is produced, used, and potentially modified. If, for instance, you understand that your informants are influenced directly or indirectly by a recent news program that broadcast negative publicity about their group, you will be able to pursue a more complete analysis of the ethnographic record. In this case, awareness of the news program as cultural product allows the ethnographer to better understand issues of social stigma and relationships between the group and the larger community. You are interested in how your informants understand and define themselves in relationship to the cultural artifact, whatever that artifact might be. Identifying important or relevant cultural artifacts is the first step in making this type of analysis possible.

Cultural artifacts can also be analyzed as proxy representations of phenomena to which the ethnographer has limited or indirect access. You may be interested in national sentiments about a recent series of events such as an election or a national disaster, but you face particular challenges in studying a concept like national sentiments ethnographically because of questions of scope and area. Localized interviews and conversations may offer some good evidence about sentiments, but you may have trouble arguing that the content of these conversations and interviews is representative of a larger whole, particularly at the level of nation, without supporting evidence. National newspapers or magazines can potentially offer such evidence, either in direct reporting on surveys and interviews or indirectly in the form of editorials or other reporting or commentary. Similarities between what you collect in the course of your research and what is contained or reported in other sources written and published at some distance for a wider readership suggest that there is a more widely shared set of ideas or understandings. In this light, the ethnographic data become especially meaningful as they offer detailed information that connects in some way to a larger whole represented by the supplemental collection of cultural artifacts. In this way, the cultural artifacts can offer corroborating or comparative data in relationship to the ethnographic record.

The ethnographer should attend meetings and performances, read the newspaper, listen to the radio, and watch television with an eye and an ear toward contextual information. These sources are not a substitute for the primary ethnographic research that involves direct experience and contact with informants, but you should also avoid thinking about your research as occurring in isolation. When you engage cultural artifacts, you provide a contextual framework.

Building a collection of cultural artifacts, such as newspaper articles, produced during the course of the ethnographic research amounts to building a sort of cultural archive representing the particular historical circumstances of the ethnographic research. With this sort of collection, the ethnographer can trace trends or abrupt shifts that might be produced by or reflected in cultural products. For example, looking at monthly letters from the manager in the company newsletter, you can look for indicators of changes in business strategies or labor relations in the course of the year of research that you have undertaken. Similarly, tapes of a preacher's sermons can be very interesting cultural artifacts that the ethnographer can mine for evidence of religious connections with politics or the preacher's development as a charismatic leader. Still, you must remember that as valuable as they might be, these cultural artifacts are not on a par with the sources of information that you collect in the course of your own ethnographic research.

Reading and analyzing the letters in the newsletter do not necessarily yield the same information and insights that a face-to-face interview with the manager does. In the letters, the manager is able to set the agenda and answer his own questions, which likely are not the same questions you want to ask. In an interview, the ethnographer can ask follow-up questions and record body language and other cues not found in a published newsletter. The newsletter is produced for a particular audience and likely has specific aims related to the success of the business, and the ethnographer has to engage the newsletter on these terms.

If recorded versions of sermons are being sold or distributed on the street, they offer a different set of insights into the study of that particular religious phenomenon than attendance by the ethnographer at the services during which the preacher delivered the sermons. In this case, it is instructive to think about at least two different ways that a recorded collection of sermons might be produced: (1) the church may have a system that records and produces copies for consumption by members of the congregation and others and (2) the ethnographer—with permission, of course—might make a point of recording the sermons at services each week during the course of ethnographic research and participant-observation at the church. The range of coverage is likely to be different. You should be trying to record as best possible the content of any particular research event; in a sense, your audience is yourself. You are recording these sermons so that you can revisit and analyze them. On the other hand, the intended audience for the church's recordings is probably the congregation and perhaps a wider listening or viewing public. The goal may very well be to present the most positive and coherent image of the preacher and the church possible, even if the ethnographer's records would suggest considerable variety in content and message. Taped sermons may very well have been edited in a variety of ways. What is available for purchase as cultural artifact may represent a sort of "best of" collection that only includes a selection of the total number of sermons delivered by the preacher. If sermons about controversial topics are excluded, the ethnographer will need additional sources of data (like a primary ethnographic record) to develop a full picture of the preacher and his sermons.

You should not simply decide to purchase taped sermons on your way to the produce market in lieu of regular fieldwork at the church, but these tapes may, for instance, allow you access to sermons preached when you were not present, before you started research, or before the preacher's following grew so large. The recorded sermons may also allow you to explore certain topics more fully than you would be able to do otherwise. In the course of their conversations about religion and the church, your informants may make repeated references to AIDS. If you have not heard the preacher deliver a sermon on the topic, you might find one among the recorded cultural artifacts available to you, in which case you can try to compare your informants' thoughts with the church's positions as represented by the preacher's recorded sermon.

EVALUATING AND ANALYZING CULTURAL ARTIFACTS

In using and analyzing historical and contemporary cultural artifacts, including documents, the ethnographer's primary rule of thumb should be to evaluate **authorship**, **context**, **audience**, and **purpose**. The ethnographer must be careful not to assume that these artifacts and their meanings are transparent. Whether created for practical, ideological, or artistic purposes, the artifacts represent the sorts of complex social and cultural processes that ethnographers know to expect. Your project may have its roots in a newspaper article you saw covering a particular event or group of people. Yet you decide to pursue the project in part because that article does not contain sufficient information or analysis. You want to learn more about the details, the causal factors, and the meanings involved. You may even be dissatisfied by the basic information or perspective offered. A recording or newspaper article is not generally sufficient ethnographic evidence in and of itself. You want to go deeper and farther in the course of your research, but you can make use of these resources to increase your knowledge and add breadth.

Imagine a newspaper article describing a political rally in the town center involving ten thousand people. If you are interested in politics as it relates to your project but were not present at the rally, you may be inclined to accept this report as a source of information. Before you do so, you should critically analyze the article before simply accepting the account as a statement of fact. This critical analysis begins by thinking about the context and source. If this article appeared in a newspaper run or sponsored by the government, that piece of knowledge is going to influence how you approach the content of the article. If the rally was held by the opposition party, there may be a strong inclination on the part of the government newspaper to downplay the significance of the event and underestimate the number of attendees. Conversely, if it is a rally held in honor of the president, there may be a clear incentive to present the event as big and successful and to report a generous estimate for the number of attendees. In either case, there is good reason for the reader of the article to treat the number of ten thousand people with some skepticism. The reader might also raise questions about the way the article's author characterizes crowd behavior and sentiment and whom the author chose to interview for the story. The interests at work here are rather obvious. In other cases, the dimensions may be less obvious, but the analytical questions should always be posed. These same sorts of questions can be asked about all sorts of cultural artifacts, be they news pieces or otherwise.

Ideally, the ethnographer wants to be able to **triangulate** between different sources of information. In this example, comparing the newspaper article to one from another newspaper published in a different venue may be a way to check the validity of the information. Collecting information from different sources can also help the ethnographer examine the social and cultural production of knowledge through artifacts. The artifacts serve as representations of larger questions of social position and perspective with which the ethnographer is almost always concerned.

ANALYTICAL SOURCES VERSUS POPULAR OR PRIMARY SOURCES

Ethnographers are usually comfortable citing and drawing from analytical sources in the course of their ethnographies. As with any other research paper, you can turn to the prior work of other researchers presented in journal articles and academic books to help frame your own work in terms of both theoretical models and empirical data. This process of citing the literature matches the work you do in constructing a literature review (see Chapter Three). The ethnographer may use a combination of theoretical and empirical works to compare, connect, and ultimately build a coherent argument and model. Generally, analysis and critical thinking are built into these types of sources; they are cultural artifacts of the academic community and have gone through a process of peer review that produces a particular type of knowledge subject to scrutiny, critique, and revision. When you use this type of resource, you are drawing on this set of knowledge and its context of production. You frame your work in terms of its relationship to an existing set of information and existing models of understanding by citing, and even quoting, academic sources.

When you utilize nonacademic publications as cultural artifacts, you approach and use them differently from academic sources. If you are writing about a physical object, such as a flute or a stool, as cultural artifact, the differences are obvious. You have to describe, analyze, and interpret in a different way—exploring issues of form, function, and meaning, perhaps. When it comes to texts or documents, however, the differences between academic sources and nonacademic or popular sources are perhaps less obvious. Generally, you should resist the temptation to use these products in the same way—that is, to quote from a newspaper in the same way you would from a well-respected ethnography. These artifacts are produced in very different contexts for different purposes and represent different forms of culturally produced knowledge. The nonacademic sources are usually primary artifacts and should be examined and used as such. The ethnographer can evaluate practical dimensions as well as symbol and meaning in working with these artifacts. They can be compared and linked to the primary sources of data represented in the ethnographic data. While they may be rich in analytical import and may represent an interesting analytical perspective, the ethnographer is ultimately responsible for framing these resources analytically. They are direct (albeit complex) representations of culture and society as primary artifacts, whereas the academic work has been refracted and refined through the lens of analysis.

SUMMARY

The nature of ethnographic research means that it is rather limited in historical and geographic scope. To widen the scope of your work, you can turn to cultural products, including documentary evidence. The ethnographer approaches these cultural products as artifacts in need of close examination in terms of authorship, context, and purpose. Archived documents represent artifacts of the past that you can mine and analyze to deepen your understanding of your research context historically and to augment your approach to continuity and change. In addition to cultural products from the past, you also frequently have access to contemporary cultural products that offer you access to events and ideas that you cannot research directly. Always keeping in mind the questions of authorship, context, and purpose, you can use these resources to broaden your scope and connect your ethnographic data to larger social and cultural contexts.

KEY TERMS

Ethnographic teams

Coverage

Perspective

Archives

Cultural products

Cultural artifacts

Material culture

Artifacts

Documents

Authorship

Context

Audience

Purpose

Triangulate

DISCUSSION QUESTIONS

1. What role does history usually play in ethnographic studies? How can archives and other sources of information be used to amplify the primary ethnographic research?

2. What is a cultural artifact? Are there different types of cultural artifacts? What are the most useful types of artifacts for ethnographers to study? Should they be particularly cognizant of particular aspects of the artifacts they study?

3. Are archives and other collections of artifacts inherently biased or imbalanced? How can the ethnographer deal with these sorts of biases or imbalances?

4. When are you most likely to find archival collections that are relevant to your ethnographic project? Are the archives likely to be readily accessible to you? What are the practical considerations in determining whether and how to use archives?

5. Can cultural artifacts be used as substitutes for ethnographic research experiences? What are the primary differences between cultural artifacts and field notes based on ethnographic research?

6. Can you analyze a cultural artifact—a text or a document, for example—in the same way you analyze an interview or a conversation?

7. Can you use this sort of cultural artifact the same way you use a text written by a fellow ethnographer, researcher, or theorist? Why or why not?

PART

3

ANALYZING AND WRITING

CHAPTER

12

SORTING AND CODING DATA

LEARNING OBJECTIVES

- Sort and code ethnographic data
- Write and analyze ethnographic data as part of an inductive process
- Connect key themes to the central research question
- Identify key research moments and experiences
- Use key moments and experiences as building blocks in a larger ethnographic presentation
- Recognize and understand apparent contradictions in the ethnographic record

At this point, you are nearing the completion of a lengthy process of field research and data collection. You have been writing and recording information from a variety of sources, and you have been analyzing your findings along the way. In following these steps, you are well positioned to complete a quality ethnography. The next step involves organizing, sorting, and analyzing the ethnographic record you have collected with an eye toward big-picture analysis and the final ethnographic project. In essence, you are beginning the process of winnowing your notes down to a core that can become the basis for an effective and informative ethnography. This chapter walks you through the stages involved in making sense of the ethnographic record through techniques that help in sorting and coding data.

WRITING FROM YOUR RESEARCH DATA

If the research questions have remained relatively stable during the course of your research, you may find it particularly easy to look back to your proposal for key concepts and questions as a way to organize your analysis. If the research focus has moved away from the original focus, you should not be discouraged; if you have done good fieldwork, you should have the opportunity to put together an informative and effective ethnography as soon as you identify key questions, themes, moments and experiences that will help you build a relevant **analytical framework.**

Because the ethnographic record you collect and produce as an ethnographer is typically extensive and varied, you need to be careful about just skimming the surface looking for examples or quotes. Your most significant insights will be rooted deep in the ethnographic research you have done. Therefore, you want to make sure your analysis grows directly out of the quality and quantity of research reflected in the ethnographic record. Since you have been the primary research instrument for your research, you have heard, witnessed, lived, and experienced all or almost all the information contained in the ethnographic record. As you prepare to build a comprehensive analytical framework, you need to make sure you return to that record. There may be words, ideas, or events contained in the ethnographic record that have faded from your memory or did not register as particularly important when you first recorded them, but when you encounter them again as you review and analyze, you may come to see the significance anew.

If you were conducting ethnographic research simply to get a good quote or to have a good story to tell, you would not have to make the long-term and intensive commitment that ethnography requires. You keep pursuing more conversations or interviews and you keep looking for additional participant-observation opportunities because you are convinced there is more than meets the eye and you want to understand both the general patterns and the unique occurrences. Ethnographers will almost always find that they have "too much" information for their final ethnographies. In fact, that is probably the single best indicator that the researcher has carried out good ethnographic fieldwork. Precisely because you have talked to ten, twenty, or fifty informants in the course of your research, you will be able to recognize a specific conversation with Javier as an important one to analyze because it contains so many key themes. You will know whether to treat a particular event as a regular occurrence or unique. You have built a body of information located in the ethnographic record, and you should aim to make the best possible use of that body of information. While not all of that information will find its way directly into the final ethnography, that information as a whole will inform the entire ethnography if you go about identifying, sorting, coding, and analyzing in the proper way.

You should always remember to **write *from* the research data.** The ethnographic research process is necessarily **inductive**. Ethnographers build their ideas and their theories from ethnographic data. They start with the specific and build toward the more general or abstract. Ethnographers can run into trouble when they choose to write *with* the data instead of writing *from* the data. When you are ready to write the final ethnography, the pressures to finish can be intense, especially if you are staring at a deadline, but you want to make sure you avoid writing without examining the ethnographic record closely. You could write *with* the data by writing a general account and occasionally turning to the record when you need a quote or a supporting example, but if you take this approach, you run the risk of simply "discovering" and writing about the things you expected or wanted to find in the course of your research. If you make sure you revisit and examine the ethnographic record as a whole, you will be much more likely to produce an ethnography that is true to the entirety of the research experience and true to the knowledge that you gained from your informants rather than to the knowledge and assumptions you brought to the research. You will be writing *from* the research data. Writing from the research data requires time and dedication. Organizing and sorting the data in terms of questions, themes, moments, and experiences can help you write from the research data in an organized and efficient manner.

IDENTIFYING KEY THEMES AND QUESTIONS

You began your ethnographic research with a set of central research questions (even hypotheses). In Chapter Eight, you identified key themes and questions emerging from your research at the midway point. At this point, as the end of your field research approaches, you need to revisit the questions and themes you identified previously. Your task now is to determine whether those questions and themes constitute a good representation of the findings and insights that your research has produced. You should keep in mind that some of the most important findings and insights to emerge from ethnographic research are completely unanticipated. In many cases, the questions and themes you have identified previously cover only part of what will eventually be incorporated into the final ethnography.

Beginning with the initial list of review questions and any revised questions you produced during the course of your research, you can revisit the issue of whether these questions still reflect your primary research interests or if your field experiences have taken you in a different direction. You can also reevaluate the priority of the questions based on intervening research experiences. Finally, you can consider whether the information that you have collected during the course of your research allows you to answer specific research questions particularly well. Ideally, the final ethnography will speak directly to the question or questions you have come to see as most important, insightful, and informative in the course of your ethnographic fieldwork. If none of the original questions you developed seem to represent or reflect the core of your research, you should aim to develop a question that captures the essence of your ethnographic work. This question may stem directly from something you learned from one or more of your informants, or it may rest in the relationship between your background research and your field research. Once you have an effective central question or focus, you can envision your final ethnography as an extended and direct exercise in answering that question.

During the course of research, you also developed a set of key themes when you made a point out of analyzing your findings along the way (see Chapter Eight). Now you can go back to that list of themes and any subsequent additions or revisions you have made and evaluate these themes' usefulness as a way of organizing and analyzing the ethnographic record. You may need to add themes that have emerged in the most recent stages of your research, and you may have changed your mind about the relative priority of particular themes. Your goal should be to produce a final list of themes that you can use to organize, search, and analyze the ethnographic record you have collected. You can identify particularly salient themes by thinking about the ones that you think absolutely need to be addressed in your ethnography. Using underlining or some other marker to indicate these central or salient themes, you can begin to develop a framework for your ethnography. The key themes can become topics, sections, or even chapters.

You will not necessarily find a one-to-one relationship between the central research questions you have developed and the key **organizing themes** you have identified, but you should expect that most, if not all, of the themes will speak directly or indirectly to your research questions. In many ways, the process of analysis begins by thinking through the meanings of themes and the way they connect with other themes. Using themes as building blocks, the ethnographer's analytical job requires bridging the gaps between specific examples of the themes in the ethnographic record to the big-picture questions.

IDENTIFYING IMPORTANT RESEARCH MOMENTS AND EXPERIENCES

Good ethnography involves insightful analysis rooted in the specifics of ethnographic data. Identifying key themes and questions will help you build your ethnography around focal questions and topics. However, good ethnography also often draws heavily on the skills of storytelling. The stories of ethnographic fieldwork can draw the attention of the reader and offer illustrative examples of the analytical ideas at the heart of the ethnography. Storytelling in the context of ethnography most frequently relays the stories of particularly important moments or experiences that occurred during the course of fieldwork.

CASE STUDY

The X-Ray as a Key Theme
When I was doing research about religion and health in southern Tanzania, I found that people repeatedly made reference to the X-ray, or *kipimo kikubwa* ("big test" in Kiswahili). This phrase or idea became an organizing theme that helped me both to understand and represent my informants' experiences with and understandings of the differences between biomedicine and traditional healing. I was able to reexamine the ethnographic notes I had made to analyze how and when Tanzanian patients talked about the X-ray as a diagnostic tool and how they used it as a symbol of satisfaction or dissatisfaction with biomedical care at the local hospital. This theme became an **organizing metaphor** for my study of the topic generally.

Identifying important moments or experiences can help you in choosing the stories you might tell in the body of your ethnography. Most ethnographers discover certain points in their research that are particularly influential in the way they come to understand their research project and their findings. These **research moments** can be influential because they offer greater clarity for you, because they lead you to perceive more complexity, because they force you to look in another direction, or because they completely change what you understand to be the primary objective of your ethnographic research. Sometimes these research experiences are obvious "epiphanies," and sometimes you come to see the true significance only after the fact, when you place it in context and have a chance to think about the ramifications.

As you near the end of the fieldwork part of your ethnographic project, you can step back and think about the moments or experiences that seem most formative or transformative from your research. Chances are good that when you look back on your research, you will be drawn to a particular conversation or a particular experience that represents a whole set of ideas or questions that you encountered during the course of your research. These may be the experiences to which you return, even months or years after the fact, because they were so fundamental to your larger understanding of your research topic.

Whether these moments and experiences come in the form of conversations and interviews or direct experiences of participant-observation, they can become the basis for strong ethnographic presentations. These moments may have been so transformative that they are the first thing you think of when you consider your research as a whole, but they will not always be that obvious. In looking back at your notes, you should look for particularly lengthy and detailed sections. Length and details can be signs of moments that prompted the need to describe and to process in extended form. You may also want to think about how you describe your research when a friend or

CASE STUDY

Recognizing a Significant Conversation After the Fact

When I think back on my research in southern Tanzania dealing with medicine and religion, I cannot help but think of a conversation that I stumbled into shortly after I had begun my research. For reasons that I understood to be important theoretical ones, I was being very careful to avoid equating traditional healing with witchcraft beliefs. I wanted to focus on the healing that went on in these contexts and to avoid relegating traditional healing to the realm of superstition or religious beliefs. In the course of this conversation, an older Tanzanian gentleman expressed great interest in my project and provided me with some good information and a lot of things to think about, but he kept turning the conversation to questions of witchcraft (*uchawi* in Kiswahili). In fact, he seemed to be substituting the Kiswahili phrases for traditional healing and witchcraft as if they were interchangeable. He also pushed me to come up with a list of practical recommendations about how the government and the local community could deal with witchcraft beliefs and the associated barriers to development.

When it came time to write my ethnography, I found that I could not write the ethnography without telling this story. The gentleman, as an unwitting informant,

colleague asks about it. If you find that you always recount a particular event or talk about a particular experience or informant, you may have already unconsciously identified important moments or experiences that help you communicate something essential about your research to an interested audience. Identifying and using key moments and experiences in the course of building your ethnography allows you to achieve that goal of communicating important ideas. These moments and experiences can serve as anchors for the overall ethnography. Detailed accounts of these moments and experiences provide you with the basis for interesting and informative analysis. The key steps for the writing process involve first identifying the key moments or experiences and then evaluating how you can use these accounts to build different components of your analysis. The accounts may tie directly into the themes and questions. If they do not, identifying the key moments or experiences may help you identify and evaluate underdeveloped analytical ideas that belong at the heart of your ethnography.

CODING AND SORTING THE ETHNOGRAPHIC RECORD

Once you have developed a list of themes based on your fieldwork, you can use this list to code the ethnographic record. This process of **coding** involves identifying each place in the ethnographic record that is related to a particular theme. In this process, you are unconcerned about the specific nature of the connection between the had challenged me to think about my topic in new and different ways—his perspective challenged my assumption that I could separate healing and witchcraft for analytical purposes, and his call for a list of recommendations forced me to evaluate my commitment to an academic (as opposed to an applied) research program. That chance encounter shaped the way that I came to understand my larger ethnographic research project, and the telling of that story helped me set the stage for consideration of important topics like the relationship between healing and witchcraft and the larger political and practical ramifications of a study like mine.

In much the same way, the first time I observed a healing ceremony that included Muslim spirits possessing Christian hosts was a formative experience in the course of my research. It led me to rethink what I understood to be the relationships between health, illness, and religion, and these instances of spirit possession ended up becoming a significant focus of my ethnographic project. In this case, that first experience rooted in participant-observation at a healing ceremony became a moment that took my research in a different direction. As a result, that moment merited extended consideration in the writing of the ethnography.

ethnographic data and the theme. You are focused simply on identifying all parts of the ethnographic record that speak to a specific theme. The same code may be associated with both participant-observation and interviews. In fact, the codes become the means by which you can sort through the ethnographic record in a systematic fashion in working toward developing both an ethnographic narrative and an analytical framework. Codes can be assigned and noted in a variety of ways. You might choose to write a representative word or phrase for each code in the margin of your field notes. In essence, you are taking notes on your notes, and after you are finished coding, you can flip through your notes to find relevant sections related to each theme. Alternatively, you may choose to code using colored tabs, with each color reflecting a primary theme. When you have finished coding your notes, your notes will be a rainbow that represents a categorized way of reading the ethnographic record.

In most cases, it is advisable to do this type of coding with copies of the original field notes. Doing so preserves the integrity of the original record and allows you to manipulate the documents without worrying about preserving the record itself. Sometimes the physical act of cutting the coded notes into smaller sections related to themes and creating stacks can offer a way of sorting that helps you find and perceive interesting analytical connections. You can experiment with different ways of categorizing and connecting the data by creating new stacks and by combining or physically shifting pieces of the ethnographic record.

If the ethnographic record is digitized, you can use computer-based tools in coding and **sorting.** Obviously, you still have to do the work of developing a list of codes and identifying parts of the ethnographic record to associate with that code. In some cases, keyword searches can help you search the record rapidly, but these sorts of searches should never replace coding through close reading of the record. Computerized searches are limited to specific parameters and will miss parts that do not match those specific parameters, but more important, computerized searches produce largely decontextualized readings of specific parts of the ethnographic record. A detailed, contextualized reading and revisiting of the record allows you to find meaning and connections in the record as you code and forces you to continually evaluate the material in relationship to the themes and codes.

The record can be coded digitally using various options, particularly databases. Once the digital codes have been assigned, you use the computer to help you sort according to themes in much the same way that you would with marginal notes or colored tabs. Especially with large ethnographic records, digitized coding allows you to move about quickly within the record in the process of analyzing and writing. These sorts of codes can also then be the basis for innovative styles of digitized ethnographic presentation. For instance, in some cases ethnographers link codes to HTML anchors in Web-based ethnographies. With the anchors, the reader can jump within the ethnographic text by clicking on the link. The result is a less linear ethnography that the reader may engage differently by following connections in various directions. When done well, these styles of presentation can produce particularly interesting ways of representing the complexity of social lives.

No matter whether you choose to use marginal notes, colored tabs, or digitized codes, the process of assigning codes enables you to sort through a diverse ethnographic record in a systematic manner. In the process, you are combining tasks of reading and writing. You are performing a careful reading (often multiple readings) of the ethnographic record, and the act of coding is a stage of writing onto or into the record. You are revisiting the record you created through writing and adding another layer of writing (in code) that structures or organizes the record along different axes. This process adds analytical dimensions to the ethnographic record and prepares you to engage in even more writing as you write from the ethnographic record into an ethnography. Coding is an essential step in the analytical process.

Coding of the ethnographic record is occasionally undertaken by more than one individual. The use of more than one coder is most common in projects employing ethnographic teams. In these cases, the ethnographic record has usually been produced by multiple ethnographers, and having several people code the record helps ensure that similar types of information are identified throughout the record. The act of coding is ultimately a subjective process of interpretation. Using multiple coders adds a check on **reliability.** The ethnographer working alone should keep in mind that another reader of the record would probably code it in at least a slightly different way. The fact that it can be coded in different ways is a sign of the richness and complexity of the ethnographic record. The main point is to make sure you are careful and systematic in the coding process. Thorough coding will enable powerful processes of sorting and lead to informative and insightful ethnographic analysis.

DEALING WITH APPARENT CONTRADICTIONS: THE MESSINESS OF ETHNOGRAPHIC DATA

Even the most thorough coding process will not make the ethnographic record clean and neat. Ethnographic data are messy, almost by definition. Trying to observe, record, and understand society and culture in action by researching human beings' thoughts, words, and lived experiences is a complex endeavor. As a result, the notes that stem from that complex endeavor are likely to be complex or "messy." The messiness of ethnographic data is one of our challenges.

The ethnographer can expect to find ideas, experiences, and pieces of information that seem to be contradictory. We often talk and write as if we expect culture and society to be logical and well ordered, but a quick examination of our own lives will probably reveal that we seldom think, talk, and act in ways that are completely rational, logical, or predictable. **Apparent contradictions** in the ethnographic record may be reflections of variation and even random chance. These contradictions can also be a product of individual differences and idiosyncrasies.

At the same time, apparent contradictions can also provide a window into different perspectives among informants, potential sources or sites of conflict or debate, and even different social roles or personae that informants exhibit in different circumstances. In this respect, these apparent contradictions can be the source of important information and insight. In fact, these can be important points of analysis as you look to develop a nuanced understanding of your research topic. You can move below the surface to examine the nonobvious and provide an important contribution in the form of ethnographic understanding in the process.

Think back to earlier discussions of your understanding of regularity and variation in the collection of ethnographic information. As you sort and analyze, your job is to make sense out of actions, words, and thoughts by placing them in ethnographic and analytical context. This means thinking carefully about how regular or special events, words, or ideas relate to the central questions and key themes. You may be able to use an instance of apparent contradiction to show a constant push and pull between masculine and feminine principles or the way your informants act and "perform" very differently, depending on whom they are interacting with and who is present.

By doing this, you are providing a sort of analytical order to the data you have collected. Sometimes, though, you will find you simply need to accept the messiness of the ethnographic record. If something seems out of the ordinary or hard to interpret or explain, you should make note of it. The next research project may need to explore that particular topic more fully. A good ethnography will provide the sort of order and structure that will allow the reader to grasp the key ideas and findings, but it should also aim to communicate as much of the complexity of informants' lives, actions, and ideas as possible.

SUMMARY

As you near the end of your field research, you turn your attention to analysis of the record. Building on previous analytical steps you have taken during the course of your research, you aim to identify a final question or set of questions to guide your analysis and your ethnographic presentation. Within the context of that central focus, you can then proceed to identify key moments and experiences that can anchor the ethnography. By applying a set of codes to the ethnographic record, you begin to construct the foundation of an analytical framework. You seek connections and patterns within the information while also recognizing the importance of engaging the full complexities of society and culture.

KEY TERMS

Analytical framework
Writing *from* the data
Inductive
Organizing theme
Organizing metaphor

Research moments
Coding
Sorting
Reliability
Apparent contradictions

DISCUSSION QUESTIONS

1. Should ethnographic analysis and writing be inductive or deductive or both? What does it mean to write *from* the data? What might happen if the ethnographer chooses not to do so?

2. Should all the key themes that emerge in the course of reviewing and coding the ethnographic record be directly related to the project's central research question(s)?

3. How can you tell whether a particular moment or research experience merits particular attention and analysis in the final ethnography? What types of moments or experiences are most likely to be particularly important?

4. What is the process for coding and sorting ethnographic data? What is the ethnographer's primary goal in this process?

5. What sorts of structures emerge in the coding and sorting process? How can these structures be translated into writing and the larger ethnography you will ultimately produce?

6. Why are contradictions a fundamental part of the ethnographic record? How can the ethnographer productively examine contradictions or apparent contradictions?

CHAPTER

13

ANSWERING QUESTIONS AND BUILDING MODELS

LEARNING OBJECTIVES

- Build a coherent analytical framework
- Identify connections and linkages between different components of the ethnographic record
- Categorize different pieces of the ethnographic record in terms of relative significance
- Determine the relevance of specific data for answering particular questions
- Connect ethnographic description and analysis
- Explain ethnography as an inductive process
- Link the specific ethnographic project to large-scale questions and issues
- Explain the connection between data and theory

The best ethnographies offer detailed and engaging ethnographic accounts at the same time that they speak to larger questions. These questions may be connected to the social and historical study of a particular place or culture as well as practical problems or concerns, but they are also linked to more abstract issues of social and cultural theory. As you begin to write by putting together the pieces of information gained through research, you should aim to build an ethnography that seeks to answer questions and contributes to larger theoretical models. This chapter examines the process that connects detailed and dedicated fieldwork to the larger picture of which it is a part.

FITTING THE PIECES TOGETHER

The analytical framework you build allows you to link the different pieces of information and analysis together into a coherent or semicoherent whole. Of course, some ethnographers are less interested in or committed to the idea of a **coherent whole.** They

CASE STUDY

Farmer's Study of AIDS in Haiti

Paul Farmer's *AIDS and Accusation* (2006) is a masterful example of a contemporary ethnography that is both compelling and clearly relevant. His consideration of the "geography of blame" that surrounds experiences with AIDS in Haiti is rooted in his ethnographic research in Do Kay, a village in Haiti, where his fieldwork includes contact with three of the first residents to develop AIDS. He devotes a separate chapter to each of these three individuals—Manno, Anita, and Dieudonné—and examines their own personal experiences with illness as well as the larger social community's responses to their illness. These individual accounts become case studies at the heart of the work that allow Farmer to examine the spread of HIV and AIDS both within Haiti and in the larger West Atlantic networks of economic exchange

and migration of which Haiti and the United States are a part.

Farmer pays close attention to the meanings produced and challenged in the context of the AIDS pandemic, particularly in Haiti. He connects the assumptions about a Haitian origin for HIV that gained great currency in the United States to local Haitian assumptions about the role of sorcery in some AIDS cases. These very different stories and meanings are connected through political and economic processes. Farmer insists that in order to fully understand the current experiences of AIDS in Haiti, the reader must understand the history of relations between the United States and Haiti as well as the economics of migrant labor and tourism, two primary means for transmission between the countries. In tracing these connections, Farmer shows that assumptions and fears in the United States that HIV originated in Haiti and then was transmitted to warn against producing ethnography depicting an **artificial whole** that presents **homogeneity** or coherence that does not exist in reality. In general, you should aim to present as much coherence in your ethnography as you think actually exists in the real-life situations you has studied. If you see significant conflict, variation, and other characteristics that do not seem suited to a model that assumes a coherent whole, you should consider how to present or represent those characteristics in your ethnography. Most important, at this point you want to tackle the question of whether and how the pieces—that is, "pieces" of data and "pieces" of analysis—fit together.

There is a variety of ways to think about **connections** and **linkages.** Starting from the data, you want to think about connections between people, events, and ideas or symbols. When it comes to people, you should consider the relationship between different informants. They may have an already existing relationship in terms of kinship, economics, or shared membership in a group, but you will also want to think about how your primary research questions link certain informants. Informants who have never

the United States were based on deep-seated cultural models of understanding that include ideas about race and political instability. The geography of blame represents the very real dynamics of the political and economic relationships between the United States and Haiti in which the United States tends to be most powerful, but the geography of blame also includes more local ideas about sorcery that play an important role in Do Kay.

The idea of a geography of blame becomes a central analytical concept that ties together rather disparate sources of information, ranging from local ethnographic fieldwork in Do Kay to historical documents. It also allows him to consider his general topic of AIDS in Haiti at a variety of geographic levels, ranging from the local to the international. This central concept ties together a detailed interpretive framework that analyzes meaning in

narratives and experiences with a focus on political economy that links events and experiences in Do Kay to Port-au-Prince, Miami, and New York.

The personal stories from Do Kay represent the foundation of Farmer's presentation and analysis. These stories make his work immediately compelling and relevant. The recurring dynamics of blame provide a framework in which Farmer can contextualize these stories and connect them to the larger picture, which is absolutely essential to a full understanding. Farmer is able to put the various pieces together into a framework that makes sense out of a big-picture problem without losing sight of local meaning and individual experiences. Farmer writes *from* his ethnographic experiences in Do Kay and connects them to much larger processes of economics, politics, illness, and meaning making.

encountered or spoken with each other may be linked analytically due to the fact that they represent a particular category or type of informant—lay members of the Roman Catholic Church or straight supporters of the movement to legalize gay marriage, for example. Highlighting connections between people in the ethnographic record can help you see shared similarities as well as internal variation and divisions within your analytical groups. If grouping informants in this manner allows you to talk about general tendencies or shared behavior and opinions, you can work from these connections to build a more general analytical framework. You may decide you need a section that examines the general characteristics and tendencies of a particular group of informants and their relationship to other categories of people. Working in this direction allows you to move from a focus on a single individual to the consideration of larger groups and to consider the relationship between individuals and the social groups of which they are a part.

In much the same way, you can connect different pieces of the ethnographic record by analyzing particular events you witnessed or participated in and placing them in categories. If you are studying a political campaign, you may want to group your notes in terms of different types of events: internal strategizing meetings, public speeches, public appearances with questions and answers, public appearances without Q&A, and private fundraising events, for example. Examining what happens at each of these different types of events and comparing the different events' components—such as who is present, types of behaviors, character of interactions, and language or rhetoric—will allow you to build a larger picture of the different types of events and behaviors that occur regularly in the course of a campaign like this one and then to examine particular events or occurrences in relation to the larger understanding you are building.

In much the same way, you can establish groups or categories of ideas and symbols that recur in the ethnographic record. Many of these symbols are probably already part of the codes you created for use in sorting your data. By following the analytical steps outlined in Chapter Twelve, you should have a working list of key themes or symbols that you can use to organize your data. In essence, this is what you are doing when you use codes to sort data dealing with a particular theme.

Once you have identified **key symbols** and the instances where these symbols occupy a prominent place in the ethnographic record, you can proceed to examine and evaluate the symbols in a number of different respects, including how and when these symbols are used, what they mean for informants (remember: symbols are often polyvalent and may be the subject of debate or disagreement), who uses them, and how they relate to the ethnographic topic. If you can identify the contexts and meanings associated with particular symbols, you can begin to piece together an interpretive framework that will add to the larger ethnographic understanding.

Evaluating the Relative Importance of Data

In developing an ethnographic record, you have recorded and collected a lot of different types of information or data. Part of the messiness of the ethnographic record stems from the fact that the information often seems to be organized haphazardly. If

CASE STUDY

The X-ray as a Key Symbol in Tanzania
I had been conducting ethnographic research on illness and healing in southern Tanzania for several months before I realized that the X-ray was emerging as a key symbol in the course of my research. Even when I did not bring up the X-ray as a topic in interviews and conversations, my informants frequently made references to it. It was clearly important to them. When I identified the X-ray (or *kipimo kikubwa*) as a key symbol in my work at that point, I had to go back into the ethnographic record and identify the places where that symbol appeared. Judging by my research experiences, I had a working assumption that patients and doctors understood and talked about

X-ray technology very differently, but I had to organize and analyze the information I had collected to confirm that this difference existed and better understand the nature of that difference and its relation to illness experiences, therapeutic itineraries, caregiving decisions, and so forth. Looking at the record in a specific and detailed way allowed me to see that patients tended to talk about the X-ray much more than doctors and nurses did (patients often brought it up in our conversations and interviews, whereas doctors often talked about it only if I brought it up as a topic of conversation) and to build contextualized understandings of this symbol—by addressing questions of who used it and in what contexts, for example.

your notes are organized chronologically (the most common and probably the most helpful way to organize notes, at least initially), you may find that very different types and pieces of information are located in close proximity and the types of information that speak to each other are relatively far apart in the ethnographic record. Sorting in (into) related categories of informants, types of events, and key symbols should help you place related pieces of information alongside each other.

Once you have sorted and connected the different pieces of the ethnographic record in this way, the next step is to think about general levels of importance or significance. If you have done a good job in constructing the ethnographic record, you will have recorded pieces of information whose significance was obvious at the time you heard, saw, or experienced them as well as pieces of information whose significance was nonobvious and may have even seemed trivial. Recording this sort of wide-ranging collection of data is absolutely crucial in producing an ethnographic record that allows you to revisit moments and ideas well after the research experience has happened, but in most cases it also means you will have a set of information whose ultimate significance is highly variable. The specific words that an informant used on the first day you met may or may not be significant when you return to them six weeks or six months later.

Now, in the process of putting the pieces together and building an analytical framework, you will need to consider the **relative significance** of the information you have collected and recorded in the ethnographic record. You had already begun to think about relative significance when you considered particularly significant moments for analysis. As you revisit the record once again, you should think about how another ethnographer would read and process the information contained in the ethnographic record you have created. You will want to consider whether there are areas of your notes that another person would immediately recognize as important and whether that person might question some of the things you understand to be significant in the data. This sort of self-check serves as a very informal check on validity.

Undoubtedly you have collected key pieces of information that would be of interest to anybody interested in general ethnography or the *general* research topic. Identifying these key pieces of information will help you think about the important contributions your research can offer to larger ongoing discussions, whether these discussions are largely practical or largely academic. The most important pieces of information often include unanticipated results, especially those results that seem to contradict or problematize previous research findings, as well as data that speak to pressing debates in the field. Usually these should figure prominently in the final ethnography. Highlighting them helps demonstrate the important contributions of your work, and these pieces can often be the foundational pieces of the overall ethnographic work.

Beyond these most important pieces of information, you can also evaluate the relative significance of other pieces of information along a continuum. Some information (like foods served as part of a meal or the score in a cricket match) may have relatively little analytical significance when compared to key interview passages or the ethnographic description of a healing ceremony that brings together a number of informants and involves a number of key symbols. Thinking in terms of this continuum of relative significance, the ethnographer can locate particular pieces of information from one pole of low significance (**small ethnographic details**) to another pole of high significance (**essential ethnographic information**). The small ethnographic details will probably play a relatively small role in the final ethnography and will not likely be the subject of sustained analysis. The essential ethnographic information will almost certainly figure prominently and be the subject of significant discussion and analysis. The pieces of information along the middle of the continuum may or may not play a major role in the ethnography, depending on the analytical focus you choose and how these pieces relate to the general research questions and key themes.

Evaluating the Relevance for This Project

The discussion of a continuum in the preceding section is generally based on an assumption that the relative significance of data can be determined independent of the specific project. This assumption probably holds most true for the two ends of the continuum, but the choice of whether or not to analyze or include the pieces of information located on the middle of the continuum depends largely on their relevance for the specific project. In collecting information, you have undoubtedly collected a lot of information that would be illuminating and essential if you were engaged in a different ethnographic project but is only tangentially related to the topic at hand in this project.

Therefore, assigning an abstract level of relative significance to different pieces of information is beneficial only if the ethnographer then proceeds to evaluate the specific relevance of different pieces for the project. This process of evaluation is likely to be an ongoing process, particularly to the degree that the ethnography is the result of an organic, inductive process. As you explore different analytical foci and frameworks, the **relevance** of a particular item for your project may rise or fall.

Ultimately, you want to produce an ethnography that is rich in both significant and relevant information. This combination of significance and relevance will help in building and supporting insightful analysis rooted in the information contained in your ethnographic record.

Telling the Ethnographic Story *and* Answering the Research Question at the Same Time

The most enjoyable and effective ethnographies are both interesting and informative. In thinking about how to make your ethnography achieve both these aims, you should consider how you can weave together detailed **ethnographic storytelling** with compelling analysis that addresses key research questions as well as practical and theoretical issues. Weaving these two elements together can be the key to a highly successful ethnography. You want to tell captivating stories that do justice to the interesting lived experiences of your informants; you also want to tell relevant stories that allow you to address your primary research questions.

The ethnographic story or stories provide the basis for a **narrative structure** in the ethnography. Whether narrating key individual moments in the research process, the course of a regular event, or the chronology of fieldwork itself, if the story or stories are told in an effective way they can both captivate the reader and lay the foundation for more analytical discussions. Effective storytelling involves the use of compelling detail as well as elements like suspense, irony, and humor. Writers of fiction have to create these elements for themselves, but luckily for ethnographers these sorts of elements appear regularly in humans' lives. The ethnographer's job is to compile, edit, and narrate these moments in ways that are faithful to the way that these events happened during the research experience and the way they appear in the ethnographic record. (This does not imply that you are not actively involved in these stories in multiple ways—as participant, interested party, editor, and so forth). These key moments identified by you can also become all or part of the narrative or narratives at the heart of the general ethnography, particularly if they are illuminating examples of analytical points you want to explore.

MOVING FROM DATA TO THEORY: THE INDUCTIVE PROCESS

Emerson et al. (1995) suggest that ethnographic research and analysis are both **deductive** and **inductive** at the same time. Their suggestion stems from the fact that the research questions and the analysis are necessarily informed by the previous work and theorizing of others. Therefore, in some ways, you are deducing what you might suspect to find and what it means based on more abstract ideas about how things like economics or political bureaucracies function. In this way, you are practicing a sort of deductive method or process. Still, ethnography as a method almost has to be inductive. You can claim to understand social and cultural lived worlds only after you have collected data about them. We should not pretend to understand the BaMbuti of central Africa, cotton farmers in the Mississippi delta, or any other group of people or set of cultural events or ideas without researching these people, events, or ideas firsthand. Deductive reasoning can take us only so far when it comes to the essential insights that ethnography offers.

At this point in the research process, you should focus especially on the inductive part of the research process, particularly the way you are building abstract or generalized theoretical ideas out of the ethnographic record. You will never lose sight of the theoretical ideas that informed your research questions and the practical implications that may have inspired your research, but at this stage you should be writing *from* the data contained in your ethnographic record *to* the more abstract or theoretical level of analysis. In other words, you start with the specific and move toward the general. You have spent considerable time researching and recording the specific. As you write with the final product in mind, you need to keep in mind the need to write from the specific. Specific ethnographic detail is the foundation of good ethnography. Analysis connects the individual pieces to answer or address larger, more abstract questions.

REMEMBERING THE BIG PICTURE AND THE BIG QUESTIONS

Your project should not only speak directly to the particular issue or problem that is your focus; it should also offer a starting point for future researchers and policymakers who confront a similar issue or problem in a different setting. The project probably started with big-picture interests and big questions. However, even if the impetus for this ethnographic project did not originate with the big picture or the abstract, when you were constructing a proposal, especially conducting a literature review and writing about the overall significance of the ethnographer's project, you were locating your project in a larger field of interest. Now is the time to revisit those questions and connections.

Ideally, fieldwork and the emerging analysis will allow you to address the general, theoretical, and abstract questions with which you started in a direct and insightful way. In this case, connecting your work to the big picture may be relatively straightforward. However, we have already seen how ethnographic research often reveals unanticipated opportunities and insights that lead you in new directions that may be significantly different from the original abstract ideas. In these cases, you often have to rethink how the research relates to your original questions and framing and consider whether it is helpful to position your work in relationship to different ideas and questions.

You can find connections between your research and bigger issues or questions by asking yourself who will be interested in reading your ethnography and why. In order to identify a particular audience that will be interested in the research, you have to consider what your audience will glean from the research. Take, for instance, an ethnographer who has been researching community relations at the local *masjid* (mosque). Given your field site, scholars of Islam and scholars of religion generally would be an obvious audience for your work, but the community interested in your work could be much broader than these two groups. For instance, if some or all of those who attend the masjid are recent immigrants, then scholars with interests in migration and transnationalism might also be a potential audience. Similarly, there may be other audiences interested in other related subjects like multicultural dialogue or community development to whom your research is potentially very helpful. You may reach a point where you lose sight of this big picture because you are so focused on the local specifics of your research. When you move toward analysis, you may be at a loss for a larger context or framework. Reminding yourself about the various audiences and communities that might be interested in your work can be a helpful way to recontextualize and bring a broader view lens to bear.

The space between the ethnographer's specific research located in the ethnographic record and these larger discussions within larger communities is the analytical space that you seek to fill. In order to fill this space, you seek to build bridges or webs of connection starting from the specific and building toward the more abstract or general. This process of building analysis is relatively hard to talk about explicitly. The process tends to be rather intuitive, but analytical skills can be developed and honed. You will benefit from paying attention to the way others build productive analyses and using their work as models. You will also benefit if you keep in mind that **analysis is a** *process.* It starts by identifying the pieces that are important and relevant and proceeds by examining connections and comparisons. Good analysis requires some imagination and creativity. It also requires a willingness to explore ideas and paths of analysis that may not eventually bear fruit. The more possible explanations or interpretations you can consider, the more robust your analytical web will be.

If the ethnography is designed to provide information and insight that can be directly related to solving or addressing a particular social issue or problem, it will be important for you to situate your research in the context of the general social and cultural phenomena (poverty, governance, communication or miscommunication, prejudice, and so on) that you perceive to be important in this situation. Problem solving depends on good, rich analysis. If you can explore models, connections, meanings, and causes in a deep and relevant way, then you have the foundation for powerful criticisms or suggestions. In order to be able to make these criticisms or suggestions, you need to be able to show why your explanation or interpretation of the situation is more appropriate than alternative ones. Evaluating models of explanation and interpretation *is* the process of analysis.

INFUSING THEORY IN ETHNOGRAPHY

Because a good ethnography is often also a good read, the theory and abstract significance of the work can often be overlooked. Still, a close examination of a wide variety of ethnographies will show that they offer important contributions that extend well beyond a specific consideration of the topic at hand. For example, Bourgois's (2003) *In Search of Respect*, which examines the social and economic dimensions of the crack economy in El Barrio, a neighborhood in New York City, is directly connected to neo-Marxist understandings of class and theoretical discussions of the relationship between structure and agency. This neo-Marxist framework comes out of his understanding of the experiences of his informants in El Barrio. He rejects largely individualized, psychological explanations for the behaviors and ideas that he encountered in the course of his fieldwork. He also rejects models that would pathologize Nyorican culture as the root of the problem. In his conversations with Caesar, Primo, and others and in his participant-observation experiences in El Barrio, he finds the foundation that supports a neo-Marxist framework concerned with questions of structure and agency. With this analytical framework, he is able to speak to questions of gendered violence, failed expectations, and a number of other things. His analytical framework provides the context that allows him to analyze and understand the ideas and behaviors of his informants in meaningful ways.

Different ethnographers find different analytical frameworks to be appropriate for their work. Aaron Fox's *Real Country* (2004) is rooted in close analyses of everyday performances of country music and conversations surrounding those performances. His analysis connects the music and conversations to larger issues of class as well as the construction of self and identity. He is able to contextualize a late-night conversation about what constitutes "real country" using his analytical framework and find deep meaning related to class, identity, and selfhood.

In *Culture and the Senses*, Geurts (2002) looks closely at everyday behavior and bodily comportment among the Anlo-Ewe in Ghana, but she is not satisfied to simply describe them and the way they move their bodies. She wants to connect bodies and bodily movements to larger questions of experience. Therefore, she turns to Merleau-Ponty's philosophical discussions of the way human beings experience and live in the world. Phenomenology provides the basis for an analytical framework that allows her to connect very specific behaviors among the Anlo-Ewe to deep questions about human experience. She does this by interpreting different pieces of the ethnographic record and comparing and contrasting those interpretations with other examples and other interpretations.

You need to be willing to explore different sets of ideas and different possibilities for analyzing the ethnographic record with which you are working. The work of analysis can be intensely rich and rewarding if you open yourself up to think creatively and imaginatively and if you keep evaluating models in terms of what you find in your field notes.

SUMMARY

The process of answering questions and building models involves a deep search for understanding in the form of explanation or interpretation. In order to be able to build these sorts of models, you need first to evaluate the general significance of the data with which you are working and then to evaluate its significance in relationship to your project. With an eye toward the data that are most significant and relevant, you can begin to look for connections and comparisons that help you construct analytical models and answer big-picture questions. These analytical steps require some intuitive and creative thinking at times, but they mostly require you to be open to different possibilities and explore the potential of different models of interpretation and explanation. You want eventually to find the model that best connects the ethnographic data to larger issues and questions.

KEY TERMS

Coherent whole
Artificial whole
Homogeneity
Connections
Linkages
Key symbols
Relative significance
Small ethnographic details

Essential ethnographic information
Relevance
Ethnographic storytelling
Narrative structure
Deductive
Inductive
Analysis as a *process*

DISCUSSION QUESTIONS

1. Choose a favorite ethnography to examine. How does the ethnographer combine description and analysis? Are some sections more descriptive and some more analytical, or is there an even balance throughout? Does the ethnographer use specific techniques to make the descriptive elements particularly effective? What basic theoretical or analytical framework does the ethnographer employ?

2. What makes one part of the ethnographic record more significant than another? Can pieces of ethnographic data be significant without being relevant? What is the difference?

3.   In what ways is ethnography deductive? How can it be both deductive and inductive? Should the analytical process be primarily deductive or inductive?

4.   How can a small-scale ethnographic study speak to big theoretical questions and important social issues? Should you always assume that your research has implications on the larger scale?

5.   This chapter mentions the work of Bourgois, Fox, and Geurts as examples of theory-infused ethnographies. What are some other ethnographies that are clearly theory infused? What are the main theories at the heart of these ethnographies? Do the authors seem to have come to these theoretical frameworks deductively or inductively? Is it easy to tell?

CHAPTER

14

CHOOSING
THE APPROPRIATE
PRESENTATION STYLE

LEARNING OBJECTIVES

- Choose a style of ethnographic presentation that is appropriate and effective
- Identify and employ common ethnographic conventions in ethnographic writing
- Take proper steps to protect informants in the writing process
- Incorporate relevant detail into an ethnographic presentation
- Link the style of presentation to the intended audience, subject matter, and analytical framework
- Adopt an appropriate tense, tone, and voice in ethnographic writing
- Decide between relatively formal and informal approaches to ethnographic writing and presentation

In order to produce the best final ethnography possible, you must find the most appropriate style of presentation. Once you have done the work of analysis and identified key themes and moments as well as areas of particular significance in the ethnographic record, the next step involves matching these components to a **style of presentation**. The subject matter and the analytical framework, as well as the intended audience, will play important roles in determining appropriate style. Presentation style in ethnography includes elements like formality of tone, the use of detail and narrative, and standard ethnographic conventions. From the very beginning, your research has involved writing as an integral component, but at this stage you will find that the craft of writing becomes particularly important. You need to be a good writer and make sound, purposeful decisions as you construct your ethnography with the aim of achieving maximum effect by providing the reader with information and a compelling analysis.

COMMON ETHNOGRAPHIC CONVENTIONS

Like any other genre of writing and presentation, ethnography often draws on a number of standard **conventions**. A perusal of ethnographies reveals that ethnographies frequently employ one or more of the following conventions: an arrival scene, stories

CASE STUDY

Presenting "Street Culture" in New York City

Sidewalk, by Mitchell Duneier (1999), opens by introducing the reader to Hakim Hasan, "a book vendor and street intellectual." In presenting a wide-ranging and largely personal account of informants that regularly occupy and carry out economic enterprises on the sidewalks of Greenwich Village, Duneier chooses a style of presentation that closely matches his ethnographic and analytical understanding of the lives and experiences of his informants. The sidewalk is associated with a strong sense of informality, from the economic pursuits of the vendors to the means of social control among those who occupy these spaces. The informality that characterizes the culture of the sidewalks is closely matched by the informal, even casual, style that Duneier adopts throughout his book.

By introducing Hakim Hasan in the very first sentence of the introduction, Duneier places his informants front and center and sets the stage with a personal and relatively informal approach. Throughout the text, Duneier offers detailed stories about particular individuals based on long-term relationships built on trust and familiarity. He wants the reader to engage his informants as real individuals with faces and names. Photographs by Ovie Carter are spread throughout the text, and Duneier refers to his informants by their real names whenever he has permission to do so.

of cultural misunderstanding as moments of serendipity, case studies, a focus on key individuals, and composite descriptions. These conventions can be combined in various interesting ways, depending on your vision for your project. The use of these conventions helps mark a presentation as ethnography and build analytical models, as well as highlighting points of particular significance. You should consider how you might use particular conventions to best effect.

Arrival Scene

Many ethnographies open with **arrival scenes** that describe the ethnographers' first experiences in their field sites. Some arrival scenes are the stuff of legend. Other arrival scenes are slightly more mundane. No matter what, the arrival scene describes the setting for the research from the outset. As you become increasingly familiar and comfortable with your field site, you may begin to take certain elements of the setting for granted. This tendency is why including detail in the ethnographic record from the very beginning of the research project is so important; you need to record your first experiences and impressions of the field site. By including an arrival scene in your ethnography, you can revisit and recount those first experiences and impressions that you recorded in your notes; these accounts often provide key pieces of information,

The friendly, casual tone that is part of Duneier's informal style invites the reader to imagine the street vendors as equals and share in their lives through Duneier's ethnography.

The stories and lives of the sidewalk vendors and those with whom they interact on a regular basis provide the common thread for the entire book. The conversations that Duneier recreates in the text frequently include the use of profanity and colloquialisms. He even devotes an entire question to the bodily functions of urination and defecation and their role in the public culture of the sidewalks. These inclusions may disarm the reader at times, but they create a tone of openness as well as a dimension of realism that comes directly from Duneier's ethnographic data and contributes to the connection between the informal style and the examination of the informal culture of the sidewalks in Greenwich Village.

Duneier clearly constructed his ethnography to make it accessible to a large general audience. He addresses important methodological, ethical, and theoretical considerations throughout his work, but the writing style is very accessible and largely free of jargon and lengthy excursions into academic or intellectual debates. Much of the more specialized discussion of methodology and the references to academic literature are confined to an appendix and the notes.

especially for the outsider who is encountering the field site for the first time in reading the ethnography. When you set the scene in this way, you enable the reader to start where you started, with similar experiences, understandings, and assumptions.

The arrival scene can also help the reader understand your position in the field site and the ways informants responded to your presence, especially when your presence may have been most noticeable at the beginning. In addition, the scene often emphasizes the human, and potentially fallible, dimension of ethnographic research, since you are particularly prone to social faux pas and moments of misunderstanding upon arrival before you settle into the routine of research. These sorts of missteps undoubtedly happen at all stages of ethnographic research, but hopefully they become slightly less frequent as research projects progress.

Despite all these reasons for employing arrival scenes as a convention in ethnography, their use raises thorny questions about ethnography as a research strategy and as a literary genre. Today most ethnographers aim to avoid or to overcome ethnography's historical roots, which link it to the context of imperialism, colonialism, and exploration. They are especially concerned about producing ethnographies that read like the accounts of explorer-adventurers or colonizers. The ethnographer arriving to study the "untouched tribe" may have been the stereotypical stuff of ethnography a long time ago, but most ethnographers work with informants who are integrated into national and international networks and systems. An arrival scene that implies the ethnographer "discovered" a place or group of people can have unfortunate consequences if it implies isolation or ignorance of the larger world on the part of informants. You are not a savior arriving on the scene, and you are usually the person with the most to learn. You want to be careful about creating an arrival scene that suggests otherwise.

Constructing an arrival scene can also be difficult if you spent time in your field site prior to beginning the research project. You may even have been born and raised in your field site. Too often we assume that ethnography is always conducted by outsiders. Increasingly, ethnography is being pursued by social and cultural "insiders" who do not necessarily "arrive" on the scene to do research; they have already been there. In these cases, an arrival scene may be inappropriate or unnecessary, and you may turn to alternative ways to open your presentation. Of course, you may be able to write about similar types of moments when you first became aware of certain ideas or behaviors in an analogous manner. Ultimately, you must decide whether an arrival scene is the most effective way to set the stage for the rest of the ethnography and whether you can communicate an appropriate image of the relationships between you, your informants, and your field site by using an arrival scene.

Stories of Cultural Misunderstanding

With luck, the potential for social and cultural misunderstanding between you and your informants is most pronounced at the beginning of a research project and shrinks over time, but misunderstanding can occur at any point in the course of research, even at the most inopportune times. Sources of misunderstanding are almost innumerable but frequently include things like misuse of a word or phrase, expecting that norms of behavior apply to a certain situation when they do not, or a lack of awareness of subtle distinctions in meaning or differences between informants. While such moments of misunderstanding can be quite embarrassing for you, many of them eventually become lasting moments of learning both because of the degree of embarrassment and the way such occurrences can bring to light social and cultural dimensions that otherwise remain implicit or hard to discern. Thus, ethnographers have made a practice of using stories about these moments to present and frame key insights gained in the course of their research.

Two of the most famous ethnographic pieces that rely on this convention are "Eating Christmas in the Kalahari" by Richard Lee (1969) and "Shakespeare in the Bush" by Laura Bohanan (1966). In the first piece, Lee describes his decision to purchase the largest and fattest ox available for a Christmas celebration as a way of thanking his informants. Instead of receiving the thanks that he expects from the !Kung, Lee discovered that the !Kung responded by insulting the ox as a "sack of bones" and suggesting that they would be left hungry at the celebration. Only later does Lee come to understand that this was a culturally appropriate response among the egalitarian !Kung, whose culture works to prevent any individual from thinking of himself as above or better than others, and that his expectation of thanks was rooted in his own cultural assumptions about individual recognition and the economics of exchange.

In her well-known piece, Bohanan describes a rainy day on which she decided to tell the story of Hamlet to a group of Tiv elders in West Africa. The elders quickly contest parts of the story by informing her that there is no such thing as a ghost and that Hamlet's uncle did the right thing by marrying Hamlet's mother because a man is supposed to marry his brother's widow. They reinterpret and retell Hamlet in culturally appropriate terms that differ significantly from Shakespeare's original version. By recounting this experience, Bohanan is able to highlight key aspects of Tiv culture— for example, the practice of the *levirate,* or widow inheritance—and explore issues related to the universality of human stories and experiences.

Like Lee and Bohanan, you may find in your own ethnographic record moments of cultural misunderstanding that eventually yielded significant insight. In these cases, you may draw on the ethnographic writing convention that involves retelling these stories of misunderstanding with the purpose of providing an avenue for greater understanding and insight. This convention turns these moments of misunderstanding into moments of serendipity. It can be a very effective way to highlight key pieces of information that emerged during the course of research. The reader may also develop some level of empathy for the researcher or informants and the practical, human dimensions of ethnographic research. Of course, including a story or stories of misunderstanding within the ethnography can draw attention to the subjective, and potentially fallible, role of the ethnographer as researcher. Doing so is more advisable in some circumstances than others and with some audiences than others. This convention works well only if it ultimately leads into a productive discussion of insight and information gained in the course of research and if it fits into a larger informative and compelling analytical piece.

Case Studies

Some research projects lend themselves particularly well to the presentation and comparison of **cases**. Different projects will use different units or levels to identify what constitutes a case. Individuals, departments, villages, and even nations can be cases. Sometimes the research plan will already be designed around comparison of specific cases, and the organization will be largely obvious. In other projects, you may come to perceive the cases only after the research has already begun. Then you may have to do significant sorting of the ethnographic record to bring together the information associated with specific cases.

Inclusion of several **case studies** can help the ethnographer pinpoint and highlight variation and differences among individuals and groups. For instance, one department in the local government may have recently reorganized its offices with the aim of improving public relations, while another department has not undergone reorganization in the past decade. Providing detailed, comparative case studies of these two departments may prove especially revealing about citizens' experiences with local government in particular circumstances. Case studies highlight the comparative dimensions of ethnographic work and have the added benefits of providing space for concentrated, detailed examination of specific examples with a specific purpose. Two or three case studies can provide a lot of content that becomes the foundation for a larger analytical framework.

Case studies are not appropriate in all projects, and you should avoid forcing your data into case studies. Your ethnographic record may include information from and about a wide range of people and events that do not readily divide into cases. In that instance, you should pursue other presentation strategies that are more appropriate for your project and your data.

Key Figures

You need to consider carefully questions of coverage and representativeness in designing and carrying out your research. You usually want to make sure you learn from as many informants as possible as you try to see your topic from multiple perspectives. Still, in many cases you come to appreciate some individuals as particularly important sources of information and knowledge and as representatives of larger groups or sets of knowledge and experience. As a result, you rely heavily on these key informants at different points in your research process. If you have relied on one or more key informants, it makes sense that they will occupy a prominent place in the ethnographic presentation. You may choose to focus on these individuals as case studies, or you may decide to give them a prominent place throughout the text.

Informants who appear as **key figures** in the ethnography serve as a sort of anchor for it. The reader has a chance to become familiar with these individuals, recognize them by name, and even identify with their personal circumstances or personality traits. In this way, the key figures can help humanize the ethnographic presentation. They can also help you present informants as experts from whom you have learned.

Composite Descriptions

While descriptive accounts of *specific* events, people, and conversations are the primary building blocks of almost any ethnography, ethnographers sometimes elect to create composite descriptions that combine elements from different parts of the ethnographic record. **Composite descriptions** allow you to focus on the shared or general characteristics you discerned during the course of your research. In this way, the composite description also represents a way to condense a lot of research into a relatively concise form of presentation. Of course, you always have to be alert to the danger of overlooking important variation and difference.

Composite accounts of events probably appear most frequently as part of ethnographies. When you have attended or participated in a number of events that follow a similar routine or structure, you are in a position to decide whether you want to construct a composite account of the general event that describes an idealized version, including all the most important and routine or standardized components of the event. An idealized, composite account of a baseball game might describe an event that begins with the national anthem, followed by a ceremonial first pitch thrown by a well-known public figure, and a nine-inning competitive contest featuring one local team and one visiting team, with regular breaks between each half-inning and an extended break called the seventh-inning stretch between the top and bottom halves of the seventh inning. This version describes a standard baseball game, but one or more element may be changed or absent at any particular game. The game might last up to thirteen innings, and various other variables, like the anthem and the ceremonial first pitch, might also change. This composite account does not describe any particular event. In fact, the ethnographer may very well never have encountered an event that included *all* of these components. Instead, the account represents the ethnographer's best field-work-based understanding of the event in general.

Composite accounts of conversations are less frequent than composite accounts of events, but occasionally you find that you have been the participant in a number of very similar conversations that seem to follow a common formula. In this case, a composite description of the general conversation may be helpful, especially since the repeated occurrence can be an indicator of widely shared ideas, perspectives, or experiences.

In some cases, ethnographers decide to develop composite descriptions of individuals. In these instances, the ethnographer describes a composite individual who represents a combination of traits from several different individuals. This approach is employed most frequently when the ethnographer wants to take extra steps to protect the individual identities of informants (especially in situations with considerable social stigma or other potentially negative consequences for the informants; see, for example, Stark 1998). These composite accounts of individuals are probably not advisable in most circumstances because ethnography usually benefits from a strong sense of informants as real people with individual experiences, dispositions, and perspectives.

CASE STUDY

Protecting Informants in the Writing Process

Ethnographic research should protect informants from the outset. Research design must include the proper steps to protect informants with whom the researcher works. These steps help to ensure anonymity or confidentiality and limit the possible negative repercussions associated with participation in an ethnographic study. Nevertheless, when you decide to present your research to a wider audience in a paper or publication, protection of informants emerges as an important issue once again. In part, presentation of the ethnography to a larger audience raises the issue because a wider community of readers now has access to the findings. Whereas during the course of research you are responsible for safeguarding the ethnographic record and the identities of informants, when you present the findings to others, you must consider how to share this information without unnecessarily exposing your informants to public scrutiny, stigma, and practical repercussions. You should be concerned about these possible effects at both the collective and individual levels.

You should carefully consider whether to use pseudonyms or composite figures to protect your informants. Whether one or both of these options makes sense depends on the research context and factors like size of population and unique identifying characteristics that might be included in the ethnography.

Ethnographers frequently assign a fictitious name to their field site to protect the privacy of their informants. This step can discourage others from trying to identify key informants by visiting the

THE IMPORTANCE OF ETHNOGRAPHIC DETAIL

Detail is an absolutely essential component of any good ethnography. A well-thought-out research plan should help you ensure you are collecting the right type of data, and therefore detail, for use in the final ethnography. The intensive and lengthy commitment to fieldwork you make proves worthwhile precisely because you can mine your extensive ethnographic record for appropriate and illuminating detail. As you contemplate issues ranging from the choice of analytical framework to tone and voice, it may be relatively easy to shift attention away from the details of the ethnographic record. However, choices related to writing style should ultimately allow the ethnographer to communicate and make best use of the details collected in the course of research.

Details fit together with elements of style like tone and voice to create a convincing ethnography. Well-told stories replete with details can contribute significantly to the overall effectiveness of the ethnography. You should not seek details for the sake of details. Instead you should focus on the way the details contribute to a larger descriptive account or provide the foundation for specific analyses. You can draw on details to field site and using deductive methods. It protects the field site from unnecessary scrutiny and should allow informants to go about their lives in relative peace, but it also raises the question of whether you control the field site and access to it and prevent others from revisiting and critiquing your research. Fictitious place names are more appropriate and more effective in some cases than others, and they may imply a degree of protection that does not really exist, since the reader may be able to figure out pretty easily that "Any Town, USA" is really Des Moines, Iowa.

Pseudonyms for informants are even more common than fictitious place names in ethnographies and can even be considered standard best practice. Some ethnographers have questioned the wisdom of using pseudonyms (see Scheper-Hughes 2001), especially if pseudonyms allow ethnographers to avoid taking responsibility for the information that they choose to share about real individuals. The ethnographer should not approach the use of pseudonyms lightly. Assigning a new name to someone is a serious and weighty task, and some ethnographers decide to ask their informants whether they want to be referred to by pseudonym and even to choose pseudonyms for themselves. Names can communicate a lot of information about individuals, and ethnographers should work diligently to convey the humanity and individuality of their informants whenever ethical considerations allow it. Referring to informants by using letters or numbers is generally not advisable since it tends to convey a relatively dehumanized image of informants.

convey the power and insight of fieldwork and to contribute to a larger sense of ethnographic realism. Along these lines, ethnographers frequently incorporate foreign or group-specific words and concepts encountered in the course of research or even accounts of fieldwork challenges to give the reader a sense of connection to the "real" circumstances of ethnographic research.

Even though details are an essential component of any ethnography, the types of details you include in the final ethnography depend on a number of factors. Too much detail can be overwhelming. The reader of the ethnography may be unable to discern which parts of the detailed information being presented are most significant and how they fit together into a larger analytical whole. Using your own evaluations of relative importance in the ethnographic record, you should aim to build on those details that emerge as most central to your ethnographic understanding. Beyond the worry of too much detail, you must also consider issues like audience, style, and subject matter. Descriptions of religious experiences will work well in an interpretive narrative account of Islam but probably will not fulfill the same function in a more formal, scientific examination of Islamic food taboos. In that case, the experiential details may seem superfluous. This sort of formal and scientific ethnography likely calls for a different type of detail, perhaps more rooted in observable behavior or even quantifiable data. Numbers and other measures can be as essential to ethnography as narrative description or specific quotes, depending on the specific goals of the ethnography.

MATCHING STYLE TO AUDIENCE, SUBJECT, AND ANALYSIS

Deciding on an appropriate style of presentation involves evaluating the research project in terms of three key factors: **intended audience, subject matter,** and **analytical framework**. Each of these factors influences the type of ethnography you want to produce. Therefore, explicitly considering each factor in turn is essential to making purposeful and appropriate decisions about how to shape the ethnography as a final product.

Intended Audience

Ethnographies are produced for a specific purpose, and that generally means they have a specific intended audience. When writing an ethnography is a class assignment, the intended audience may be limited to the instructor or professor, but ethnography, like all other research and other academic endeavors, is usually meant to be shared with a larger audience. When shared with an audience, the ethnography can inform and motivate its audience. Readers can also critique and evaluate the ethnography as they connect it to other sources of information. Different audiences will have different expectations of the ethnography and will be prepared to engage it in slightly different ways. Ethnographies may have multiple intended audiences. Good ethnographies can speak to a wide range of audiences, but evaluating the primary intended audience helps ensure that the ethnography is as effective as possible in fulfilling its main purpose.

You should consider whether the primary intended audience for the ethnography is an academic one. If so, the audience will probably expect you to employ standard academic conventions in terms of organization and citations. All ethnographies should be based on rigorous research, but knowing whether the audience is primarily academic can help you decide how much detailed consideration of theoretical debates related to the academic discipline to include. An academic audience will want to know how you situate yourself and your work in relationship to these debates. A less academic audience may be less concerned with these issues and more focused on the empirical findings or policy implications, for instance. Therefore, knowing whether the audience is an academic one can aid you in deciding how much discussion of academic theory and debate to include in the body of the ethnography.

Along similar lines, knowing whether you are writing for a general or a specialized audience can be helpful, especially when you think about the readability of the ethnography. You should always aim to make your ethnography readable and accessible, but the style and type of discourse appropriate for a specialized audience may be relatively inaccessible when presented to a general audience. If you intend for your ethnography to be available to the general public, you will want to write it to be accessible to a nonspecialist. Making the work accessible in this way involves avoiding jargon or specialized terminology and considering word choice and sentence structure.

In evaluating whether the intended audience is academic or not and specialized or general, you are considering what specific sets of knowledge the audience brings to the ethnography. You should also consider how much knowledge of the culture and society in question the audience already possesses. If the ethnography introduces the audience to a culture or a cultural phenomenon for the first time, you will need to make sure you provide all the necessary information to explain the symbols and behaviors involved. However, if the intended audience is familiar with the setting and the culture under consideration, you may be able to assume some basic knowledge and move more immediately into the specifics of the research. Ethnographies are most frequently written with the assumption that the reader as audience comes to the topic as an "outsider" and possesses little to no prior knowledge of the subject. However, in some cases you are writing the ethnography for an audience that includes your informants. In these cases, it is unnecessary, and even potentially condescending, for you to write as if your audience knows nothing about the topic and the culture in question. Awareness of the types of knowledge the audience brings to a reading of the ethnography helps you ensure you provide appropriate and sufficient information within your ethnography.

If your intended audience is particularly practically minded, you will want to keep this fact in mind. Administrators and policy makers often look to ethnography as a source of information in making decisions. They may expect to find clear recommendations for policies or programs within the ethnography. If the ethnographic research is practical or applied in focus or if you know your audience is particularly practically minded, you should make sure your ethnography clearly delineates practical ramifications and recommendations stemming from the research.

In summary, critically evaluating the intended audience can help you make a number of stylistic decisions. Based on the audience, you can make decisions about relative formality or informality and whether to emphasize practical or intellectual dimensions to the project.

Subject Matter

Besides the question of audience, you should consider carefully whether your subject matter lends itself to a particular style. In this instance, subject matter refers to the cultural and social phenomena being researched, but also to the specific types of data that your research strategies have produced. Research focusing on behavior and relying heavily on participant-observation as a method lends itself to a writing style that features descriptive accounts of specific moments or events. Conversely, research aimed at studying ideas and values and depends on interview data and its analysis might usefully incorporate dialogue and excerpts from interviews. Because ethnography relies on a combination of research techniques and ultimately investigates both ideas and behavior, the differences are typically differences in degree, but you should aim to develop a writing style that emphasizes your primary data and the most illuminating elements of the ethnographic record in the most appropriate manner.

Subject matter also influences the tone of the ethnography as a key component of the overall style. The subject matter and the analytical framework being employed can determine whether the tone should be more or less formal and whether a more scientific or creative approach to writing is appropriate. In this case, the writing style can help frame the content of the ethnographic record. A logical discussion of social structures may lend itself to a rather formal, scientific tone, whereas if you are examining the playful, creative elements of subversive ritual you may be able to communicate some of that playful subversiveness in your own use of language in the course of your ethnography. The best ethnographies seem to have styles that match the subject matter in especially interesting ways.

Analytical Framework

Once you have chosen an analytical framework that allows you to produce the best analyses or interpretations, the next step is to consider how that analytical framework requires or suggests a particular style of presentation. If you feel that a postmodern approach is the most helpful theoretical entry into the ethnographic record, then you will almost certainly want to produce an ethnography that is postmodern in style—perhaps producing a pastiche of fragments that overlap and even contradict, and avoiding the creation of a single master narrative. On the other hand, an ethnography rooted in the theoretical school of cultural ecology will likely rest on a rather coherent narrative of explanation that ties the ethnography together into a rather neat, coherent package. Whether you rely on a Marxist, feminist, or functionalist theoretical framework (to name a few), you will want to choose a style that is most effective at communicating the insights of that framework in relationship to your specific ethnographic data. Familiarity with ethnography as a genre is important when you are looking to match your analytical framework to a writing style. If you have read multiple examples in feminist or functionalist ethnography, you are much better positioned to consider how you can model your work after the work of others, especially those who employ a similar theoretical model. Analytical models based on *explanation* and a commitment to scientific objectivity tend to be closely linked with relatively formal styles of interpretation. On the other hand, *interpretive* analytical models with a more humanistic inclination tend to be more informal.

A FORMAL TO INFORMAL CONTINUUM OF STYLE

Compared to many other types of writing related to serious research, ethnographic writing tends to be *relatively* informal. The strictly objective and neutral tone and stance characteristic of much scientific writing is not necessarily the most common approach in ethnographic writing. Ethnographers frequently find ways to incorporate first-person accounts, emotions, and subjective interpretations into their ethnographies. The **relative informality** of ethnographic writing is directly connected to the methods employed in ethnographic research and to the types of data collected. The very

The Ethnographic Present

You should also carefully consider whether to write in the past or present tense when presenting ethnographic findings. The "ethnographic present" is a longstanding convention in which you write in the present tense about fieldwork data and the culture or society being studied. At its most effective, this writing technique can produce a sense of immediacy as if the conversation or event is happening right then and there in front of the reader. It provides a sense that the events, ideas, and behaviors are persistent and ongoing. However, this use of the present tense can also imply that a particular culture is unchanging and elide the historical circumstances of ethnographic research. Even though a group exhibited a particular set of behaviors or employed a particular set of symbols when you were doing your research, that does not mean the group has always behaved in the same way or used the same symbols or that what you have recorded will stay the same indefinitely.

If you write in the past tense about your research, you can emphasize the historically situated nature of your research and the potential for change. The past tense may be particularly appropriate if you want to include consideration of social and cultural change in your ethnography. On the other hand, if you want to highlight constancy and cultural continuity or if your ethnography focuses on what can be taken as very general defining characteristics of a group or culture, the present tense may be particularly effective, especially if you want to communicate a particular sense of immediacy. You may want to remind the reader that the content of the ethnography is directly related to the current lives of the readers, and the present tense may be the most effective way to create that sort of immediate connection between the reader and the subject matter. The present tense implies a sense of tangible reality and presence in this case.

fact that you rely on yourself as the primary research instrument means that you have a directly personal stake in the research data that is impossible to deny. Therefore, the formal style associated with a purely objective stance in research may seem inappropriate. Still, the model of a continuum representing a range of relatively formal and informal approaches to ethnographic writing seems apt when considering the question of formality in ethnographic writing. Ethnographies exhibit significant variation in their relative formality and informality. In constructing your ethnography, you should decide where you want your ethnography to fall on that continuum and how to achieve that goal with specific writing techniques.

One of the choices you face concerns the questions of voice and perspective. You have to decide whether to write in the first or third person about your research. In the early years of ethnography, most works were written in the third person from a perspective that positioned the ethnographer as a sort of omniscient observer. In more recent years, though, many ethnographers have turned to the first person in their writing, in part because writing in the first person allows them to include their own experiences as researcher and research instrument, and also because of increased recognition of the subjective dimensions of ethnography. In fact, use of the third person has been criticized because the idea of the ethnographer as an omniscient observer hides the influence of personal characteristics and access to particular perspectives. Nevertheless, ethnographers sometimes decide that the third person perspective is most appropriate for their projects. Generally, the first person sets a more informal tone than the third person, and the choice should be made in the course of considering related issues like audience, subject, and analytical framework.

The tone you strike in your presentation can help by communicating a sense of shared empathy or even common cause with informants, but that sort of tone is not always possible or advisable. Still, you should be wary of an overly objectifying tone that creates or communicates distance between you and your informants. However, even the most empathetic tone does not carry the necessary protection of informants.

SUMMARY

Different writing conventions can be very effective pieces of the final ethnography you produce. The conventions typically involve the presentation of specific ethnographic details organized in such a way that they support sustained analysis of the ethnographic data. The space in between these parts of the ethnography based on one or more ethnographic conventions is the space of analysis and building connections. Your choice of writing conventions should be directly connected to your larger understanding of your project's purpose and audience. These factors will help you decide where to position your ethnography along a range of relatively formal and informal presentation styles.

KEY TERMS

Style of presentation
Conventions
Arrival scenes
Cases
Case studies
Key figures

Composite descriptions
Intended audience
Subject matter
Analytical framework
Relative informality

DISCUSSION QUESTIONS

1. What sort of tone is set in the opening of Duneier's *Sidewalk*? How does this tone relate to the overall style of presentation that Duneier employs?

2. Name the common ethnographic conventions mentioned in this chapter. In the ethnographies with which you are familiar, do some conventions seem to be more common than others? How can you decide if a particular convention is appropriate for your work?

3. What does an arrival scene help you accomplish or convey in your ethnography? Are there potential pitfalls you should try to avoid when you elect to include an arrival scene?

4. What are the common intended audiences for ethnographies? Can you match these different types of audiences with appropriate styles of presentation? Are there particularly appropriate conventions?

5. How does the ethnographer choose between the past and the present tense? First and third person?

6. Should you always employ pseudonyms to protect your informants' anonymity? What are the ethical implications of using pseudonyms?

7. Should ethnographies strive for a relatively casual tone? Can an ethnography be too casual or informal? Can an ethnography be too formal?

CHAPTER

15

PUTTING THE WHOLE ETHNOGRAPHY TOGETHER

LEARNING OBJECTIVES

- Decide whether the hourglass model is appropriate for a specific ethnography
- Evaluate alternative models for ethnography
- Incorporate relevant literature effectively in an ethnographic presentation
- Incorporate maps, charts, and photographs
- Demonstrate the relevance of an ethnographic project
- Develop a plan for sharing ethnographic results and incorporating responses and critiques

Once you have developed an analytical framework and made appropriate choices about how to present your ethnography, you are ready to put the pieces together into a final product that can be shared and critiqued. In writing throughout the process, you will already have produced written drafts and fragments that you will be able to pull together into a coherent whole. Constructing the whole involves interweaving descriptive accounts, visual representations like maps and tables, citations of other works, and analytical insight. You can work with one of several different models in building this whole, but the most important concerns at this stage are the effectiveness with which you communicate your ideas and findings and the coherence of the ethnography as a unit. Ideally, the different components of the ethnography should work together to convey most effectively the key ethnographic ideas.

THE HOURGLASS SHAPE AS A MODEL

Many ethnographies follow a model that matches the shape of an hourglass: wide at the ends and narrow in the middle. These ethnographies are wide at the ends in the sense that the broadest, most general questions and topics receive consideration in the opening and closing sections, while the middle of the ethnography focuses on specific ethnographic detail and analysis. This model is very common in many forms of academic and scientific writing, and the standard research proposal follows this general model. In fact, a research proposal can often be relatively easily transformed into the **hourglass model** for the final ethnography if fieldwork has followed the research plan relatively closely. For example, many of the sources cited in the literature review of a research proposal will be cited in the introductory section of the hourglass model. This introductory section situates the general research project within larger contexts of history, theory, and empirical research. It clearly lays out the central research questions and the import of the research to a larger audience. With this foundation, the focus of the ethnography shifts to the specific research project you have completed. This part of the ethnography is full of ethnographic detail and seeks to present a rich and nuanced account of the main findings produced in the course of ethnographic fieldwork. Once the most important detail and specific analysis are presented, you then turn back to the big picture at the end of the ethnography. At this point you connect the specific findings you have presented and the analytical framework you have built to larger questions and debates. You may argue for a new understanding of the social or cultural phenomenon, a new theoretical model, or a policy change as a result of your research. At the end, the reader leaves the ethnographic presentation with a firm sense of how the research relates to the work and ideas of others as well as practical programs and policies.

This model is likely familiar to many audiences and may make reading and interpreting the ethnographic findings particularly easy. It is a relatively straightforward model of presentation that can include a lot of information and ensures that you relate your work to the larger picture at several points. This model is probably the best default organizational model. However, ethnographers often turn to other models to meet their various needs and goals in presenting the results of their ethnographic work.

ALTERNATIVE MODELS FOR ORGANIZING AN ETHNOGRAPHY

In following an **alternative model**, ethnographers frequently choose to dive right into ethnographic detail at the outset of their ethnography. The most common approach along these lines involves opening the ethnography with a story or narrative account. An arrival scene often fills this role. The story or narrative helps set the scene for the project and connect the reader to the specific project from the very beginning. A well-told story with compelling detail can be a very powerful opening that connects with the reader through various elements, including humor, irony, human interest, or even surprise. Once the reader has entered the field site along with you and is engaged, then you can widen the lens or scope to consider the work of others by showing how this detail relates to or differs from what others have found or argued. With this model, the ethnographer starts with narrow detail and then gradually or abruptly widens the scope. You may then return the focus to detailed description and analysis, producing a sort of modified hour-glass model with a narrow, detailed focus attached at the beginning, or you may work from a model that starts with the specific and gradually moves to the wider, more general perspective in the end. In this second case, the larger questions and debates appear most prominently only at the end of the ethnography. The model produces a sense that questions and answers as well as solutions emerge out of the ethnographic data themselves. This can be an effective way to present the significance of the ethnographic record, but it may not meet all audiences' expectations for the ethnography, especially because the opening story generally sets a rather casual tone.

An increasingly common model for ethnographic writings incorporates significant attention to historical sources of information and historical context. When you have access to substantial historical data and find that they illuminate your ethnographic data in particularly productive ways, you can decide to include a substantial historical section. More often than not, these ethnographies follow a chronological model with the historical information preceding the bulk of the ethnographic information, though the two are frequently intertwined in various important ways. In much the same way that an arrival scene or opening story can set the scene for the ethnography, historical information can provide an absolutely essential basis for understanding and analyzing the ethnographic data being presented. With this model of an opening historical section followed by an ethnographic section, the focus almost necessarily turns to change and **causal relationships** that connect the ethnographic and historical records. The model can be particularly effective if you choose to focus a great deal of attention on historical changes and you have the data to construct your ethnography along these models.

Ethnographers who want to emphasize the variety of perspectives and relative lack of consensus they have found in the course of their research sometimes construct ethnographies that forgo any of these models. Instead, they produce an ethnography that relies on **fragments** and the juxtaposition of disconnected or dissimilar pieces from the ethnographic record. The model here is a pastiche or a collage, though referring to it as a "model" runs counter to some of the underlying theoretical ideas that give rise to these choices. In many respects, this approach is quintessentially postmodern and involves a rejection of master narratives and assumptions of coherence. The approach offers a counterpoint to the tendency to interpret cultural groups as coherent and homogeneous and recognizes that the ethnographer frequently encounters contests of power and authority as well as serious debate and disagreement about meaning.

When done well, an ethnography that adopts this approach can convey the rich textures of ethnographic fieldwork and the variety that almost all ethnographers encounter in the course of their research. You should carefully consider how much **variety** and **contestation** you perceive in the ethnographic record and how you want to convey these aspects. Readers as an audience for the ethnography may be frustrated by a seemingly chaotic mess if they are unable to glean particular pieces of information and key ideas from the ethnography generally. If you choose to adopt this approach, you should be very clear in your own understanding of what you want to communicate to the reader and how your approach builds on the ethnographic record and highlights items of significance. Conflict and contradictions *can* be items of significance if they emerge from the ethnographic record. However, this sort of fragmented ethnography may not satisfy the expectations of audiences looking for practical recommendations or scientific explanations. A composite option involves interspersing case studies or profiles of key figures throughout the text to highlight diversity and variation but placing these elements within a larger, more coherent narrative.

INCORPORATING RELEVANT LITERATURE

The majority of data or information included in any ethnography should come directly from the researcher's own ethnographic record. The power of ethnography stems in large part from its ability to draw on these sets of *primary* data. However, ethnographic research does not occur in isolation. The ethnographer's choices about what and how to study are shaped by the work of others, and ethnography almost necessarily depends on a comparative dimension, which is often rather implicit but involves comparing the ethnographic data to other sources of data. In order to situate your work and make the most of this comparative dimension, you must incorporate the work of others into your ethnography. Luckily, in building a literature review for your research proposal, you have already identified many of the relevant sources on which you are likely to draw, though you may find there are also unanticipated areas of research and theoretical literature that you want to examine.

In the process of writing the final ethnography, you will insert references to relevant literature primarily as a way of building a larger framework and emphasizing the relevance, importance, and uniqueness of your own project. You can use references to relevant literature to show how your findings parallel or diverge from the findings of others, how your research has employed new methods and answered new questions or addressed longstanding questions that have not yet been adequately answered, and how your findings and analysis support particular models or suggest the need for new or revised models. You might occasionally cite literature in considering specific parts of the ethnographic record, but most references to relevant literature appear at the points where you move from the level of the ethnographically specific to a more abstract or generalized level. The literature helps contextualize and fill in the gaps as you shift from the specific to the general or abstract.

For most ethnographies, citations of relevant literature are concentrated in the opening and closing sections. This distribution of references makes sense in light of the popularity of the hourglass shape as a model. Other models may mean that the ethnography shifts between specific and general or abstract at different points in the text. Therefore, concentrated citations may be appropriate at various points in the text. You want to make sure you draw on relevant literature at these points to lend weight to your own work and show that your work is part of an attempt to build understanding and answer questions within a larger community of participants, observers, researchers, and thinkers. Ethnographies that include limited reference to relevant literature tend to indicate a relative lack of awareness of the larger context for the research. You should not limit yourself to considering only those sources that directly address your topic or field site. Literature can be relevant if it allows you to further your thinking about your own topic; those connections may manifest themselves in similarities in form, function, structure, meaning, or a number of other elements. Some of the most innovative and insightful ethnographic works build on nonobvious connections in the literature that give rise to new perspectives on a given topic.

INCORPORATING MAPS, CHARTS, AND PHOTOGRAPHS

In constructing the ethnographic record, you frequently produce a number of different types of visual representations, including maps, charts, tables, and photographs. You can frequently incorporate one or more of these items into the final ethnography in a way that makes the ethnography as a whole more effective than it would be without them. For instance, a photograph will provide a mental image to accompany your description of standard dress, and a map of a home's interior will allow the reader to visualize movement, spatial relationships, and spatial distances that are absolutely essential to ethnographic understanding. In moving toward producing a final ethnography, you must decide which visual representations to include and how to incorporate them into the larger ethnographic presentation.

You have probably produced some visual representations in the ethnographic record that function primarily as ways to stimulate your memory or think through a set of analytical ideas. These sorts of representations are largely for your benefit and your own thinking process, and they usually ought to remain in the ethnographic record, though a refined version might occasionally become a useful addition to the final ethnography. Ethnographers also produce visual representations that represent a condensed version of ethnographic information and help them communicate their ideas and findings to their audiences most effectively. These representations are the most beneficial additions to ethnographic texts. They are most helpful if they communicate information that is hard to communicate adequately with a verbal explanation alone and if they help the reader to understand the basis for analysis and larger models. A map of interior space may help the reader understand why the basic distinction between male and female space is so important (see Wood 1999 on Gabra), and a chart or table might clearly lay out the conceptual categories that the ethnographer takes to be fundamental to an understanding of behavior and structures. The chart or table can show the relationships between categories and subcategories and offer brief examples of each category, among other things. Well-integrated visual representations supplement the text directly. Ideally, the text will make direct reference to the figure or table and utilize the visual imagery to maximum descriptive and analytical effect. Therefore, the integration of visual forms involves connecting them to specific parts of the larger ethnographic presentation.

Maps that locate the field site geographically typically appear at the very beginning of the ethnography. Like the arrival scene, these maps provide context and set the stage for what follows, so they usually belong in the introductory sections. However, other maps (both geographic and conceptual) can appear throughout the ethnography. They are most effective when inserted at those points where you turn your attention to these particular spaces and the relationships between those things depicted in the map.

When you use tables and charts, you usually place them in the central body of the ethnography. In much the same way that the maps support discussion and analysis of spatial relationships and the perception of space, the tables and charts support ethnographic treatment of topics such as conceptual categories, structures, social divisions, and rates. Therefore, strategic placement of these tables and charts can help you provide a complete ethnographic picture, especially if you refer the reader to the table or chart in the course of your description and analysis in the text. When comparing groups, time periods, or other things, tables and charts can be particularly powerful if supported by structurally similar charts or tables that highlight key similarities and differences.

Photographs can also appear throughout the ethnography. Ethnographers frequently place some photographs at the very beginning to set the stage and offer visual images for the reader that anchor textual descriptions. If you have a particularly good photograph of a person, event, or item that you examine in the body of the ethnography, you should include the photo at that point. Photographs, however, are often less connected to the text of the ethnography than maps, charts, or tables. Ethnographers frequently use photographs to provide a general, supplementary picture and only loosely tie them to the specific content of the ethnography. Photographs add a particular sense of realism to the work, but you should be cautious about expecting your audience to glean too much from photographs. Your verbal description and analysis should always be the primary focus of the ethnography, and photographs should be chosen for inclusion based on what they add directly to the text.

DEMONSTRATING THE PROJECT'S RELEVANCE

Ultimately, you want to communicate the **relevance** of your work. You do this by contextualizing your work in terms of existing questions, ideas, and information. The best way to demonstrate the relevance of the project depends on the intended outcome and the intended audience. You lay the foundation for a project's relevance in the way you address and contextualize your work from the very beginning of the ethnography, but the question of relevance most often comes to the fore in the concluding sections of the ethnography, as the focus shifts toward the big picture and the larger ramifications of the research project. You will want to consider how you can best communicate the relevance of your project to your reader.

An ethnography can be directly relevant if it has **practical ramifications** and makes the implications of the research clear in a series of **recommendations** or proposals. In this case, relevance resides in the process of problem solving and the researcher's ability to produce outcomes like reform or advocacy. If the project is practically oriented, you should keep those practical dimensions front and center in the final presentation of results. In fact, you may want to end your ethnography with a practical list of recommendations or proposals as the final takeaway from the ethnography.

If the ethnographic research is less focused on practical problem solving and more oriented toward the collection of information and the answering of **intellectual questions**, demonstrating the project's relevance involves showing how the research has contributed to current understandings and ongoing debates centered around these intellectual questions. You want to draw attention to the unique ethnographic findings you have been able to document, but you also want to show that you have done more than simply contributing to a catalog of cultural and social phenomena. You want to connect your work to big-picture questions that have wide relevance. Therefore, the more you are able to connect your work to discussions of power, inequality, gender, social change, and other major topics that interest many people, the more effective your ability to demonstrate its relevance. You may want to conclude your ethnography by highlighting these connections and might consider suggesting interesting cross-cultural comparisons and directions for future research that can build from your own work. If others use your work as a starting point in building knowledge and understanding and it inspires others' research endeavors, then it is relevant.

Ethnographies can be both practically oriented and intellectually inclined and frequently are both. You do not necessarily have to choose one focus at the expense of the other: you simply need to highlight the most relevant aspects of your research so that readers can appreciate its significance. If the work has both practical and intellectual relevance, that makes it particularly significant, and you should seek to communicate both dimensions to your readers, but you should always do so with an eye to your primary purpose and your primary audience.

EVALUATING AND REVISING ETHNOGRAPHY

After you have produced a complete ethnography that is ready for presentation to your audience, the processes of **evaluation** and **revision** begin in earnest. Writing and rewriting are indispensable parts of the ethnographic process, and you should expect your ethnography to go through various stages of revision in which you refine your work and draw on the responses of others. This process of revision will require you to make clear decisions about the quality of your ethnographic record and the most important elements of your ethnographic presentation. The ethnography is, after all, ultimately *your* work based on your experiences, your analysis, and the models or theories that you understand to be most insightful. Another ethnographer might produce a very different ethnography about a similar topic. Such diversity does not diminish the value of either ethnography, as long as the works are based on good ethnographic information and well-reasoned analysis. A wealth of ethnographic information and ethnographic perspectives contributes to our overall understanding of social and cultural phenomena. The wider reading public ultimately has to decide which ethnographies are best researched and analyzed and which ones are most relevant in addressing pressing issues and questions.

You can start the process of evaluation and revision by revisiting your original research proposal. You will want to consider how well your final ethnography matches the ethnography envisioned in the proposal, especially in terms of the central research questions and research methods. Considerable differences between the proposal and the final ethnography do not necessarily indicate problems in the final ethnography. Instead, this stage of review allows you to evaluate how well your final ethnography represents the results of the research that you undertook.

Placing the ethnography alongside the proposal may allow you to see that you have neglected an important section of the ethnographic data that you intended to include and to consider. Or this comparison may remind you of reasons that prompted you to adapt and modify your original plans in the course of your research. In fact, the questions you ended up researching and answering may be more interesting and productive than the ones at the heart of the original research proposal. In this case, you will want to make sure the final ethnography communicates the significance of these questions; you may even want to describe the evolution of your project and your thinking within the ethnography. This sort of explanation can help readers understand the choices that informed the research process.

Looking back at the research proposal also helps you evaluate specific components of the ethnography. You can compare the literature cited in the research proposal with citations in the ethnography to see if you have neglected an important piece or segment of the literature in the ethnography. You can also use the methods section of the proposal to evaluate your discussion of methods in the ethnography. Some of the specific research techniques may have been modified as the project evolved, but you should consider whether you have included important and adequate information about research methods in the ethnography itself. You should make sure that the reader understands how the ethnographic information was collected and what it represents.

SHARING THE ETHNOGRAPHY

Once you have undertaken your own personal process of evaluation and revision, the next step involves **sharing** the ethnography, as a representation of the research process and the findings, with a larger audience. Chapter Fourteen details how different characteristics of the intended audience can influence choices related to style of presentation. At this stage, the question becomes how the audience responds to the content of the ethnography as well as the presentation. In most cases, you can benefit tremendously from sharing your ethnography with your informants and others interested in the topic.

Careful review of responses and critiques can help you consider your contribution to knowledge building and practical decision making, as well as your responsibilities to your informants. Ethnographers cannot pursue ethnography without tremendous help from informants, who are asked to share their knowledge and their lives in numerous ways. In doing ethnographic research and writing the ethnography, you should always keep your informants' interests in mind. You should aim to produce an ethnography that both informs and respects the humanity of the informants at its heart. Inviting response and evaluation helps ensure that you avoid conveying unintended meanings and producing unintended consequences. As researcher and writer, you need to be able to question, analyze, and critique. Precisely because you are questioning, analyzing, and critiquing your informants' ideas and behaviors, you need to be aware of how they respond. This approach involves thinking about ethnography as collaboration or dialogue. You may occupy a privileged position as researcher and author of the ethnography, but openness to other ideas and potential critiques will help you produce the best ethnography possible.

For a variety of reasons, seeking evaluation and **critique** from informants is both most important and most unnerving for many ethnographers. Because you seek to represent the lives, thoughts, and behavior of your informants in the ethnography, a positive response to the final product from informants can be affirming and reassuring. If informants confirm all or part of the ethnography, this response constitutes an important form of validation for the ethnographer. However, informants' responses are not always positive.

Sometimes informants respond with seeming indifference to the work of the ethnographer (for example, Behar 2003), and sometimes they respond with sharp critique. Indifference may be linked to a feeling that the research does not have a direct impact on their everyday lives, especially if the primary audience is socially or geographically distant from the field site. Critique can originate in a number of different experiences and sentiments. Informants may feel that the ethnography misrepresents them as individuals or as a group, or they may take issue with specific accounts of events or conversations that they remember differently. They may also feel that the ethnography ignores or underemphasizes the most important parts of their lives by focusing on the trivial or sensational. Receiving these sorts of critiques can present a challenge for you, especially since you have taken it as your primary task to present the most significant pieces of the record that you produced in the course of your work with informants.

In some instances, critique from informants may prompt you to return to the ethnographic record and help you see pieces or dimensions that you overlooked or underestimated. This situation probably represents the most productive outcome when critique emerges. In other cases, you may decide after considering the critiques that your perspective and presentation are defensible and important. Informants' critiques may reflect differences between the ethnographer's practical understanding of social and cultural phenomena in action and informants' desires to present idealized versions of society and culture to a wider public audience. These critiques may even reflect informants' own political and social concerns about how the research findings reflect and affect interpersonal relationships with other informants. Like any other audience, informants will always respond to the ethnography from their own perspectives, and your challenge involves determining how best to evaluate these socially produced responses. An ethnography that pays close attention to the interests and wishes of informants is most likely to be a rich ethnography that is true to the context of research, but you ultimately have to decide how to present and represent information and which perspectives and interpretations can be usefully included. You may decide to keep sections and ideas that prompt significant critique from informants, but you should always remain cognizant of the connection between critiques and ethical concerns. Sometimes critiques communicate serious concerns about what will happen when particular forms or pieces of information are shared with a particular audience.

In addition to seeking responses from informants, you should also seek evaluation and critique from other interested parties, especially other ethnographers and those with longstanding interests in the research topic. These individuals will be able to provide invaluable feedback about the ethnography as a whole and about specific elements, ranging from style of presentation to analytical framework. Evaluation of these different elements from individuals who have significant experience with similar projects and similar topics can offer invaluable assistance in revising and refining your ethnography.

These individuals may be able to identify gaps in the research or presentation that you are unaware of. They may also raise questions by suggesting alternative interpretations or explanations, and they may offer interesting ideas about connecting the ethnography to specific studies or theoretical frameworks that you have not considered previously. All these sorts of responses can be very helpful, though sometimes a detailed critique will suggest that you construct a very different ethnography from the one you have worked so hard to produce.

Like informants, other individuals bring their own perspectives, experiences, and biases as they respond to the ethnography, and you should carefully evaluate the responses to see which suggestions and critiques seem most valid and helpful. You should avoid being overly defensive of your work; you want to be open to improving your ethnography through feedback. At the same time, in evaluating the responses of others you will find that you are committed to certain elements of your ethnography as foundational or essential, and you are unwilling to change them. This process of evaluation and critique involves a delicate balance of being open to suggestion and critique while claiming ownership or authorship over the ethnography as a whole, especially its key parts.

INCORPORATING RESPONSES AND CRITIQUES

Responses and critiques from informants and others offer you stimulating impetus for revision. Occasionally, the responses and critiques will prompt you to rethink your project and your ethnography radically. You may find that you need to adopt a different organizational model or that a different style will more effectively communicate the important parts of your ethnographic findings. In these cases, you will then need to undertake a major revision of the ethnography as a whole. The result can be a radically different ethnography that emphasizes different elements of the ethnographic record, a different analytical framework, or a different understanding of the field site.

More often you find that response and critique motivate you to revise a particular section or rethink a particular element in the style of presentation. You may also decide that you need to augment what is already included in your ethnography to provide a more complete picture. This sort of approach is easy if there is a general consensus among the responses and critiques you receive. If there is considerable variation or disagreement among the responses, you will have to decide which ones are most helpful and how to incorporate these suggestions and critiques into the ethnography.

In some cases, you may find a particular response or critique important even though it does not lend itself to incorporation through revision of the ethnography. You may decide that the main ethnographic presentation as it stands represents a valid and important way of presenting the information and that the response involves taking the ethnography in a completely different direction. Still, you may want to acknowledge and share the valid response and critique. You can do this by adding a section to the ethnography that presents the response and connects or compares it to the ethnographic presentation as a whole. These sections can appear anywhere in the ethnography that makes organizational and analytical sense, but they most frequently appear near the end, following a chronological model of organization that places at the end of the ethnography the responses that emerged at the end of the research period. Ethnographies that are republished after some time often include a preface or epilogue that includes follow-up information about changes in general and about responses to the ethnography itself (Bourgois 2003 and Scheper-Hughes 2001, for example). A good ethnography should produce a wide variety of responses that extend well past its original presentation. The responses give life to the ethnography and the information and ideas that it contains. The more you can invite and build on responses in the revision process, the stronger your ethnography will be in the end.

SUMMARY

In the final stages of bringing an ethnographic project to completion, you need to make choices related to writing and sharing the ethnography. In accordance with the choices you have made about writing style and writing conventions, as well as your overall understanding of the underlying nature of your ethnographic analysis, you have to choose between models that range from the rather standard hourglass shape to an intentionally asymmetrical collage. Whichever model you choose, you need to make intentional decisions about when and where to incorporate literature citations and visual representations as key components of the ethnographic presentation and analytical framework. Once you have fitted the pieces together into a complete ethnography, you then need to consider how to share your work and get feedback from your informants and oth-ers interested in your work. This feedback is an invaluable asset in continuing to refine your ethnographic understanding.

KEY TERMS

Hourglass model
Alternative models
Causal relationships
Fragments
Variety
Contestation
Relevance

Practical ramifications
Recommendations
Intellectual questions
Evaluation
Revision
Sharing
Critique

DISCUSSION QUESTIONS

1. What factors should the ethnographer consider in deciding between different overall models of presentation? If the hourglass model serves as a sort of default, what sorts of situations call for alternative models? Should there be a default model for ethnography?

2. Should the ethnographer always aim to present a coherent and comprehensive framework?

3. How does the ethnographer know when and how to cite relevant literature? Can the reader of an ethnography expect to find consistent citations throughout, or are citations likely to be concentrated in specific sections of the ethnography?

4. What is the best way to utilize visual components in an ethnographic presentation? Can inclusion of visual components ever be counterproductive in building an effective ethnography?

5. Are there particular individuals or groups you should be particularly interested in sharing your ethnography with? Who is most likely to provide the most helpful feedback? Are there ethical responsibilities to share results with certain groups?

6. Should informants be granted editorial control over the ethnographic presentation? What are the ethnographer's responsibilities in terms of presentation and editorial decisions?

GLOSSARY

Access Practical ability to carry out research in a particular site and to collect necessary information

Analytical Perspective focused on addressing questions related to abstract concepts and building explanation or interpretation

Analytical focus Specific questions related to variables, causality, explanation and interpretation; more specific than a general research topic

Analytical framework Ethnographer's approach to data rooted in specific questions and theories; ethnographer should choose a framework that helps her to make sense out of her specific data; allows her to move from specific to general and to synthesize data

Anonymity Protection of individuals' identities in conducting research and disseminating results

Apprentice A person (or researcher) who learns from an expert by gaining practical experience and training to become an expert

Archives Collections of documents and other objects that represent specific time periods, individuals, groups, and institutions; an invaluable supplemental resource for many ethnographers

Arrival scenes Descriptive accounts of moments when ethnographers enter a field site; often serve to provide key details and highlight researcher's first experiences and impressions

Artifacts Objects that are produced in specific social and cultural contexts and become part of the material record

Audience Primary individual or group that will receive a document or artifact; knowledge of audience informs researcher's ability to analyze meaning and purpose; same document or artifact may be used or understood very differently by different audiences

Authorship Question of who prepared a particular document and for what purpose; helps researcher to evaluate perspective and utility of a document

Behavior Activity and actions engaged in by individuals and groups; often shaped socially and culturally; can be studied using ethnographic methods

"Being there" Important commitment on the part of the ethnographer; allows the researcher to employ appropriate research methods, especially participant-observation and to collect experiential data

Benefits Positive results (of research) to be compared to potential risks of conducting and participating in research

Bias Personal influences that shape an individual's perspective and prevent the achievement of objectivity

Bilateral descent Kinship system that traces familial relationships through both the mother and the father's sides of the family

Case studies Detailed examinations of specific individuals, groups, or events chosen as exemplars worthy of close examination; often chosen to represent a larger whole

Causal relationships Associations between different variables or factors that suggest one does or does not have an effect on the other; can be analyzed through ethnographic data

Charts Visual representations of various types of information and the relationships between people and pieces of information

Coding System of marking and organizing field notes in order to easily search and identify connections in sets of data

Comparative data Data collected from various, comparable sources that shed light both on the regularity of social and cultural phenomena and on similarities and differences across cultures and societies

Composite descriptions Ethnographic accounts that combine details from various individuals or individual cases; can be used to protect anonymity in certain circumstances; also used to highlight general tendencies that crosscut individual situations

Conceptual maps Representations of mental understandings of relationships between people, things, and ideas; attempt to examine the dimensions of society and culture that are neither physical nor visible

Confidentiality Respect for and protection of personal information

Context Important consideration in evaluating and analyzing artifacts and documents; helps ethnographer to understand connections, purposes, and meanings

Conventions Common elements of ethnographies that researchers can choose to employ in constructing ethnographies; include arrival scenes, case studies, key figures, and composite descriptions

Critique Feedback that helps ethnographer to identify areas that need revision and data or analytical ideas that she may need to revisit

Contestation Disagreement over meaning or significance that often emerges in the course of research; highlights the variety and complexity of cultures and societies; important arena for analysis

Conversations Informal opportunities to collect thoughts and words from informants

Cultural products Anything that is produced in specific social and cultural contexts and represents the contexts of its production; may or may not be tangible

Data collection Research stage focused on using appropriate methods to acquire information related to research question(s)

Deductive Process of reasoning that starts with major theories and assumptions and uses them to build a logical model for an entire phenomenon

Descriptive Perspective focused on detailed recording and representation of ethnographic data

Documents Written records that the ethnographer has access to in archives or other locations; one type of cultural artifact

Egalitarian System of social organization based on relative (but not absolute) equality; limited opportunities for one person to exert power or authority over another

Emic Insider's perspective

Ethics Key concern for ethnographers and all researchers; involves considering the researcher's responsibility to informants and others

Ethnography Firsthand study of society and culture in action

Ethnographic storytelling Using narrative skills to present evidence and highlight key moments and themes in the research; utilizes detail and sets the stage for analysis; ethnographer should make intentional and purposeful choices about narration

Ethnographic team Group of ethnographers working together to accomplish the goals for a specific research project

Etic Outsider's perspective; a perspective that influences how someone from outside perceives and analyzes information from a particular site or situation

Evaluation Key part of ethnographic process; should occur throughout the research project, but especially important during analysis, presentation, and revision

Event Activity that constitutes an object of study; often present important opportunities for participant-observation

Experiential data Data gained through direct experience; participant-observation often involves collecting and analyzing experiential data

Exploitative relationship Unequal relationship where one party benefits at the expense of the other; ethnographers must be careful to avoid building such relationships

Exploratory research Research undertaken to collect information without a well-defined question or plan; usually pursued at the beginning of a project and designed to lead to an analytical focus with a specific question and plan to guide future research

Feedback Response to research and analysis that the ethnographer receives from informants and other audiences; invaluable in refining final ethnography and checking validity of both data and analysis

Field sites Locations for ethnographic research

Fragments Pieces of ethnographic data that seem incomplete or disconnected from the rest of the ethnographic record; can signal variety within social phenomena, the complicated nature of human lives and social interactions, or gaps in the data collected

Gatekeepers Individuals who control access (both formally and informally) to particular field sites and to other sources of information

Hierarchical relationships System of social organization that entails significant differences in power, status, and prestige; places some individuals in a position of authority over others as a result of their place in the organizational structure

Homogeneity Uniformity across a group of people, things, or events; the ethnographer should always be cognizant of the degree of homogeneity that she finds in the course of her research

Hourglass model Specific manner of organizing an ethnography where general theories and comparative data figure prominently at the beginning and end and specific ethnographic detail is the focus of the main body of the ethnography

Household surveys Survey technique that allows the researcher to collect data at the household level; distinct from surveys aimed at collecting individual data

Hypotheses Informed predictions about what research data will reveal, especially about the relationship between different variables under consideration; a particularly scientific way of presenting ideas about research topics and the data to be collected

Inductive Process of reasoning that builds models of understanding from the primary data that is collected

Informants The participants in ethnographic research who provide the bulk of the information that ethnographers collect through their words and behaviors

Insider's perspective Point of view of a member of a particular culture or society; frequently referred to as the emic perspective; in groups without firm boundaries and characterized by heterogeneity, identifying an insider's perspective may be difficult or problematic; there are often multiple insider's perspectives in any situation

Instrument Any tool used to collect data; ethnographer often serves as a primary research instrument

Intended audience Ethnographer's understanding of the primary group to which she will present her findings; important in determining an appropriate style of presentation

Interviews Key ethnographic method in which ethnographer collects information by asking questions of informants; focuses on words as a way to access ideas and information

Interview schedule List of questions to be asked in the course of an interview; a strict schedule details the specific order of questions

Key figures Individuals that figure prominently in an ethnography as important sources of information and insight; sometimes represent or speak for a larger social group

Key informants Informants upon whom ethnographer particularly relies; often offer unique insights or occupy a specific social position that offers an important perspective

Key methods Primary means for collecting ethnographic data; participant-observation, interviewing, and mapping are some of the key methods in ethnography

Key themes Patterns in ethnographic data that emerge in the course of data collection and analysis; represent social and cultural elements that seem particularly interesting or important; basis for analytical framework

Kinship charts An ethnographic tool used by researchers to collect and to present information about familial relationships in different settings

Knowledge Information and ideas learned through a variety of avenues; most knowledge is socially and culturally shaped and connects the thoughts and words of individuals to the societies and cultures of which they are a part

Literature review Overview of relevant literature for project under consideration; covers existing research data and theories and sets stage for proposed research project

Local Refers to a specific area that has particular defining characteristics the scope of the local can vary depending on the circumstances and the research question

Mapping Key ethnographic method that allows the researcher to document and to analyze the social and cultural dimensions of physical (and conceptual) space; mapping also allows the researcher to record and present evidence on spatial relationships and movements

Maps Ethnographer's representations of spatial relationships and movement, especially as they relate to social and cultural phenomena

Material culture Complex of objects that are produced in a particular cultural context can be analyzed in terms of circumstances of production and use as well as symbolic significance

Matrilineal descent System for tracing familial relationships through the mother's side of the family

Methods Specific means for collecting research data; key ethnographic methods include participant-observation, interviewing, and mapping

Methods section Portion of research proposal that details specific methods and techniques researcher intends to employ in the course of her research

Moments Specific points in the course of fieldwork that represent critical insights for the ethnographer or that bring together various elements of the research; can be the basis for effective ethnographic presentation

Narrative storytelling A way of presenting information that follows conventions of storytelling; often chronological; one way to present ethnographic data

Object of study Specific item or concept that researcher seeks to examine

Objectivity A perspective that assumes the ability to perceive and to analyze without bias; if objectivity is possible, everyone should be able to perceive the same thing and to collect comparable data

Observer Researcher who collects data without engaging directly with research subjects or objects; distinct from a participant or participant-observer

Open-ended Refers to questions that do not limit the possible answers; allow the informant or interviewee to construct their own answers

Open-ended questions Questions that the ethnographer asks without providing possible answers; allow the interviewee to interpret the question on her own terms and to answer in a variety of ways

Organizational charts Visual presentations of social relationships in a specific setting; focused on mechanisms and relationships of authority and information and responsibilities for specific tasks

Participant-observer Researcher involved in engaged research with a commitment to trying to meld the benefits of participation and observation; can collect primary and experiential data and connect to comparative data from other contexts

Participant-observation Unique research position of the ethnographer; seeks to combine and to juxtapose the different benefits of the perspectives of an engaged participant and a relatively detached observer; a challenging position to adopt; directly connected to ethnographer's role as research instrument

Patrilineal descent System for tracing familial relationships through the father's side of the family

Patterns of behavior Trends or tendencies in actions and activities that emerge in the course of collecting and analyzing ethnographic data

Perspective Viewpoint; ethnography often highlights and examines the different perspectives involved in research situations (including the perspectives of ethnographers and informants)

Practical ramifications The applicable dimensions and consequences of ethnographic research that speak to related fields like policy, implantation, and advocacy

Privacy A key concern in ethnographic research, especially related to the need to protect and respect information collected from individuals during the course of research

Process Ethnography is a process; the project evolves during the course of data collection and analysis; embracing the processual dimensions of ethnography allows the researcher to engage in the most productive research

Proposal Complete explanation of research that ethnographer plans to undertake; includes literature review, research question(s), methods, and plans for analysis and presentation

Purpose Goal of individual or group responsible for producing document or artifact; important for understanding larger significance of these cultural products

Rapport An established interpersonal relationship (often between ethnographer and informant) that makes specific research activities such as interviews or participant-observation possible; good rapport generally requires openness and honesty and is often established over an extended period of time

Recommendations Suggestions that the ethnographer makes as a direct result of data collection and analysis; often a key component of applied or practical ethnography

Relative significance The amount of import that the ethnographer assigns to a particular piece of information; determined by evaluating importance to key questions and building insightful analysis

Relevance Measure of the direct applicability of a specific piece or set of information for the ethnogapher's project

Reliability Degree of confidence in a particular piece of information

Replicability Ability to reproduce research and collect comparable results; an important way to check validity and reliability of data

Representative Standing for or reflecting a larger whole; individuals may or may not be representative of larger groups; data may or may not be representative of more general trends or relationships

Research instrument Object or technique used to collect and record data; in ethnography, the ethnographer becomes a primary research instrument

Research plan Methods and techniques intended to be used to collect information directly related to research topic or question

Research plan Specific objectives and schedule for collecting relevant data and completing successful analysis of data

Research process Different stages for collecting and analyzing data from start to finish; ethnographers need to consider carefully the different stages in research

Research project A well-defined endeavor to research a specific question or topic; project may include multiple researchers and multiple methods

Research question A specific question that guides the research project and forms the basis for a research plan; focuses on important analytical concepts and variables and relationships among them

Research strategy A general approach for conducting research; ethnography is a research strategy along with surveys and experiments; research strategies can encompass a range of methods and techniques

Research subjects People who participate in research projects, including experiments and surveys

Research topic Focus of a research project; usually formulated in terms of studying an analytical concept in a particular site or sites

Revision Key stage of ethnographic process; allows the ethnographer to collect feedback and to identify areas that need to be refined in the final ethnography

Sharing Essential to ethnography as a collaborative endeavor; ethnographers ask informants to share a lot and should be prepared to share thoughts and results with informants; important source of feedback at various stages in the research process

Social interaction The conversations and activities that occur when two or more people meet and that are informed by cultural expectations and understandings

Social or cultural empathy A degree of understanding that can be achieved in the course of ethnographic research

Spatial relationships Dimensions of space and time that reflect social connections, activities, and movements

Structures Systems of organization that constitute larger wholes; can be mental, physical, or social

Style of presentation Manner in which ethnographer chooses to write her ethnography and deliver it to her audience; includes level of formality, organization, and various ethnographic conventions

Symbols Words or visual forms that represent things or ideas; meaningful when shared by a group; key to communication; essential part of culture and social interaction; meanings often debated or shared imperfectly

Techniques Very specific research steps for collecting information; techniques often require researchers to utilize specifically honed skills

The non obvious Dimensions of society and culture that are not immediately clear before investigation and analysis; highlights the complex nature of human thought and behavior

Transcript Detailed written recounting of interview or conversation; process of transcription typically involves carefully revisiting taped interviews to produce transcripts

Unilineal descent Kinship system that traces familial relationships through only the mother's or the father's side of the family

Validity Degree to which research data provides an accurate reflection or measure of the topic or variable under consideration

Variety Key dimension of virtually all social and cultural contexts; ethnographer should be aware of variety within groups and across circumstances; can provide insight into multiple perspectives, debates, and contested meanings

REFERENCES

Altork, Kate. 1995. Walking the fire line: The erotic dimension of the fieldwork experience. In *Taboo: Sex, identity, and erotic subjectivity in anthropological fieldwork,* ed. Don Kulick and Margaret Willson. London: Routledge.

Anderson, Nels, and Council of Social Agencies of Chicago. 1923. *The hobo: The sociology of the homeless man.* Chicago: University of Chicago Press.

Askew, Kelly Michelle. 2002. *Performing the nation: Swahili music and cultural politics in Tanzania.* Chicago: University of Chicago Press.

Behar, Ruth. 2003. *Translated woman: Crossing the border with Esperanza's story.* Boston: Beacon Press.

Benedict, Ruth. 1946. *The chrysanthemum and the sword: Patterns of Japanese culture.* Boston: Houghton Mifflin.

Bluebond-Langner, Myra. 1978. *The private worlds of dying children.* Princeton, NJ: Princeton University Press.

Boas, Franz. 1920. The methods of ethnology. *American Anthropologist* 22(4):311–21.

Bohanan, Laura. 1966. Shakespeare in the bush. *Natural History.* Available at http://law.ubalt.edu/downloads/law_downloads/IRC_Shakespeare_in_the_Bush1.pdf.

Bourgois, Philippe I. 2003. *In search of respect: Selling crack in El Barrio.* 2nd ed. New York: Cambridge University Press.

Bradburd, Daniel. 1998. *Being there: The necessity of fieldwork.* Washington, DC: Smithsonian Institution Press.

Chagnon, Napoleon A. 1997. *Yanomamo.* 5th ed. Fort Worth, TX: Harcourt Brace.

Clifford, James. 1983. On ethnographic authority. *Representations 1*(2):118–46.

Comaroff, Jean, and John L. Comaroff. 1991. *Of revelation and revolution.* Chicago: University of Chicago Press.

Duneier, Mitchell. 1999. *Sidewalk.* New York: Farrar, Straus and Giroux.

Emerson, Robert M., Rachel I. Fretz, and Linda L. Shaw. 1995. *Writing ethnographic fieldnotes.* Chicago: University of Chicago Press.

Engebrigtsen, Ada I. 2007. *Exploring gypsiness: Power, exchange and interdependence in a Transylvanian village.* New York: Berghahn Books.

Evans-Pritchard, E. E. 1940. *The Nuer: A description of the modes of livelihood and political institutions of a Nilotic people.* Oxford: Clarendon Press.

Farmer, Paul. 2006. *AIDS and accusation: Haiti and the geography of blame.* Berkeley: University of California Press.

Fox, Aaron A. 2004. *Real country: Music and language in working-class culture.* Durham: Duke University Press.

Frank, Katherine. 2002. *G-strings and sympathy: Strip club regulars and male desire.* Durham: Duke University Press.

Freeman, Derek. 1983. *Margaret Mead and Samoa: The making and unmaking of an anthropological myth.* Cambridge, MA: Harvard University Press.

Geurts, Kathryn Linn. 2002. *Culture and the senses: Bodily ways of knowing in an African community.* Berkeley: University of California Press.

Ghannam, Farha. 2002. *Remaking the modern: Space, relocation, and the politics of identity in a global Cairo.* Berkeley: University of California Press.

Gifford, Paul. 2004. *Ghana's new Christianity: Pentecostalism in a globalizing African economy.* Bloomington: Indiana University Press.

Hodgson, Dorothy L. 2004. *Once intrepid warriors: Gender, ethnicity, and the cultural politics of Maasai development.* Bloomington: Indiana University Press.

Hurston, Zora Neale. 1990a. *Mules and men.* New York: Perennial Library.

———. 1990b. *Tell my horse: Voodoo and life in Haiti and Jamaica.* New York: Perennial Library.

Hutchinson, Sharon Elaine. 1996. *Nuer dilemmas: Coping with money, war, and the state.* Berkeley: University of California Press.

Katz, Pearl. 1999. *The scalpel's edge: The culture of surgeons.* Boston: Allyn and Bacon.

Landau, Paul Stuart. 1995. *The realm of the Word: Language, gender, and Christianity in a southern African kingdom.* Portsmouth, NH: Heinemann.

Lee, Richard Borshay. 1969. A naturalist at large: Eating Christmas in the Kalahari. *Natural History.* Available at www.naturalhistorymag.com/htmlsite/index_archivepicks.html.

Lester, Rebecca J. 2005. *Jesus in our wombs: Embodying modernity in a Mexican convent.* Berkeley: University of California Press.

Lois, Jennifer. 2003. *Heroic efforts: The emotional culture of search and rescue volunteers.* New York: NYU Press.

MacLeod, Jay. 1995. *Ain't no makin' it: Aspirations and attainment in a low-income neighborhood.* Boulder, CO: Westview Press.

Malinowski, Bronislaw. 1922. *Argonauts of the Western Pacific.* London: Routledge.

McCurdy, David W. 2008. Family and kinship in village India. In *Conformity and conflict: Readings in cultural anthropology,* ed. James P. Spradley and David W. McCurdy. Boston: Pearson.

McCurdy, David W., James P. Spradley, and Dianna J. Shandy. 2005. *The cultural experience: Ethnography in complex society.* 2nd ed. Long Grove, IL: Waveland Press.

Mead, Margaret. 1928. *Coming of age in Samoa: A psychological study of primitive youth for Western civilisation.* New York: Morrow.

Nanda, Serena. 1999. *Neither man nor woman: The hijras of India.* 2nd ed. Belmont, CA: Wadsworth.

Nathan, Rebekah. 2005. *My freshman year: What a professor learned by becoming a student.* Ithaca, NY: Cornell University Press.

Nordstrom, Carolyn, and Antonius C.G.M. Robben. 1995. *Fieldwork under fire: Contemporary studies of violence and survival.* Berkeley: University of California Press.

Ortner, Sherry. 1978. *Sherpas through their rituals.* New York: Cambridge University Press.

Robben, Antonius C.G.M., and Jeffrey A. Sluka, eds. 2007. *Ethnographic fieldwork: An anthropological reader.* Malden, MA: Blackwell.

Scheper-Hughes, Nancy. 2001. *Saints, scholars, and schizophrenics: Mental illness in rural Ireland.* 20th anniversary ed. Berkeley: University of California Press.

Sluka, Jeffrey A., and Antonius C.G.M. Robben. 2007. Fieldwork in cultural anthropology: An introduction. In *Ethnographic fieldwork: An anthropological reader,* ed. Antonius C.G.M. Robben and Jeffrey A. Sluka. Malden, MA: Blackwell.

Spradley, James P., and David W. McCurdy, eds. 2008. *Conformity and conflict: Readings in cultural anthropology.* Boston: Pearson.

Stark, Cathy. 1998. Carrying out HIV-related research in an area of low prevalence: Issues for researcher and researched. In *Meddling with mythology: AIDS and the social construction of knowledge,* ed. Rosaline S. Barbour and Guro Huby. New York: Routledge.

Suggs, David N. 2001. *A bagful of locusts and the baboon woman.* Belmont, CA: Wadsworth.

Turnbull, Colin M. 1968. *The forest people.* New York: Simon & Schuster.

Watson, C. W. 1999. *Being there: Fieldwork in anthropology.* Sterling, VA: Pluto Press.

Watson, James L. 2006. *Golden arches east: McDonald's in East Asia.* 2nd ed. Palo Alto, CA: Stanford University Press.

Weiner, Annette B. 1976. *Women of value, men of renown: New perspectives in Trobriand exchange.* Austin: University of Texas Press.

Whyte, William Foote. 1943. *Street corner society: The social structure of an Italian slum.* Chicago: University of Chicago Press.

Wood, John Colman. 1999. *When men are women: Manhood among Gabra nomads of east Africa.* Madison: University of Wisconsin Press.

Reference

INDEX

Page references followed by *fig* indicate an illustrated figure.

119–120; descriptive, 39; ethnographic storytelling and answering, 176, 189; follow-up,
110; good versus bad interview, 109–111;
hypotheses relationship to research, 40; interview use of hypothetical, 110–111; linking
methods and research, 40–41; open-ended vs.
closed-ended, 109–110; project's answering
of intellectual, 217; research plan on how to
use, 57–58; revising your research, 120; that
shouldn't or can't be asked, 111–112; turning
an idea or topic into research, 38–39

R

Real Country (Fox), 192
"Real" culture or society, 104
Recommendations, 217
Recorders/recording: for ethnographic record,
72–74; interviews, 105–107; pragmatics of
using technology for, 75–76
Relationships: causal, 213; charts used to represent, 144; culture manifested through inter-
personal, 144–146; hierarchical, 146; kinship
basis of, 146; kinship charts to examine, 7,
44–47, 89, 91; research-informants' exploit-
ative, 58; social interaction connecting, 45;
spatial, 45. *See also* Connections; Linkages
Relative informality style, 206–207
Relative significance, 188
Relevance: demonstrating project's, 216–217;
including literature with, 214–215; information, 188–189
Reliability, 180–181
Religious phenomenon studies, 165
Remaking the Modern (Ghannam), 136–137
Replicability goal, 13, 15
Representative informants, 44
Research: descriptive versus analytical, 38;
exploratory, 38; presentation of, 196–208;
recommendations based on, 217; relevance
of, 216–217
Research design: historical or personal perspectives impacting, 40; tweaking the, 121
Research instruments: data collection, 72; different types of, 72–74; ethnographer as primary, 13–15
Research methods: early approaches to ethnographic, 6–8; ethnographic, 4; examining
key, 41; issues to consider when selecting,
47–49; linking questions and, 40–41; participant-observation, 26–28, 41–43; research

plan on using specific, 58; tools used for, 58,
133. *See also* Interviews/interviewing;
Methods section; Participant-observation
Research moments: identifying important,
176–178; writing about revealing, 124
Research plans: description of, 26, 56; issues to
consider for, 47–49; proposal inclusion of
detailed, 56–58. *See also* Methods section
Research process: analysis as, 191; deductive,
190; inductive, 175, 190; revising questions
and focus during, 26
Research projects: demonstrating relevance of,
216–217; selecting topic of, 21. *See also*
Research topics
Research proposals. *See* Proposals
Research questions. *See* Questions
Research strategies: collaborative, 15–17; different methods and techniques of, 4; ethnography as, 4; using the Internet, 24
Research subjects: critique of Mead's work with,
10; ethnographer involvement with, 4; gaining
access and building rapport with, 7; human
subjects review to protect, 59–61; power balance between researchers and, 5; pseudonyms
to protect identity of, 62, 202–203; risks for, 60.
See also Informants; Participant-observers
Research techniques: ethnographic, 4; household surveys, 7; kinship charts, 7, 44–47, 89,
91, 147–148, 150*fig*–152. *See also*
Ethnographic maps
Research topics: benefits of relatively specific
focus for, 23–26; cautions regarding, 33–35;
choosing an appropriate, 21; formulating
research questions from, 38–40; issues of
accessibility on, 29–31; issues of privacy
related to, 31–32; object of study focus of,
23; where to look for possible, 22–23. *See*
also Field sites; Research projects
Revising, 217–218
Risks, 60

S

Samoa studies (Mead), 4, 5, 7, 10
Scales (ethnographic map), 131–132
Sensory experience, 72
"Shakespeare in the Bush" (Bohanan), 199
Shapes (ethnographic map), 131–132
Shared sets of symbols: patterns of, 95; repeti-
tion of, 95–96; variation of, 96–97
Sharing ethnography, 218–220